Where The Road Ends

A Guide to Trail Running

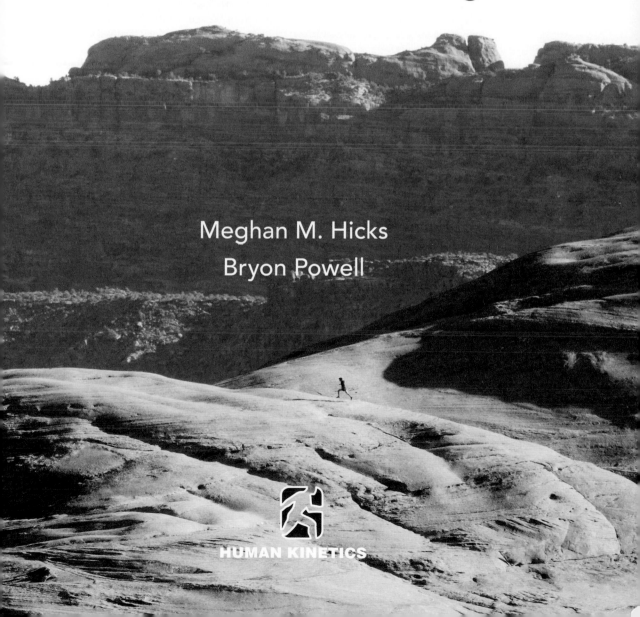

Meghan M. Hicks

Bryon Powell

HUMAN KINETICS

Library of Congress Cataloging-in-Publication Data

Names: Hicks, Meghan M., 1978- author. | Powell, Bryon, author.
Title: Where the road ends : a guide to trail running / Meghan M. Hicks and
  Bryon Powell.
Description: Champaign, IL : Human Kinetics, [2016] | Includes
  bibliographical references and index.
Identifiers: LCCN 2015042715 | ISBN 9781492513285 (print)
Subjects: LCSH: Running. | Trails--Recreational use.
Classification: LCC GV1061 .H47 2016 | DDC 613.7/172--dc23 LC record available at http://lccn.
loc.gov/2015042715

ISBN: 978-1-4925-1328-5 (print)

The web addresses cited in this text were current as of **December 2015**, unless otherwise noted.

Acquisitions Editor: Tom Heine; **Developmental Editor:** Laura Pulliam; **Managing Editor:** Nicole Moore; **Copyeditor:** Bob Replinger; **Indexer:** Katy Balcer; **Permissions Manager:** Martha Gullo; **Senior Graphic Designer:** Joe Buck; **Graphic Designer:** Tara Welsch; **Cover Designer:** Keith Blomberg; **Photograph (cover):** © Kirsten Marie Kortebein; **Photographs (interior):** Photos courtesy of: **Lloyd Belcher**: 203; **Alexis Berg**: 11, 52, 76, 111, 205; **Tim Bergsten/PikesPeakSports.us**: 143; **Jeff Browning**: 84; **Gretchen Brugman**: 12; **Marc Chalufour**: 25; **Simon Green**: 189; **Meghan Hicks**: vi, viii, x, 29, 33, 36, 83, 92, 122, 160, 167, 168, 171, 173, 180, 191, 213, 216; **Max Keith:** 102; **Tim Kemple**: 3, 58, 145; **Kirsten Kortebein**: i, xiii, 7, 8, 13-23, 32, 35, 51, 56, 60, 81, 96, 105, 126, 132-140, 159, 207; **Fred Marmsater**: 114, 183; **John Medinger**: 155; **The North Face**: 85; **Bryon Powell**: iv, 1, 9, 27, 28, 30, 39-47, 63-74, 78, 87, 103, 104, 107, 109, 115, 118, 120, 148, 152, 157, 162, 175, 186, 195, 197, 208, 210, 215; **Raymond Skiles**: 169; **Glenn Tachiyama**: 116; **Matt Trappe**: 80; **Photo Asset Manager:** Laura Fitch; **Visual Production Assistant:** Joyce Brumfield; **Photo Production Manager:** Jason Allen; **Art Manager:** Kelly Hendren; **Associate Art Manager:** Alan L. Wilborn; **Illustrations:** © Human Kinetics; **Printer:** Versa Press

Human Kinetics books are available at special discounts for bulk purchase. Special editions or book excerpts can also be created to specification. For details, contact the Special Sales Manager at Human Kinetics.

Printed in the United States of America   10 9 8 7 6 5 4 3 2 1

The paper in this book is certified under a sustainable forestry program.

Human Kinetics
Website: www.HumanKinetics.com

United States: Human Kinetics
P.O. Box 5076
Champaign, IL 61825-5076
800-747-4457
e-mail: info@hkusa.com

Canada: Human Kinetics
475 Devonshire Road Unit 100
Windsor, ON N8Y 2L5
800-465-7301 (in Canada only)
e-mail: info@hkcanada.com

Europe: Human Kinetics
107 Bradford Road
Stanningley
Leeds LS28 6AT, United Kingdom
+44 (0) 113 255 5665
e-mail: hk@hkeurope.com

Australia: Human Kinetics
57A Price Avenue
Lower Mitcham, South Australia 5062
08 8372 0999
e-mail: info@hkaustralia.com

New Zealand: Human Kinetics
P.O. Box 80
Mitcham Shopping Centre, South Australia 5062
0800 222 062
e-mail: info@hknewzealand.com

E6615

To those who choose the crooked trails.

Contents

Foreword

"Bryon Powell and Meghan Hicks of iRunFar, here with . . ."

The passionate souls of trail running hear this introduction in the video interviews that Bryon and Meghan do with the world's top trail runners before and after any big race. Those opening words have become the reference when talking of trail running. Anyone who considers him- or herself a trail runner knows who Bryon and Meghan are, and we impatiently wait for their race previews and articles.

Kilian Jornet enjoys running the 2014 Hardrock 100.

It's early autumn in California, I think around 4 a.m., and the first proper meeting between Bryon and me. We are running together and using the time to get to know each other. We start running north on easy footing from Tahoe City. Not many words are spoken, just ones to get to know each other a little more. Talking seems over-rated—we are doing what we love: running in nature, absorbing the silence, and looking forward on the endless trails. The dark disappears and the reddish atmosphere of dawn invades the old tree bark of the giant forest through which we run. Our long shadows flirt with the trees and sandy rocks as we move with a light pace. We are more floating than running. Some hours later, with a heavy sun and flat light, Bryon stops and I turn right and then down, contouring this big lake. I meet and run with Bryon several times during the next 40 hours as I run nonstop the 165-mile Tahoe Rim Trail around Lake Tahoe, while Bryon and others join me as pacers. From then on, I have continued to meet Bryon and Meghan frequently, always with some trails in front of us.

On this first meeting back in 2009, I, Bryon, Meghan, and a few more humans were the misunderstood people who loved to run on the trails as long as our bodies could. We are part of a generation of runners who train and compete in a serious way for trail running, exploring year after year how the body reacts to long distances. We have been learning and acquiring the knowledge that we hope can help future generations of trail runners run better and have more fun exploring the trails.

Where the Road Ends is a journey among this community of trail runners, a community that, despite growing professionalism and a search for performance, stays strong in values such as passion, altruism, connection with nature, volunteering, and companionship. This book links the search for performance, the knowledge about how our bodies and brains can run longer and faster, and the connection that trail running gives us to nature and the other runners of this wonderful community. Enjoy this journey!

—Kilian Jornet

Acknowledgments

Thanks to my parents for taking our family to wild places and to my brother who played endlessly with me in the woods behind our house.

Thanks to my dad, who always countered my mother's "Be careful" admonitions with equally important "Be wild" reminders.

Thanks to those who had the foresight to establish America's national parks and wilderness areas and to those who are dedicated to their continued preservation.

Thanks to all the people who get out early, stay out late, and push boundaries in experiencing the wild.

Thanks to Bryon, my partner in life, for making ours a life of adventure.

—*Meghan*

Thanks to Poppop for taking me on long walks in the woods as far back as I can remember.

Thanks to the Parkers for encouraging a young neighbor to run and to Coach Hoch for sharing the joy of trail running.

Thanks to Scotty and all the Virginia Happy Trailers for stoking my love of trail running.

Thanks to all the trail builders and maintainers, for yours is a sweaty, often-thankless toil.

Thanks to my parents for never failing to encourage me along whatever path I've gone down.

Thanks to Gretchen, Maya, and Norah for giving me three reasons to inspire someone.

Thanks to Meghan for taking my hand and running down life's crooked trails with me.

—*Bryon*

Introduction

A Sense of Adventure

Very little light has crept into the sky as my good friend Kristin Zosel and I, Meghan Hicks, greet each other with a still-sleepy hug in the trailhead parking lot. What light has arrived is yellow, the precise color that the sun burns into your eyes if you make the mistake of looking straight at it, and it is pressing its way across the electric-blue sky of waning night. Tall, black silhouettes looming up from the ground are the giant mountains that surround us. We meet this morning to run the famed Four Pass Loop in Colorado's Maroon Bells–Snowmass Wilderness. It's a 26.5-mile (42.6 km) loop outside Aspen that features a bold 8,000 vertical feet (2,400 m) of climbing (and as much descending), largely through high-altitude, alpine terrain.

We head up the trail where a rock garden greets us for the first stretch of running. Our feet tap a staccato rhythm on the small spots of bare earth between the rocks, and our knees rise high to lift our legs over the obstacles. Our arms swing hard, instigating more forward propulsion than normal because our legs are busy with tasks beyond just moving forward. Moving requires the full attention of our minds and bodies, a natural wake-up call.

Colorado's Crater Lake wakes up.

The trail leads to Crater Lake, its surface a perfectly still mirror that reflects everything: the conifer trees on its shoreline, North Maroon Peak and its companion mountains glowing pink in alpenglow, and a pale blue sky containing poofs of white clouds. We stand silent for a moment before jogging on.

We turn left at the trail junction and head up the West Maroon Creek drainage on a well-established trail that traces the valley bottom uphill. Here and there the trail is briefly muddy. I concentrate on making sure that my feet land right beneath me and straight into the ground so that the lugs on the soles of my shoes can grab the gook. With a little attention, good traction comes easily.

Kristin and I alternately jog and powerhike up the large valley. When the trail steepens, our heart rates spike, and we temporarily slow to a power-hike. As the trail moderates again, we switch back to a jog. Our bodies naturally seek the most efficient way to move across the dynamic terrain. The hillsides are choked with wildflowers—Indian paintbrush, lupine, and dozens of other species. Strokes of red, purple, yellow, and orange flash up the hillsides before giving way to the coral pink and rust-colored bare cliffs above. Simply said, the scene is stupendous.

We reach the first of the four namesake passes on this loop, West Maroon Pass, which acts as the topographical divide between two drainages. We've watched the clouds grow big and gray, expanding from separate units into a continuous layer. At the top of West Maroon Pass, we see an ominous curtain of rain falling a couple miles off and headed our way. We stop for just a moment—to take photos and don our rain jackets—before bulleting downhill.

Raindrops come first; they patter gently against my jacket. Then tiny pieces of hail begin to tap Morse code on my hood. Next comes a soaking rain. But just as the curtain of rain envelops us, we see through to the other side. The rain ends within 15 minutes, just long enough to soak our shoes.

The second pass, Frigid Air Pass, comes unexpectedly fast. At a little pond, the trail makes a quick, signed jog to the right and then pitches into the sky. Just a half mile (800 m) to the top, the steep grade forces us to hike every step. I remind myself to inhale deeply with each breath to give myself access to as much oxygen as possible and to engage my core muscles, which act as the support structure for this hard work. We leave the bounty of wild-flowers and ascend through rocky terrain devoid of nearly all vegetation.

Another trail runner climbs the opposite approach to the pass. We watch him tackle the switchbacks with command. He mostly jogs, although occasionally he switches to a powerhike for a couple steps, pressing his hands down on his thighs to add extra, upper-body oomph to each step.

In the valley after the pass, we encounter one backpacking group after another, maybe 75 people total over the next 10 miles (16 km). We also intersect another pair of trail runners sauntering together. The Four Pass Loop is a mecca for outdoor enthusiasts of many kinds.

Meghan and Kristin run together on the Four Pass Loop.

The 2,000-foot (600 m) climb to the third pass comes in what seems like two giant stair steps. First, the trail steepens as we snake up a forested hillside on switchbacks. Just past tree line, the grade flattens as we meander past another unnamed pond. Trail Rider Pass is now in view, a V dipping into a ridge of rocks maybe 800 feet (240 m) above us, the second of the two big stairs. In the nook of the V, humans who are already up there appear as wee dots, like ants.

We make it to the top, but not without hard work. Trail Rider Pass lies on the shoulder of a mountain made of white igneous rock called Snowmass Peak. Although the pass is above 12,000 feet (3,600 m), the summit of the mountain is a couple thousand feet higher at over 14,000 feet (4,200 m). The walls of white that rise from the pass are so reflective of the sun that they are almost blinding.

Below Trail Rider Pass and Snowmass Peak lies a giant lake, suitably named Snowmass Lake. It's turquoise and glittery. Sunlight flashes off thousands of ripples as if a massive tropical fish were laid out on its side.

Somewhere below the pass, we stop for a snack. Before this morning, Kristin and I hadn't seen each other for more than six months. But our conversation and friendship easily picked up where we last left it. All day we've chatted away, catching each other up on the comings and goings of life and then lapsing into the kind of comfortable silence that only two people who get along well can share. The ease of being with Kristin is a highlight of the day. As we stand there, under the hulking peak and above the sparkling lake, laughing and crunching on energy bars, I feel levity— about life and our friendship and this wild place. It's a runner's high.

Ahead of us looms one more pass, Buckskin Pass but the trail makes us dip lower still before we climb again. We cross Snowmass Creek and start the 1,500-foot (450 m) ascent. There's no way to describe this point in our journey other than grinding. Kristin and I have been moving conservatively all day, so although it hurts a little, we are able to powerhike and jog hard. When we get to the top, we hug and high-five. We're four for four, and the hardest work of the day is done!

Down Minnehaha Gulch we go, some 3,000 feet (900 m) back toward Crater Lake, where things began this morning. There's no way around it; the final downhill of many long trail runs is a challenge. The eccentric muscular contractions that come with simultaneously bending our legs and supporting our body weight makes our already tired quadriceps burn. Our brains are tired, so although the trail is buffed out enough in some places that we can cruise, in others we have to concentrate hard so that we don't trip over exposed rocks and roots.

After what seems like a long time, we finish off the descent, rolling through the trail junction near Crater Lake, taking one last left back toward the trailhead. We're back in the rock garden, our final segment of the day, and we play. We dance. We leap from rock to rock. We are completely joyful. We move efficiently, lightly, even picking up speed in this human version of smelling the barn.

At the trailhead, we peel ourselves out of our dirty, damp socks and shoes, grab our recovery drinks, and make our way to a cold creek to soak our tired legs.

"Now that was a ladies' day out!" we hoot about our frolicking, rollicking day.

About This Book

Whether Colorado's Four Pass Loop sounds like your ultimate adventure or will serve as inspiration for more moderate outings, give trail running a chance and it will invigorate your mind and body. Trail running is exertion and exhilaration, fitness and friendship, challenge and change. Trail running is a means of exploring the landscape, our connection with it, our lives, ourselves. If you want to start your trail running journey or take your trail running to new heights, you've come to the right place.

You may already know this, but wherever you live—from a medium-sized city to a rural hamlet, from a mountain village to a major metropolis—there are trails near you. Perhaps you run them all the time but have never thought of yourself as a trail runner. Maybe you know the trails are out there but you've never ventured on them. Or maybe you've already competed in several trail running races. From someone looking to take his first strides down the trail to the experienced trail runner seeking to improve her considerable skills, *Where the Road Ends: A Guide to Trail Running* is a comprehensive how-to for trail running designed to assist you.

In this book, we the authors, Meghan Hicks and Bryon Powell, combine our more than 35 years of trail running experience with the expert advice of other experienced runners and educators to explain the ins and outs of trail running in a no-nonsense, let's-get-on-the-trail fashion.

The book kicks off with chapter 1, "Stepping Off Road," which delves into the basics of trail running by answering the questions most often asked by those considering or just starting trail running:

- What is trail running?
- How does it differ from road running?
- How do I locate trails to run?
- Do I need different shoes and gear for trail running?
- Is it safe?
- Where can I meet other trail runners?

In "Trail Running Techniques," the second chapter, we jump into the nitty-gritty of exactly how to run on trails. The core of this chapter (and trail running) is foundational trail running techniques such as running with an active body position, fixing your gaze in the right place, using quick turnover and nimble feet when obstacles arise, and more. Along the way, you'll learn some drills for acquiring trail-worthy agility.

Chapter 3, "Finding Footing," discusses the ground beneath our feet, one of the most variable conditions that trail runners encounter. On the same run, you can run over dirt, sand, roots, and rock, and each substrate might be dry, wet, icy, or obscured by debris. Learn how to read and react as you pass over and tread on a multitude of surfaces. A trail runner must also respond to the dictates of the broader terrain. In chapter 4, "Techniques to Match Terrain," you'll learn how to approach climbs and descents (both steep and gradual), conquer curves in the trail, and overcome major obstacles like boulders and logs. Be ready for it all! If chapter 2 is the classroom driver's ed class, chapters 3 and 4 are driving with your learner's permit, when you learn how to deal with real-world scenarios.

Even the most simple of trail runners uses equipment to facilitate single-track sessions. Other personal preferences and scenarios call for a more extensive set of gear when hitting the trail. In chapter 5, "Trail Tools," you'll learn all about the physical tools that can facilitate your sport: shoes, apparel, hydration systems, gear haulers, lighting, safety equipment, navigation tools (GPS units, maps, compasses), and more. You'll learn about everything from matching shoes to terrain and footing to how to carry enough water for a trail run, from what tools to take to find your way back home to the best lighting options for night running. We also address gear use more generally, including when you might be able to pare down your pack.

Sometimes, a mile on the trails can take two or three times as long as it does on the roads, even at the same effort. On the other hand, a more relaxed approach to trail running often facilitates longer outings (time wise)

The authors Bryon Powell and Meghan Hicks run in Utah's La Sal Mountains.

than your typical road sessions. As such, adequate hydration and nutrition come into play more often in the wilds. Chapter 6, "Hydration and Fueling," lays out the ingredients for staying happy and healthy out there.

Tips for successful trail running are provided for a wide array of conditions such as heat, cold, rain, snow, sun, high altitude, darkness, and more in chapter 7, "Conquering the Conditions." For example, you'll learn the basics of layered clothing systems, what to wear in wet weather, options for keeping feet dry and warm, and more.

Chapters 8 and 9, "Training for the Trail" and "Creating a Training Plan," both take broad and in-depth looks at trail running training. Chapter 8 first explains some well-known training theories for endurance running such as long runs, hill repeats, various forms of speed workouts, and more. It then discusses other activities you can use as cross-training for trail running as well as specific trail running drills you can use to get faster, stronger, and more comfortable. Chapter 9 focuses on how to combine these different types of running into short- and long-term training plans. Finally, the chapter wraps up with discussion points about the importance of full-spectrum health for your running.

Trail running exposes runners to new and sometimes dangerous risks, so chapter 10, "Trail Safety and Stewardship," focuses on those plausible risks and ways to minimize and address them. Some of the risks discussed include wildlife, water crossings, thunderstorms, steep terrain, crossing snow, dangerous humans, getting lost, and more. We also address the fundamental nonrunning skills needed for safe trail running such as effective navigation, obtaining and purifying water in the backcountry, and more. This chapter also introduces the ethics of running through wild spaces.

In chapter 11, "Health and Injuries," you'll learn how to prevent, identify, and mitigate common backcountry bad happenings such as blisters, cuts, bruises, altitude sickness, and sunburn.

The final chapter, "Trail Racing," serves as a how-to for becoming acclimated to trail racing. From course maps to aid stations, markings to finish-line environments, you'll find out what to expect at a trail race and how such events are likely to differ from their bitumen-based brethren. We also clue you in on how to make the most of your big day.

In each of the chapters you'll find a sidebar titled "Places and Races to Inspire." Each of these takes you to an inspiring trail race or locale. The hope is that you'll want to experience some of them, or places like them, someday.

Although you can feel free to skip around the book to meet your interests, this book is designed to be read front to back the first time you read it. We establish and expand on a knowledge base from chapter to chapter, so you may find yourself better understanding something later in the book if you've read the beginning first. Perhaps most important, this book is meant to act as a resource that, over the years and as your relationship with the sport grows, you'll keep coming back to.

We hope that every time you shut this book you'll have a new skill, drill, task, inspiration, or nugget of knowledge to take with you onto the trail—something that will enhance your experience.

Thank you for choosing *Where the Road Ends*!
Happy trails,
Meghan and Bryon

Sunrise views like this one of Wyoming's Salt River Range answer one of the whys of trail running.

Chapter 1

Stepping Off Road

Short, long, fast, slow, dirt, rocks, snow: It's your turn to step on to the trail. You've found *Where the Road Ends* because something about trail running speaks to you.

The basic beauty of trail running is that it's at once a simple and dynamic sport. Its simplicity is based on the facts that running is a natural human motion—one of the first things we figure out how to do as toddlers—and that it doesn't require much preparation or gear for each outing. On the other hand, the sport is dynamic because of the diversity of places you'll run, the obstacles you'll work your way through, the wildlife you might encounter, and the people with whom you'll share the trail.

For some, the appeal of trail running goes even deeper. Many people find that trail running helps them navigate an interesting, new way of experiencing the world. As the population grows, humans gather themselves into cities for the convenient concentration of workplaces, schools, supermarkets, doctors' offices, family, and friends. Although humans live inside homes and apartments, in close proximity to more buildings and many people, some are still called by something inside themselves to spend time outside. Many people say they need to breathe a little fresh air, to let sunshine fall on their faces, to see some greenery, and to move their bodies to feel, well, human. An hour or so on the trail makes many people feel refreshed in returning to the rest of life.

Trail running might speak to you in other ways, too. Perhaps you are already a runner who revels in your daily dedication to mind and body. You take to roads, bike paths, and treadmills. Maybe you race, entering local 10Ks and marathons to help sate the competitive fire inside you or to satisfy your desire to spend time with likeminded people. Maybe you're on the hunt for a new venue for the sport you love, and you've heard about trail running through Twitter, a magazine, or a neighbor.

Maybe you've gravitated to *Where the Road Ends* because you already spend time beyond this point. You are a hiker, mountain biker, backpacker—someone who already spends a good amount of time on the trail. You don't need anyone to sell you on how enjoyable time spent in wild places is. Chances are you've seen another breed of trail lover in your explorations, trail runners, and you're curious about becoming one, too.

Maybe you're a competitive gymnast or tennis player who has ended your career but is looking for a place to play with your competitive drive. You might be a new mom or dad who's seeking quick access to quiet and calm, and a way to reconnect with yourself. Perhaps you're coming off an injury from another sport and have heard that the soft surfaces of trail running might cradle your delicate body. There are almost endless reasons to try trail running.

As you begin your journey into this sport, you might find that you have some questions about what to do and expect. In this chapter, you'll find basic answers to the very first questions you might have about trail running. What follows in this chapter should be enough information for you to enjoy your first trail runs. Let's do this!

What Is Trail Running?

The short answer is that trail running is the sport of running off paved surfaces. The longer answer is that trail running is the act of running on an unending diversity of substrates: dirt, gravel, grass, wood chips, roots, rocks, sand, and more. Across flat ground, along rolling hills, up steep climbs, or down bomber descents—trail running is traveling over whatever terrain Mother Nature delivers. Trail running can include traveling short distances very quickly and long distances somewhat slower. It's a sport in which your sweat comingles with dirt and mud. Trail running allows you to flow through shady forests, over treeless alpine terrain, atop steep cliffs, and through endless grasslands. It's a sport whose community is strong and gritty but also filled with warmth and welcome. The sport is as much about running with interesting people or in beautiful places as it is about minutes-per-mile paces.

Rory Bosio running at night during the 2013 UTMB®.

Why Trail Running?

Wow. That's a great question, and, perhaps, the least straightforward one of all to answer. We are all uniquely motivated in life, aren't we? A survey of all of us trail runners about our motivations for spending time off road would yield widely varied results. Some of us trail run to be fit and fast, and to win races. Others trail run as means to relieve stress, to carve out "me time" from each day, and to instill confidence in ourselves. Still, more of us trail run so that we can spend time in nature, away from highways and skyscrapers. And some trail run to enjoy the company of the amazing people who do our sport.

As a two-time winner of the UTMB® (formerly the Ultra-Trail du Mont-Blanc®), a highly competitive race that circumnavigates Mont Blanc in the European Alps, Rory Bosio is one of the fastest female trail runners out there. However competitive she is, Rory finds deep joy in the act of running along a trail: "I love the simplicity of running. The act of putting one foot in front of the other is such a natural movement that one doesn't need to be taught how to do it. Do you remember someone teaching you how to run? Probably not. As toddlers we progress from an unsteady walk to a full-on trot, no instruction needed. Running is ingrained in our DNA. Running outdoors provides an intimate connection with nature that at times feels magical. I live for that feeling of flow: speeding down a trail, opening up the stride, the worries of everyday life evaporating with every step, the clarity of the mind that comes from being truly in the moment, feeling enmeshed in the natural world as opposed to just being an observer of it, the body moving in harmony with the earth."

Is Trail Running Safe?

The sport of trail running has a small amount of inherent risk. We can fall on some types of terrain, and a normal trip and fall is always a possibility. Heat, snow, and other weather variations challenge us to keep our bodies warm, cool, or dry. Wildlife such as snakes or large predators add some risk when we run through their habitat. And as in life off the trails, dangerous humans always pose a small risk.

But anyone can acquire the knowledge, skills, and abilities to keep the risks of trail running very low. Chapters 10 and 11 of this book are devoted to giving you some of the knowledge you need to be a safe, smart trail runner.

How Does Trail Running Differ From Road Running?

It depends. Some kinds of trail running look and feel fairly similar to road running, whereas other kinds of trail running couldn't be more different from running on pavement. Let's consider a couple examples.

Have you ever seen or gone for a run on a wood-chip or packed-dirt trail at your local park? Or maybe you've seen the local high school's grassy cross-country course? A run on any of these routes is trail running! On these trails, you'll experience gentle terrain deviations—ups, downs, and shifts to the left and right. The dirt or grass substrate, in comparison to blacktop or concrete, will probably feel soft and impact absorbing. If you wear a wrist-top GPS, you might notice that your average running pace is 15 or 30 seconds per mile (10 or 20 seconds per kilometer) slower than the pace you run on roads as you slow to navigate hills, curves, and tree roots. Overall, however, the differences between this kind of trail running and road running are subtle.

Next, imagine a giant mountain range with peaks that claw high into the sky and fall away into steep valleys, like the Appalachian Mountains, the Rocky Mountains, or the Alps. Mountain ranges like these have thousands of miles of trails that spider through them. These trails are replete with rocks and roots that chop up trail surfaces, have climbs and descents that can take an hour or more to go up or down, and possess twists, turns, and constant changes to their direction. These trails might require you to cross snow or wade through a creek. The trails might be difficult to detect in places, disappearing into a big meadow and reappearing some distance later. Sometimes, when two trails meet, you'll find no sign to indicate which way to go, so you'll need the ability to navigate on your own. A mile on these trails can take triple or quadruple the time it does on roads at the same effort.

Trails like these require the continuous attention of your mind and body to help you dance among the rocks, to know which way is north, to not give up when you feel like you've been climbing forever, and to keep you safe for the journey to come. Complex and burly, this sort of trail running looks and feels like an entirely different sport than road running.

I've Heard of Ultrarunning. Is That the Same as Trail Running?

Ultrarunning is the sport of running distances in excess of a marathon, that is, more than 26.2 miles (42.2 km). Common ultramarathon race distances are 50 kilometers, 50 miles (80 km), and, believe it or not, 100 miles (160 km). Ultramarathon distance runs and races take place on both roads and trails, although the vast majority of ultramarathons occur on trails. In this way, ultrarunning can be thought of as one kind of trail running.

How Do I Find Trails?

We bet you already know of trails near where you live. And if you don't know about them, we bet they are not far away. Many urban and suburban parks have unpaved trails, sometimes extensive networks on which you can run for hours. Meghan, for instance, grew up in the suburbs of St. Paul, Minnesota, near a couple of parks. She ran on the paved bike path through one of these parks dozens of times before she noticed singletrack trails diverging into the woods from it. The trails weren't marked and didn't appear on any maps, but they were there. Bryon was raised in Titusville, New Jersey, northeast of Philadelphia, Pennsylvania. Washington Crossing State Park is located there. Its 3,500 acres (1,400 ha) are filled with the singletrack on which Bryon cut his trail running teeth as a youngster. Even in these developed areas, trails abound. Thus, our first words of advice for finding trails are to keep your eyes open. A bonanza of trails may already lie very close to your everyday haunts—you just have to discover them.

> Did you know that Google Earth and Google Maps contain hundreds of thousands of miles of trails all over the world, with more being added every day? Plan a trail run anywhere with these online tools.

Next up, ask the experts at your local running store for trail information. Even if the store has a road running focus, surely at least one of its employees runs frequently on trails and will be happy to tell you about her or his personal playgrounds. If a visitor center or tourism office is located nearby, stop in. These places collect and collate all kinds of information for locals and visitors, and they may have trail maps and descriptions.

If you've exhausted your local, in-person resources and are still seeking information, check the websites of nearby conservation or recreation nonprofits and the websites for the agencies who manage any open spaces in or near your home.

Finally, the last (and sometimes best) source is Google Earth and Google Maps or even paper maps. No kidding! These are truly wonderful tools for exploring your local landscape. You might find trails and a whole lot of other things you never knew existed in your town. Find the green spots and go.

Do I Need Special Shoes for Trail Running?

On the most fundamental level, you absolutely do not need special shoes to trail run. You can wear whatever athletic shoe you like on your feet to trail run, and chances are you will have an enjoyable outing. The simplicity of running is one of its greatest gifts, and trail running is no different.

That said, dozens of trail-specific shoe models are on the market, and they have all been designed to help your feet and body navigate the challenges of the trail. For instance, some shoes are meant to provide increased traction through mud or on wet rocks, whereas other shoes have been made to drain well if they take on water in a stream crossing. Some shoes offer waterproofing technology that can help keep your feet dry and warm while running on a snowy trail. Still other shoes offer protection for the bottom of your feet or the front of your toes in case you step on or kick rocks. Depending on the complexity of the terrain and substrates on which you trail run, you might find that such specialty shoes improve your experience by allowing you to run faster, safer, and with greater confidence that you're going to keep the rubber side down.

As you start trail running, we recommend keeping things simple. Go for a run in a pair of sneakers you have lying around the house—maybe a pair of road running or hiking shoes. If you decide that trail running is up your alley, consider investing in a basic pair of trail shoes. Just as you would when buying athletic shoes, take the time to do your research and try on shoes at the store. First, buy a pair that feels good on your feet. Next, look for shoes that possess some basic trail running features that will improve your performance and confidence. Consider a trail shoe that offers protection to your toes with a toe bumper on the front of the shoe and to the bottom of your feet with a rock plate or extra cushioning. A rock plate is a device embedded in the sole of the shoe that prevents rocks from bumping or bruising the bottoms of your feet. Also, choose a trail shoe with some lugging on the outsole, the bottom of the shoe. This lugging should help you maintain traction on mud, wet rocks, or snow.

Be sure to check out chapter 5, "Trail Tools," to learn more about trail running shoes in much more detail.

Do I Need Special Gear to Trail Run?

Just as with trail shoes, special gear isn't a prerequisite for trail running. You can take your standard athletic apparel on the trails for a 30- to 90-minute run, and as long as the weather isn't extreme, you'll be perfectly happy.

But as with trail shoes, certain pieces of gear can enhance your experience. For example, a hydration pack to carry water, a bit of food, and a jacket will go a long way in making your body happy on a trail run that lasts a few hours. A waterproof jacket can extend your comfort on rainy or snowy days. Some runners find gaiters, which fit on your shoes to keep debris or snow out, a bonus in some conditions. A wrist-top GPS or a map and

A small hydration pack and water bottle aids this runner's trail experience.

compass allow you to venture safely farther into the backcountry. To learn more about various fun-extending gear, check out chapter 5, "Trail Tools."

Do People Run on Trails at Night?

We sure do! In fact, trail running at night can be one of the most enjoyable aspects of our sport. We race at night, too. An appropriate lighting system is necessary for safe night running. Those starting out with night running may want to run in groups of two or more to minimize risk and to share in the experience. Check out chapter 5, "Trail Tools," for an advanced discussion on lighting systems for night running.

How Do I Meet Other Trail Runners?

We think you'll really like getting to know other trail runners and being part of the trail running community. Right now, the sport is in explosion mode. Interest in trail running is increasing in almost every country of the world. With that expanding interest comes the development and growth of robust trail-running communities.

Almost every decent-sized city or metropolitan area has a trail running group or at least an organized running group that spends part of its time on trails. All you need to do is find them. Many trail running groups are active on social media and the internet with a website, Facebook group, or Twitter feed. A quick Google search can link you with them.

A headlamp lights up a night run.

Your local running store will also be a font of community information, as could be your local community or recreation center, gym, yoga studio, or CrossFit box. Many of these health-centered ventures have their own running groups or organize group runs, including trail runs.

Finally, perhaps the easiest place to meet trail runners is at a trail race, which leads to the next question.

How Do I Find Out About Trail Races?

In general, the same places that offer information about trails and trail runners will likely be able to inform you about trail races. Additionally, if the town you live in hosts trail races, the race director will likely advertise with posters on the bulletin boards of coffee shops, outdoor stores, libraries, and community centers.

Online, *Trail Runner* magazine's website has a robust trail-race calendar that provides information on races out of town, out of state, and, sometimes, in other countries. Also, Google is a solid tool for locating the websites of nearby trail races.

You've unearthed the desire to run with dirt underfoot, you've found a pair of shoes that will get you out there, and you've discovered a place to run and perhaps a couple fellow adventurers with whom you'll travel. All the pieces have fallen into place. Don't delay! Go test a piece of singletrack and read on in this book to learn more about how to be your own best trail runner. Let your trail running adventure begin!

MOAB, UTAH, UNITED STATES

Caution! The unusual beauty of the fire-red slickrock surrounding Moab, Utah, will burn itself into your soul. It will captivate your senses and call you back for visit after visit. We, the authors, speak about the slickrock's siren song from personal experience. Once vacationers to the red rocks, we now live here. The red rocks enchant! Located in southeastern Utah at the edge of the mighty Colorado River, what's now Moab has been a home to Native Americans for thousands of years. Now, Moab is largely a tourist town full of folks flocking to the region's unique geology.

Fully surrounding the town is federal land of various kinds, including Arches National Park, Canyonlands National Park, the Manti-La Sal National Forest, and more. What this means is that there are literally millions of acres of protected wildlands and thousands of miles of trails to explore. Out there you will find arches, fins, and towers of rock improbably resisting gravity, miles of road-less terrain in every direction that imparts a sense of solitude little found in America today, all forms of wildlife, and even mountains exceeding 12,000 feet (3,700 m).

Trail runners have discovered Moab and you can enjoy the fruits of their finds. More than a half dozen trail races take place over the course of each year, from one that's just 6.5 miles (11 km) long to a six-day stage race. As locals, we endorse all the trail races around Moab, but we're especially partial to the Moab Red Hot 33 km (Bryon) and 55 km (Meghan) races each February and the Moab Trail Marathon and Half Marathon, which occur in the fall. Their courses don't fail in either their challenge or aesthetic.

(continued)

Moab *(continued)*

If you wish to run instead of race, your singletrack choices are endless. However, may we politely direct you to Canyonlands National Park. Take heed, this is a remote corner of the U.S. so you need to be smart and self-sufficient out there with a map, water, food, appropriate clothing, and more. The trail running you'll do there will transport you into a whole new world.

Proper technique will help you surpass all of the trail's challenges.

Chapter 2

Trail Running Techniques

Running is about as natural an act as we engage in as humans. Whereas you learned to talk and to read, running is something that just came when your body was ready for it. To explain how to run, well, that would be as unnecessary as telling you how to blink or swallow. Instead, you can recall any time you've run to play a sport, to catch the bus, or to follow your child. You know how to run.

At its simplest, trail running need not be any more complicated than that, an act you've done thousands of times. Most trail running, however, requires at least minor adjustments. In this chapter we'll look at those basic modifications. The subsequent two chapters, "Finding Footing" and "Techniques to Match Terrain," will explore variations on the foundational concepts introduced in this chapter.

An Effective Mindset

Before getting to the physical adjustments required to run trails, you need to look at another set of adjustments: the mental ones. If you've long been a road runner, this adjustment might be the most important one you make. On the other hand, if you've previously run only when the situation has called for it, then you're necessarily more accustomed to running the obstacle course that is the world around us.

Be Aware

Let's stop beating around the bush and, instead, observe it. To trail run effectively, you'll need to see the bush, the rock, the downed log, and anything you might encounter from the top of your head to the bottom of your feet. That's not meant to sound overwhelming. You have to be alert when walking around in new and changing environments every day of your life. As your pace increases, however, the consequences of tripping on a stone or running headlong into a branch multiply.

To trail run successfully, you have to be aware of what's around you. Open your eyes and ears and actively take it all in. At the beginning, you should focus, on average, about 20 to 30 feet (7 to 10 m) down the trail. If you have road running experience, this focus might seem too close, but the shorter distance will help reduce the time between when you spot an obstacle and when you have to react to it. If you focus farther out, you'll occasionally start piling up multiple obstacles between when you spot them and when you have to react to them physically.

You should think of those 20 to 30 feet as your average focal point. If you're running a straight, flat trail with few obstacles, your focal length should lengthen. On the other hand, if you're running across a jumble of wet rocks or a tangle of downed branches, you'll bring your gaze in closer. Your speed will similarly cause an adjustment in focal length; the length increases as you run more quickly and have less time to react for a given distance. Physical therapist and trail running coach Joe Uhan suggests, "even when technical terrain has your focus zoomed into the terrain immediately in front of you—as little as 10 to 15 feet (3 to 5 m)—you should still glance up to a 100-foot (30 m) horizon, so your brain has a vague idea of what's coming up."

More generally, you'll find yourself reading the ground ahead of you. In doing so, you'll scan ahead, catch sight of an obstacle, and track it until your glance skips outward again, just as your gaze leaps and refocuses while reading.

Over time, you'll shift to looking for the positives rather than the negatives. That is, your vision will gravitate toward the one or more lines that you can run with the most efficient effort and track those lines more than the obstacles you're trying to avoid. You'll be looking for where you can put your feet rather than where you can't.

(a) If the trail isn't technical, you can set your gaze further out on the trail. *(b)* On rocky, technical terrain, focus your gaze on the obstacles you will encounter in the next several footsteps.

You'll also need to engage your peripheral vision. Catching a bit of motion out of the corner of your eye can alert you to a mountain biker coming around the bend or an animal in the trailside brush. Taking in the broader view will also cue you in on upcoming variations in terrain as well as any nearby streams, cliffs, or roads.

Although your peripheral vision works well, you should also actively glance around at your surroundings for just a few moments every minute or two. This approach will not only further inform you of the terrain, weather, and other potential concerns, but also let you take in the natural beauty that surrounds you, which is, after all, one of the primary benefits of trail running. Of course, you'll only want to take this look around when you're comfortable that you have a corresponding bit of easily negotiated trail for a few seconds longer than the time you take to peek at the scenery.

Over time, as you become more comfortable with trail running and more familiar with a particular trail or type of terrain, you'll find yourself looking farther down the trail as you run. You'll also find yourself being able to be less consciously alert, at least on familiar terrain, as the rhythm and reaction of trail running becomes second nature. You'll find beauty in reaching this point both in your trail running career and on individual runs.

Believe it or not, part of being alert on the trails includes listening. While you're getting into the sport and becoming familiar with what you'll encounter and how often you'll encounter it, lose the headphones on the trails. They're not anathema to the sport by any means, but, depending on where you're running, you'll want to know how often you might encounter other pedestrians, mountains bikers, equestrians, pets, and wildlife that you might be able to hear before you can see. Over time, you'll know when wearing headphones in both ears is appropriate, when you might want to have only one ear bud in, and when you're best off nixing the noise completely.

Be Engaged

Watching and listening to what's going on around you is not enough. You need to take that information and actively process it. We'll get into details on how to deal with various footing and terrain in subsequent chapters, but in all situations you'll want to read changes and adjust your stride and gaze accordingly. If you're engaged, changes in daylight, weather, and other aspects might lead you to change your hydration, your clothing, or even your overall plan for the run.

Because of the constantly changing variables on trails, trail running is a little like the ball sports that require you to be energized and ready to move in any which way, at any moment. Stay engaged.

The flip side of this is that you don't want to be overengaged. If you're nervous or rigid, you're less likely to find the fluidity that helps you negotiate obstacles, tackle variation in terrain, and enjoy trail running overall. In short, be engaged, but not uptight.

Be Prepared

Aside from reading and reacting, being ready for the trails also means being prepared. As we'll describe in later chapters, you may have to plan for bodily needs, weather, and the run itself. For the most part, planning trail running is more significant than planning for a run of comparable distance or duration on the road. A mental shift is needed. You'll be taking care of yourself out there, often with limited access to outside assistance.

An Effective Body

As mentioned at the outset, running is an instinctual act. At its easiest, trail running can be as simple as running on a road, treadmill, or ball field. But even when running slightly more challenging trails (and most are), you will benefit from making some basic adjustments to your gait. As with running in general, given enough time you would instinctually figure out how to adjust your approach in various circumstances. But in this and following chapters, we aim to help you make that process a whole lot less time consuming and less painful. We've even included a couple easy drills here to help you practice a couple of trail running's basic movements.

Pick 'Em Up!

One quick adjustment you can make as a new trail runner to save some unpleasant learning experiences is to pick up your feet a bit higher than you'd expect. The reason is obvious enough. Lifting your feet higher means you're less likely to catch your foot on a rock or root. The extra height usually comes from lifting the knees, rather than kicking your lower leg forward or flexing your ankle to raise your toes.

Now, if you catch yourself prancing like a horse in a dressage competition, you might be taking this concept a bit too far. This extra lift is meant to be a small adjustment to your stride, not a switch to an entirely different gait.

> When trail running, lift your feet just a little higher than you might expect to avoid most obstacles.

As with the adjustments in mental awareness, you'll find yourself gradually transitioning back toward a lower foot swing over time. This adaptation is natural and, from an efficiency standpoint, beneficial. Still, the most experienced trail runners switch to a higher foot swing when low lighting, poor visibility, or other obstructions limit their ability to see their footing.

Pick-Up Game

Head to a yard or park and find half a dozen fallen logs or branches that stick up 3 to 4 inches (8 to 10 cm) when on the ground. Obstructions about 3 feet (1 m) long are ideal so you'll have some width to cross the log or branch, but the item should be light enough to give way easily should you catch your foot. Drop these logs parallel to one another at approximately both arms' length (5 to 6 feet [1.5 to 2 m]) apart on a soft, even surface (grass is perfect). Some variation in distance between the logs is helpful.

The pick-up game helps train you to lift your feet higher to clear trail running's obstacles.

Now, go run the length of this branch-strewn path, crossing the branches. Run it a few times at an easy effort. Run it a few more times, varying your pace and starting point, such that you have to clear the logs at different points in your stride. If you're catching your feet on the branches, adjust your stride by lifting your feet a bit more.

Pick Up the Tempo

In addition to picking up your feet, you'll improve your trail running by picking up your cadence, at least occasionally, without necessarily picking up your pace. With a long, loping stride, you're more committed to your path and less able to react to the obstacles that might be in it. With a shorter, quicker stride, you have many more chances to push off the ground to alter your body's path. Joe Uhan notes that a quick stride also enhances energy conservation: "A quick stride rate allows for instantaneous energy transfer from the ground into the leg, then back to the ground. This quick energy reversal creates a plyometric effect wherein the muscle stores the energy only for an instant before releasing: like a bouncing ball."

You don't need to feel like a hummingbird out there, but modestly picking up your stride rate from 160 strides per minute to 180 strides per minute or more will make you more nimble. Likewise, a runner whose cadence is normally 180 strides per minute will be more agile at 200 strides per minute. This faster cadence is beneficial in a variety of situations, such as when the trail is strewn with obstacles or when obstacles come at you more quickly while running downhill.

According to Uhan, on most flat terrain, 180 strides per minute is ideal: "This allows for maximal energy storage (through a long, strong, hip-driven stride) yet is quick enough to pop off the ground. Any slower and that energy is absorbed by the muscles; too fast and the legs don't achieve maximal range of motion."

Uhan, however, advises a quicker stride rate on climbs and descents: "Upwards of 240 steps per minute might be ideal on the steepest, most technical terrain."

Besides enabling you to pick your way through nature's obstacle course, a quicker turnover is safer and more effective when the running surface becomes loose, uncertain, or slippery. In such circumstances, the smaller you can make your incremental changes in direction and speed, the better off you'll be. That's enough for now, because we'll discuss dealing with poor footing in more depth in the next chapter.

Naturally, you can resume your normal stride rate after the reason for picking it up has passed.

Hot Feet

Grab your shoes, a friend, and a stopwatch and step outside. You can complete this drill without outside assistance if you have a count-down timer with an alarm so that you can focus on counting rather than watching the timer.

Find an open, flat, obstacle-free area where you can easily run up to 200 yards without distraction. Start running at a comfortable pace. After you're up to speed, have your friend say, "Go" as he or she hits start on the stopwatch. When your friend says go, continue running as

Understand and increase your stride rate with the hot-feet drill.

you were, but start counting every time either your right or left foot hits the ground. Have your friend yell, "Stop" after 30 seconds. Multiply the number you counted by four to get your number of strides per minute.

Many folks come in at around 160 strides per minute. If you naturally hit 180 strides per minute, you're in a sweet spot for trail running. If you're much over 200 strides per minute, that's quicker than needed for all but the steepest or most technical terrain.

No matter what your baseline stride rate was, try the drill again with a somewhat faster stride rate but with what feels like the same pace. Note what that feels like. Be ready to make a similar adjustment when a trail becomes more treacherous.

If you have difficulty adjusting to a faster turnover, download a metronome app on your phone and run in time to the beat.

Be Ready

Now that you have your feet moving higher and faster, you need to pay attention to the rest of your body. If you've played a ball sport such as baseball, softball, or tennis, you may remember being told to stand in the ready position. In this position, you were up on your toes, engaging your leg and core muscles, and putting yourself in a position to move as quickly as possible in any direction.

Similarly, trail running requires that you be ready to react in any direction, and you'll need to do so while you're already moving. Therefore, soccer, basketball, lacrosse, and field hockey are more apt analogies. In each of these ball-based team sports, players spend much of their time in motion without the ball. Throughout, the player's body is in a responsive, athletic position.

So how do you get into a ready position for trail running?

Before thinking about how you hold this or where you swing that, you need to engage your core. You'll want to activate your abs, lower back, and even your butt to some degree. This action isn't superficial, as if you are posing for a photo on the beach. You want to firm everything up from the inside out.

To help get a feel for this, imagine that you're surrounded by friends who are going to surprise you at random with pushes at shoulder height. Your goal in this exercise would be to keep standing as upright as possible. What happens? Your entire midsection firms up. It's strong, stable, and able to respond to movement in any direction, just as you want to be able to do while trail running. If this mental exercise has you conjuring up yourself as an immovable mountain, relax, literally. You'll want to be fluid and limber, not rigid, while trail running, but you will use all those muscles that you would use to brace yourself.

Activating your core is a subtle but intentional act. First, your pelvis should be in a neutral position. (A neutral pelvis is explained in depth in

It takes intention and practice to achieve good running form.

"Getting Technical: Powerful Pelvis".) Next, to activate the muscles on the front and the back of your core, draw your belly button in. Do this with your deepest abdominal muscles, not your breath. This might take a little practice, but if you can teach yourself to draw your belly button muscularly back toward your spine an inch (2.5 cm) or so, you will activate your core in a way that will benefit your running.

Although most of your torso should be nearly still as you run, you may notice a bit of rotation in the middle of your back, just below your shoulder blades. During nonreactive running, this location is the rotational pivot point between the movement of your lower body and upper body, which are always swinging in opposing directions. This motion is subtle. Allow it to happen.

Most of the muscles you use in your upper legs during the running motion attach to the bones of your pelvis or vertebral column. For those muscles to do their job, their origin and insertion points—where the muscles attach to bones—must be able to resist the powerful forces placed on them when those muscles are in action. An example of this is the psoas major muscle, a hip flexor. One of its main jobs in the running motion is to lift your knee. The muscle originates in your low back and inserts on your femur, the big bone of your upper leg. When you lift your knee, the psoas major contracts and pulls forcefully on your lower back and femur. In this example, if one side of your core is weakened and cannot hold your low back in its natural position, then the psoas major on that weakened side may have to work harder, opening up your body to injury.

Getting Technical: Powerful Pelvis

The pelvis is the skeletal structure that connects your spine and your legs. The structure is complex, but it's composed primarily of the sacrum and the tailbone, which are the bottom couple of segments of the vertebral column, as well as the two hip bones. To get a feel for the extent of your pelvis, feel for the bones that jut from the front outside edge of your hips. These are the hip bones. Now place one hand on the lowest part of your back in the center, where the crease between your buttocks begins. Underneath your hand is your sacrum and lower down from that is your tail bone.

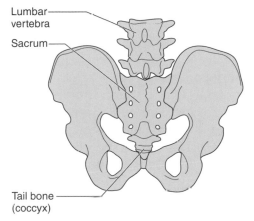

This whole structure needs to remain in a neutral position as you run. Your pelvis can move in almost any direction, but the pelvic motion over which we have the most conscious control is anterior or posterior tilt. A posterior tilt is like tucking your tail as if you are a dog. An anterior tilt is just the opposite, the sticking out of your buttocks. To practice this movement, put your hands on your hips and tilt your pelvis back and forth. Runners often let the pelvis lapse into a posterior tilt when they are fatigued (although a few runners introduce anterior tilt when tired). Too much tilt in either direction while running can create injury.

Structure of a pelvis.

(*a*) Posterior pelvic tilt and (*b*) anterior pelvic tilt.

(continued)

Getting Technical: Powerful Pelvis *(continued)*

    How do you keep your pelvis in a neutral position? It's all in the core, baby! When we say core, we are referencing the soft tissues of your pelvis, low back, and abdominal cavity. The fundamental function of all those muscles is to hold your vertebral column and pelvis in their natural alignment. All the muscles play off each other, sometimes in tandem and sometimes in opposing motion. But the result of the engagement of your core muscles in their natural and balanced way is that the bones in the center part of your body are supported.

    How exactly do you engage the core? The simple act of drawing the belly button in, as previously described, helps you get there. If you draw your belly button back toward your spine muscularly, not with your breath, you will be using one of the deeper abdominal muscles, the transversus abdominis. The transversus abdominis, along with a couple other deeper abdominal muscles, when engaged, will hold the pelvis and vertebrae in their natural positions.

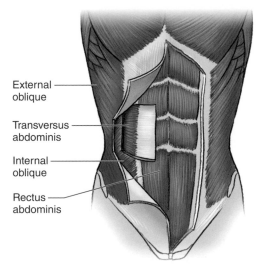

External oblique

Transversus abdominis

Internal oblique

Rectus abdominis

The relative position of the transversus abdominis to other abdominal muscles.

    Engaging the transversus abdominis can be an easy process or a difficult process for someone trying it for the first time. If you're trying this for the first time, lie flat on the ground with your palms on your abdomen below your belly button. Lightly contract the muscles beneath your hands. Use those muscles to draw your belly button back toward your spine, about an inch (2.5 cm) or so for women and perhaps two inches (5 cm) for men. You may instinctually want to use your breath to draw in your belly button. If so, muscularly draw in your belly button as you exhale. Getting the hang of this might take a while, or it may come very easy. If it's a bit of a struggle, practice until it comes naturally. This practice, in relative isolation from the other abdominal muscles, will train your transversus abdominis to engage with all the abdominal muscles to help create your stable core which puts your pelvis into a neutral position, the basis of the runner's ready position.

    In the imaginary bracing exercise discussed earlier, you may have also noticed that many of the muscles in your legs activate as well. These weren't just the major propulsive muscles—the glutes, hamstrings, quadriceps, and calves. You may have noticed the front and side of your hips engaging. Likewise, the outside of both thighs energize. That's great, because these muscles are major players in any lateral movement. Although you might not be able to articulate exactly how it happens, the entirety of your lower legs is ready to go. Each of the muscles in that muscular quiver is ready to fire in whichever direction your feet demand (they're ready to go, too).

Your feet are your interface with the uneven, ever-changing ground around you. If you're a longtime road runner, you might be used to a thought-free foot-on-the-ground transition that varies only with pace and the mild inclines you encounter on pavement. That all changes on the trail. Yes, you'll have a neutral stride to fall back on, but you'll need to be ready both to absorb the constant small tilts, pebbles, trail undulations, and a million other things thrown at your feet and to push off in any direction to adjust your course.

In running on an undulating surface, you'll constantly have to ask different parts of your feet to do different things. For example, say you land on a small rock on your outer forefoot. The outer toes will need to relax and spread out around those rocks, whereas the big toe may need to engage more heavily than usual to support the body's weight. A thousand other scenarios will require a thousand different active reactions from your feet. As such, your feet might feel a little worn out after a trail run. Give your feet the time they need to adapt.

In recent years, the broader running community has been engaged in an intense dialogue, and at times a fanatical debate, about whether runners should first strike the ground with the forefoot, the whole foot (midfoot), or the heel. We'll skip that debate entirely by suggesting that whichever foot-strike pattern you run with, trail running will, at times, necessitate striking the ground with your forefeet first. When? Whenever you feel like you need more agility to negotiate obstacles. You don't want to be caught firmly and decisively back on your heels when you're descending hazardous terrain.

Now, take a step back. When you put the length of your body—your feet through your head—into action, think of standing upright in a straight, unbroken line. Now, take that straight line and bend forward a few degrees from your ankles. That stance is the general body position you'll want to return to as you're trail running.

Focus on the "return to" in the previous sentence. As you negotiate obstacles and oscillations, your legs will go this way and that, while your arms and torso instinctively react as counterbalances. Let this happen. Then bring yourself back into the active, ready position as soon as you can so that you're ready for the next adjustment.

As you run, your torso will stay relatively stable compared with your arms and legs, which will be busily helping your body cover ground. No matter what your arms and legs are doing—and no matter what the terrain is requiring of your body—maintain the gentle forward tilt of your whole body, including your torso, from your ankles. Avoid trying to achieve that tilt by bending at the waist or rolling your shoulders forward.

Whenever your legs and torso move side to side to navigate obstacles, your head automatically recenters itself toward your center of gravity. Likewise, your head instinctively retains upright position relative to the horizon. Let those two reactions work as they do. Don't feel as if your head needs to be mounted atop your spine with a metal rod. Like your torso, your head should and will return to a neutral position in a line down through your spine, pelvis, and beyond after you've cleared the obstacles at hand.

As for the horizontal aspect of your head, you'll generally want your head and chin upright. Adjust your gaze by tracking with your eyesight rather than adjusting the angle of your head. Tilting your head forward a bit in the diciest of sections is OK if doing so allows you a better look. If you do this, tilt your head forward from the top of your spine rather than droop from your shoulders or torso.

As your torso reacts to keep your center of balance over your feet, your arms move about to maintain your balance. Most of the time, you'll want to keep your arms at your sides, bent 90 degrees at the elbow, swinging back and forth in a relaxed manner. Generally, put as much effort into the back swing as you do the forward swing. Keep those arms relaxed so that they can aid you in balancing as needed. You'll often see experienced trail runners carrying their arms a little higher and a little wider as they descend difficult terrain so that the arms can react quickly to counterbalance the

In navigating obstacles, the head stays upright and the feet seek landing spots while the arms counterbalance.

movement of their legs and torso even more quickly. We'll get more into this topic in chapter 4.

Be aware that as you tire you might start to hunch your shoulders. This posture breakdown will impede your ability to use your arms to balance. If you catch yourself doing this, remember to keep your torso tall and your shoulders back.

Walk the Walk

It's OK to walk. Yes, you read that correctly. Here's a running guide that gives you permission to walk. If something feels too steep or rocky or muddy or whatever to run, walk it out. Sometimes slowing yourself down is the most efficient, not to mention most prudent, means of covering a given stretch of ground.

Although walking is all good, so is testing your limits, whether you're out on one of your first trail runs or three decades into hitting the dirt. You'll often find that what you once thought was unrunnable has become a new running playground. This transformation is one of the gifts of trail running.

So you're running down the roads of your neighborhood when you decide to turn down that path you've seen countless times but have never explored. You look ahead at the trail before you. It's not much different from the road you were just running except that it's dirt rather than asphalt.

As you enter the forest, you start to see tree roots stretching across the trail. Don't worry; you've already started picking up your feet a bit more than usual and you easily clear the roots.

A few minutes later, you notice the trail is studded with a constellation of tennis-ball-sized rocks. As you approach, you follow them in with your gaze and easily pick your way through with a stride rate that has naturally quickened. Your pace now quickens a bit, too, as you find yourself descending. The rocks grow in size, but decrease in frequency. With your active body position, you find yourself playfully ricocheting side-to-side down the trail as you deftly maneuver around the rockstacles. You land on your forefeet gently but quickly, padding the earth almost silently.

Half an hour later, you are cruising down some buffed-out singletrack when . . . Boom! The next thing you know, you're on the ground, hands stretched out in front of you superman style. You pause for a moment, pick yourself up, brush yourself off, and carry on. No matter how aware, engaged, and well adjusted physically you are for trail running, you will fall. It's OK. (You'll learn more about how to minimize injury when falling in chapter 10, "Trail Safety and Stewardship.")

The trail pitches down, and you pick up the pace. Off to the right, you catch a flicker of light. You listen carefully as you continue running. Noise comes from that direction, and it's getting louder. Your senses heighten.

A moment later a mountain bike whips around a turn 15 yards in front of you. You sense an opening in the brush on your left and quickly step off the trail, giving the rider a friendly nod as she carries on. So do you.

A few minutes later you're back on the roads of your neighborhood. You look to the right at the expanse of trees. Instead of seeing a tangle from which deer can dart in front of your car, you see a vast playground to explore. Congratulations: You're a trail runner!

APPALACHIAN TRAIL, EASTERN UNITED STATES

Spanning 2,180 miles (4,520 km) between Maine and Georgia in the eastern United States, the Appalachian Trail (AT) runs through its namesake mountain range. If one word can collectively describe those several thousand miles of trails, it would be diversity. From the thick deciduous forests of the south end of the trail to the high, treeless balds over which the trail travels in North Carolina and Virginia, from the remote, rocky terrain of New England to places where the trail passes very close to civilization, the AT has all this and more. Although most famous for its thru-hikers, those who travel the entire distance of the trail in a multimonth trip, the vast majority of those who use the AT are day trippers who tackle short sections of the trail, including many trail runners.

If you're looking for a race on the AT, you'll find just one, the JFK 50-Mile Run, which occurs in November each year in Maryland. Some of the early miles of the race are run on the trail. The National Park Service, the federal agency responsible for protecting the trail, generally disallows racing on the AT—with the exception of this one race that is grandfathered in because of its half-century-long existence—to help preserve the peaceful and wild nature of the trail.

But that's good news for trail running adventurers. Nearly 2,200 miles of secluded singletrack await along with even more miles of side trails running off the AT over its entire length. Although it's impossible to go wrong with any trail run that's on or incorporates the AT, a couple of emblematic destinations are where the AT traverses the rocky terrain above tree line in New Hampshire's White Mountains and the trail over the grassy balds of Great Smoky Mountains National Park in Tennessee and North Carolina.

High alpine meadows melt out late in Colorado's San Juan Mountains.

Chapter 3

Finding Footing

Now that you've learned the basics of trail running technique in chapter 2, you are ready to embrace change—the changing surface under your feet, that is. One of the joys of trail running is the stimulus it provides to both the body and the mind. One source of this stimulus is the trail itself or, rather, the surface that the trail is made of. Depending on when and where you run, you might run over compacted dirt, loose sand, sloppy mud, wet rocks, deep snow, or slick ice. In fact, you may encounter many of these conditions, along with others, in a single run.

> Each type of trail surface reacts differently under your feet. As you trail run, you'll get to know what is required of your body to negotiate various surfaces.

As you change from one surface to the next, you'll want to adapt your stride and approach accordingly. This chapter explains when and how to do so.

A runner cruises hard-packed trails in Sonoma, California.

Terra Firma: Hard-Packed Dirt Trails

Trail runners will often find themselves running on relatively even, firm, dirt trails not dissimilar to paths worn through the grass in a park or on a school campus. If measured, the surface is softer than asphalt or cement, but there's no noticeable give underfoot. The trail is firmly compacted, meaning that when you brush your hand over the trail, little to no debris slips across the surface.

This surface is about the easiest on which a trail runner can trod. You could easily enough just turn off your brain and run. But you'll still want use those trail running basics you learned in chapter 2. Be alert, be engaged, and be in a position from which you can react quickly. The most experienced trail runners will tell you that most of their falls aren't on the gnarliest bits of singletrack. Instead, they fall when they relax their concentration on the easy stuff and the smallest of obstacles takes them down.

That said, if you have long stretches of well-packed, low-obstacle trail, you can aim to be a bit more efficient. If you're coming from a road running background, you can move close to the gait you're used to. For example, you can lower your foot swing a bit, so long as you're ready to pick up your feet a bit higher when you next approach an obstacle. Likewise, you might relax your arms and shoulders while you try to use as little unnecessary energy as possible.

Squamish, British Columbia has famously plush forest trails.

Holy Grails: Soft Dirt Trails

Somewhere out there lies trail nirvana—an endless singletrack spider web, soft and smooth. These buttery, buffed-out bonanzas are most often found in the forest, particularly conifer forests. Their gift? To give ever so slightly with each step while not noticeably sapping energy.

Like the hard-packed paths mentioned earlier, these tempting trails call for basic trail running technique. But the possibility of variable underfoot give from one footfall to the next requires a bit more overall engagement from head to toe.

Although not meant to be the defining characteristics of this section, the fact that these trails are most often found in conifer forests warrants two cautions. First, if you're running through a forest, you'll likely encounter roots, possibly quite a few of them. You'll learn how to approach these and other foot-level obstacles later in this chapter. Second, you may find pine needles or loose soil on the surface of the trail. Keep reading to find out how to deal with loose trail surfaces.

Volcanic pumice yields to each footfall on Spain's Canary islands.

Slip Slidin' Away: Loose Surfaces

Just like a bag of marbles emptied on a wooden floor, any loose material that can roll atop the surface of a trail can cause your feet to slide beneath you. Among the plethora of particles that can lubricate your landings are dust, loose dirt, pebbles and gravel, pine needles, pine cones, and many other items.

Although each such surface may behave slightly differently, the same general principles apply to all of them. In fact, what you learn in this section applies in large part to all slippery surfaces, such as mud, ice, and wet rock. Pay attention, because this is one of the key lessons in this book.

Minimize Sudden Moves

The most important thing to remember when running on slippery surfaces is to minimize sudden moves. The best way to do this is to be observant and to change your direction or speed gradually. If you don't do so, you and your foot will tend to continue traveling in the direction you're moving, just as a car continues in the direction it's been traveling when it hits an icy patch of road at too fast a speed. But a car traveling smoothly through a turn at 15 miles per hour (24 kph) is much more likely to retain enough traction to avoid careening off the road than one traveling at 45 miles per hour (72 kph) or another car traveling much slower but making an abrupt turn. When asked how to maximize traction, 2015 Scottish Hill Running champion Tom Owens said quite simply, "Straight line it." That's certainly one way to minimize sudden moves!

Travel at a Safe Speed

If you're ever feeling out of control or otherwise unsafe on a slippery sub-strate—be it a loose surface, mud, wet rock, ice, or something else—your default option is to slow down. You might downshift from a run to a jog or from an easy running pace to a walk. Yes, you should cautiously test your skills and limits from time to time, but in general, slower is safer.

If you do continue running on a slippery surface, travel at a speed at which you can maintain solid contact with the trail. Just as cars going too fast or too slow on slippery roads will be unable to maintain their course because of lost traction, there's a near-perfect speed for trail running on slippery surfaces. You will find that each surface is different, however, and you will need time and testing to find your right speed on these variable surfaces. Avoid slowing down or speeding up too rapidly, because doing so is a recipe for a fall. Again, remember that you can walk as needed.

Brake With Caution

If you have to turn or brake quickly on a loose section of trail, try to plant your whole foot evenly on landing and while applying pressure. If you contact the ground solely with your toes or your heels, you're applying pressure over a smaller surface area than if you apply that pressure with your whole foot.

Land Whole Footed

Landing with your whole foot will also help you add a more vertical component to your footfall than usual (see figure 3.4). Horizontal motion is the real culprit when you keep sliding on a slick surface. Accordingly, you want to minimize the horizontal component of your footfall. When running on a slippery surface, you might add a little prance to your trail running stride. Take care to generate this action via knee lift rather than adding vertical motion above your waist.

In such situations, you might also want to experiment with a faster cadence, as described in chapter 2. A faster cadence will give you more steps per length of trail and, therefore, allow you to make smaller incremental adjustments as you turn or brake. You can also think about planting your foot under your center of gravity. This technique will help prevent over-striding, when your foot falls in front of your body, bringing the dangerous, horizontal-motion component into play.

Anton Krupicka, two-time winner of the Leadville Trail 100-Mile Run in Colorado, is no stranger to tackling uncertain footing:

"In order to maintain traction on the variable surface that a trail provides, I find it best to run with a short, quick stride where each foot plant is landing roughly under my center of gravity and on my midfoot. By doing this, I'm never 100 percent committing all of my body weight and momentum

When landing on potentially slippery surfaces, try to hit the ground with your whole foot.

to any one footfall, so if that surface or foot plant ends up being unstable I can quickly shift my weight onto the next foot. Running with these less-committing strides lets me respond instantaneously to the trail surface."

If you do start to slide, go with it. Ride it until your other foot is able to swing forward for your next footfall. Your instinct to correct your motion will be to push against the motion, but that only further sends your foot in the errant direction. Your instinct will also be to raise your arms for balance amidst the slide. This reaction can help you stay upright until you can get your other foot back on the ground.

Life's a Beach: Sandy Trails

A little dust on the trail is one thing, but running on sand is something completely different. What's more, you might find yourself running on a huge variety of sandy surfaces.

The most benign sandy trails will be firmly compacted. You can run them more or less like the hard-packed trails described at the start of the chapter. The caveat is that sections of well-compacted sandy trails are likely to have areas with enough loose sand to warrant an approach outlined in the preceding section for when a small amount of debris reduces traction.

Running on Loose Sand

If the sand isn't cemented together yet it's moderately compacted, you'll notice some give underfoot as soon as you hit it. This sand may slip if you try to turn or stop quickly. If you're likely to run on this type of loose, sandy

The Sahara Desert's loose, shifting sand will challenge runners to adjust their technique.

surface for very long, test how well the ground holds together underfoot with such actions and act accordingly. If you're running quickly or running uphill, you might notice the toe of your shoes digging into the sand each time you toe off. There's nothing particularly wrong with or perilous about this. In fact, you should just go for it if you're charging up a short, steep, sandy hill.

But if you'll be running on this soft sand for a long time, especially if you're new to this type of surface, you'll want to adjust your footfall. That sand giving way under the front of your foot wastes energy and is an invitation for sore calves, Achilles tendons, and more. As with slippery surfaces, you'll again aim to have a flatter footfall than usual. You do this not so much for traction as for flotation. You want to maximize the surface area of your shoe's outsole and thus minimize sinking, just as you would use snowshoes to float on snow. Focusing on planting your feet under your center of gravity can help flatten your footfall. One nice thing about the sandy surface is that you have instant visual feedback on whether your adjustment is working based on whether that toe-off divot has shrunk or not. Be aware that you will be slower and will tire more quickly when running on a surface like this. That's normal.

Now, imagine that you're running on a sand dune, or at least trying to. Depending on where you run, you might encounter similar stretches. Heck, you could even seek out a run across the dunes the next time you're at the beach or you travel to a dune-filled desert. Away from the beach proper, this sand becomes windblown, and running through it is often difficult because it readily gives way underfoot. To run efficiently on flat stretches of extremely soft sand, you'll again want to adapt to a more up-and-down, whole-foot landing. If you look back and see much of a toe divot, you're wasting energy. When ascending, you'll want to focus even more on having your foot hit the ground parallel to the surface of the sand. If the sand has any sort of crust or cohesion, you might be able to scoot up the climb this way. That said, if you've got a short climb on sand, sometimes it's best just to put your head down (figuratively), dig your toes in, and power up the hill. On the other hand, running down a trail or bank of unconsolidated sand is a simple joy. It's one of those times that you can let your guard down and just play. Using an aggressive heel strike is fine (good luck doing much else), because the sand will give enough to absorb the shock.

Running on Wet Sand

Wet sand can act like anything from the most compacted to the loosest of sands. You'll find out what sort of sand you're dealing with after stepping on it. At one extreme, think of the breakwater along many ocean beaches. Along the edge of the water, the surface is firm to slightly yielding, and you can run on it as if you were in a grassy yard. At the other end, firm-looking damp sand might turn out to be an aqueous sludge that easily parts below your feet, quicksand style. If the latter happens and running becomes impossible, just laugh as you walk through it.

Sticks and Stones: Obstacle-Strewn Trails

Although this chapter has so far discussed the primary trail surface, we need to change directions for a minute, both literally and figuratively, and discuss how to tackle trails strewn with obstacles such as rocks and roots, secondary objects you'll need to get safely around. While trail running, you should always be aware of and prepared for obstacles on the trail, but on some trail sections, obstacles will be frequent and significant factors.

The more obstacle filled the trail is, the more important it is to be aware, engaged, and in the active body position outlined in chapter 2. You want to be able to go both over low objects and around taller objects.

Low-Lying Obstacles

On trails with lots of low obstacles like roots and small stones, raise your feet a bit higher than you do when running on obstacle-free trails. At the same time, be ready to step even higher as needed. Often, the best approach is to try to clear an obstacle in the middle of your stride, when your lead foot is naturally at its highest. To do this, you'll likely have to adjust the length of your preceding couple of strides so that only a small shortening or lengthening of your stride is necessary on the crucial step.

Sometimes, the best way to clear a low trail obstacle is to step on it. You may be able to add efficiency by carrying on in a straight line without altering your stride length or speed by turning an object like a stone into a stepping-stone. For obstacles likely to provide good traction on a stable surface, you can often land with most of your weight on the object. You should usually land with your forefoot on the object so that you can react more quickly if it moves or doesn't provide sufficient traction. The same applies if you're landing on a small object. If the object might be either slippery or unstable, touch down on the object quickly and softly. Treat this step as a way to keep the rhythm of your stride intact without relying on the obstacle for significant propulsion or weight bearing. However adequate an obstacle might be for landing on, it's still best to exercise some caution by not aggressively pushing off it.

Weaving Between Obstacles

Higher obstacles or the desire for a more obstacle-free path might call for you to weave among the obstacles. If this is the case, you should be scanning the trail ahead, looking for the best route more than one obstacle in advance. If the trail surface isn't slippery, you can weave about at will so long as you can find a spot to plant your feet firmly. This running technique can be one of the great joys of trail running after you get the hang of it. If you're looking to be most efficient, try to minimize sudden lateral movements and generally maintain a straighter course. Regardless of whether you take the playful or practical option, you'll want to be up on your toes with the outsides of your legs feeling energized so that you're ready for the next side-to-side movement.

If you're aiming for efficiency, keep your torso laterally upright and moving forward down the trail in as straight a line as possible. Your feet and legs can be dancing off to your right and left while your center of gravity continues moving forward without pause or deviation.

Don't forget you can use the lateral plane to move around obstacles.

Heads Up!

Finally, keep your eyes peeled for high obstacles like tree branches and rock overhangs that you'll need to duck under or around to pass. Because these sorts of obstacles are uncommon, we trail runners sometimes neglect to watch for them. Almost every longtime trail runner has a story about a painful brush with some sort of high obstacle. Although your attention might be focused on obstacles near your feet, use your peripheral vision and regularly glance up to scan the trail ahead for higher issues if you are in the forest or on closed-in terrain with rock exposure. When pushing through areas of tall, thick brush, you can either alternately use your hands to push away the brush from side to side or elevate one forearm parallel to the ground at eye level to act as a blocker to protect your face.

Getting Dirty: Muddy Trails

More than any mountain or forest, the image of a mud splash is probably most evocative of trail running. In some places, muddy trails are inevitable almost daily whereas they're a rare occurrence elsewhere. Still, running on mud is a basic trail running skill that you should have in your arsenal.

Heavily lugged shoes can aid greatly while running in the mud, but they have their drawbacks, as well. They'll be discussed separately when we tackle gear in chapter 5.

Before jumping into a discussion of appropriate techniques for running on mud, note that important ethical considerations are involved in when, where, and how you run if the trails are muddy. We encourage you to read "Dirty Politics: The Ethics of Muddy Trails" so that you're aware of the effects you have on muddy trails and ways to minimize them.

Learn to move efficiently through mud to prevent slips, falls, and frustration.

After a good, soaking rain, your trails might be covered in garden-variety mud. Anywhere from a fraction of an inch to an inch (up to 2.5 cm) of gloppy mud could cover the trail, and the ground as a whole will have more give than normal. Just as when you encounter loose debris on top of the trail, you'll want to moderate your sudden adjustments when running on mud, whether you are moving laterally, braking, or accelerating.

Less mud can mean less traction. Such can be the case when you encounter a thin coating of mud on hard-packed dirt. That thin layer of mud is like grease on tile floor; it doesn't take much to reduce traction to nothing. What's more, even the luggiest rubber-soled shoes won't bite into the ground because of the hard pack directly under the thin mud layer. You need to exercise a great deal of caution when traversing such sections. Don't act quickly when changing direction or stopping. Pick up your cadence so that you can make additional and, therefore, smaller adjustments as needed. You can either stay up on your forefeet in a ready position or land whole footed. With either style, but especially with the latter, try to contact the ground with light feet—just tapping and going. Add more of a vertical component to your footfall and more lift than normal. In this scenario, you definitely want to avoid a heel-striking stride.

More mud means more problems. Sometimes you'll encounter progress-stopping, shoe-sucking mud. It can act like shifting sand, except that it grabs onto your feet and holds tight. The best advice for this type of mud? Avoid it. (Refer to "Dirty Politics" for information on when you should or shouldn't run through a muddy stretch of trail.) If you can't avoid it, concentrate on landing with your whole foot simultaneously flat against the ground. As with running on sand, you do this primarily to increase flotation rather than to improve traction. Tread softly and quickly to minimize how far you sink in. If you do find yourself getting stuck, drive your legs forward and exaggerate your arm swing for a little more oomph. If your feet are getting stuck in deep, shoe-sucking mud, you can try pointing the toe of your stuck foot while driving ahead with your other foot.

If you're wearing lugged shoes, you might build up some mud in the tread. Even if the mud makes your shoes a bit heavier, taking the time to stop and clean off the mud is rarely worth it. That said, if the mud has clogged up your shoes' lugs to the point that you've got comically bad traction (and an extra half pound per foot in mud weight), it might be time to clean the bulk of the mud out.

If you find yourself in something more closely resembling a bog than a trail, perhaps it's time to stop and walk. We'll tackle water crossings in the next chapter.

Dirty Politics: The Ethics of Muddy Trails

Oh, the muddy waters of running on muddy trails. Yes, countless advertisements, articles, and inspiring videos prominently feature imagery of people splashing down muddy trails. But that kind of running is not always the right thing to do.

If heavy rains, snowmelt, or a major thaw means that a significant portion of your planned run will be on muddy trails, simply choose another route. You will damage the trail if you run on it by unnaturally displacing or removing the trail substrate. This damage self-reinforces by collecting and holding water. The sloppier the trail is and the more people who pass over a muddy stretch of trail, the more damage occurs. Good trail ethics begin with each person making the right call every time.

But that's not to say you can never trail run when it rains. Hardly. Many trail systems drain incredibly well. Other trail systems are packed hard enough that clear water pools on top and the ground remains firm under foot. Dirt roads and doubletrack (parallel trails that are, in fact, tire tracks) are also fair game. If any of these situations apply, run on.

At times when you come upon muddy singletrack, it's appropriate to carry on. For example, you may encounter a few short, muddy sections on a trail that is 99 percent mud free, or the trail may have brief muddy stretches where it transitions to snow and back to dry trail. In both examples, a vast majority of the trail is mud free. Trail races are almost always held rain or shine, whether the trails are bone dry or muddy slop fests. In these cases, the organizer decides whether holding the race is the right call. For a multitude of reasons, we should all hope that the race organizer mitigates any negative effects the race may have on the trails on which it's run.

Likewise, at times you may honestly think that a trail will be runnable, but it turns out to be muddier than expected, and you're not reasonably able to backtrack to avoid causing damage. This happens. It's OK. If anything, ponder the conditions and signs leading to the mud so that you can better avoid damaging a trail in the future.

If you do encounter mud, mitigate the damage you cause. If the existing trail is wide and you can avoid the mud while staying entirely on the trail, go for it. But if the mud spans the entire trail, go straight through the middle of mud. Do not go off the trail to avoid the mud, because doing so will widen the trail without resolving the underlying problem. The same holds true in avoiding standing water on a hard-packed trail. Stay on the trail!

Increasingly, trailheads signs, community websites, and trail-user forums issue guidance on trail use in muddy conditions. When available, please refer to these resources and adhere to their advice.

On the other hand, in some waterlogged communities slogging through mud is accepted practice. Indeed, in such places the trails might never be suitable for running if held to general standards. Think of the United Kingdom or the wetter areas of the Pacific Northwest. When in doubt, ask a local.

Steep terrain can often mean rocky trails.

Rockin' It: Rocky Trails

Rocks are trail running's box of chocolates; you never know what you're going to get. OK, that's only true in that the huge variety of rocks out there all offer their own flavor of traction. Some rocks are extremely grippy under all conditions. Others offer adequate traction when dry but might as well be banana peels in a comic book when wet. And some rocks never offer enough traction to be trusted.

The best advice for running on rocky surfaces—be it the endless slickrock outside Moab, Utah, a talus pathway over an alpine pass, or a trail in the Appalachian Mountains that's got more rock than dirt for tread—is never to trust the rocks until you've tried them under similar conditions. The marble floor of a grand public building is a worry-free luxury on a sunny day. If you visit on a rainy day, however, the lobby is likely to be filled with freshly unfurled carpets and signs cautioning you to watch your step, because the marble is slippery when wet.

When running on rock or a trail that requires you to step on stones, you can minimize the risk of slipping by looking for places where the exposed rock is generally flat and aiming your footfalls there, if possible. That said, a little bit of surface variation can help with traction. If you have doubts about the grippiness of a rock, avoid landing on rock surfaces slanting in the direction that you're traveling. Whether you strike with your forefoot or your whole foot is a matter of personal taste, but you should make quick, light steps with an increased cadence. Touch down and lift off right away.

Don't let this talk of slipping keep you from running on rocky terrain. Rocky travel offers playful, adventurous, and challenging opportunities. Sometimes you'll find that the rock over which you're traveling offers incredible grip, better than any other trail surface, even if the rocks are angled steeply in different directions. Using your increased traction to run up and down very steep pitches is amazing fun. In other words, rock play rocks!

Hidden Obstacles

What can you do when grass, brush, dry leaves, or another obscurer prevents you from seeing the trail surface? Keep on running! But do so with caution, and possibly a bit slower. Remember the kinds of obstacles you've encountered in the preceding minutes and how frequently you encountered them. In addition, try to read the clues from the surrounding terrain. If a big tree of a species that tends to have large, exposed roots is growing right next to the trail, adjust your stride to account for these obstacles. Likewise, if you're running below a cliff face that ends in a talus slope, prepare to encounter rocks.

If obstacles have been infrequent or low to the ground, you can slow your pace while lowering your stride to a "worm-burner" motion that feels more horizontal than vertical. This technique allows you to kick up against any low obstacles rather than land unpredictably atop an uneven or unstable

Fallen leaves can mean tricky running.

one, possibly leading to a sprained ankle or fall. One way to visualize this stride is to think of a thin covering of dry leaves on the ground and try to swish through those leaves continuously with your feet. An alternative to the worm-burner method is to increase your stride rate, land delicately, and be ready to react immediately to what happens underfoot. You should experiment and find which method works best for you.

If you encounter a section that presents frequent, high obstacles, your best bet is to walk until you have a better view of your footing.

Water and mud can also obscure underlying footing. If you encounter shallow puddles or mud patches, you should adhere to the general advice given earlier about running on concealed trails (as well as the advice on mud running). If you've come to a full-scale water crossing, you can find advice on how to tackle that in chapter 4.

Snow can also hide what you trod upon. We talk more about that in the following section.

Winter Wonderland: Wintry Trails

Winter trail running can be magical. It's quieter. Fewer people are on the trails. The transformed landscape provides new challenges. Let's see how you should tackle some of those challenges.

While it can be slower going, snow can enhance the silence and stillness of the trails.

For starters, if your trails aren't snow covered and it's below freezing, you're likely to encounter more hard-packed trail than usual. If they're damp when temperatures drop, normally soft trails and even sandy trails can firm up. This harder surface can make them faster to run than usual, although at the cost of a bit more pounding. Occasionally, a soft trail with good grip can become a bit more slippery if it freezes up with a little loose debris on top.

Freeze and thaw cycles can sometimes leave the surface of a trail honeycombed. This frozen lattice might be an inch or two thick at times. Such stretches are rarely very long. The most notable attribute of this footing is that it will intermittently collapse underfoot. You're not in any danger, but you should be prepared to drop perhaps an inch more than expected, so keep your legs and core engaged and be ready to balance things out with your arms.

Let It Snow!

Oh, snow! The Inuits have myriad words for it, and, as a trail runner, you'll find that there are, in fact, countless kinds of snow and that each reacts differently under your feet. By its very nature, snow also obscures what lies below, thus adding additional complexity. Nevertheless, if you can learn just a few techniques, you can unlock a winter wonderland.

The biggest issues with shallow snow, from a trace to half a foot (15 cm), are the possibilities of slipping and of encountering obscured obstacles. When snow makes the trail very slippery, you should focus, of course, on not slipping. Use a more vertical footfall and land more on your whole foot. Have your core engaged and your arms ready to react. On the other hand, if the snow only minimally hampers traction, go into obstacle-protection mode. In snow up to a couple inches, you should be able to pick up clues about the location of snow-covered obstacles and pick your way around them. As the snow gets thick enough to obscure small obstacles, try landing with a flat footfall to provide some extra flotation so that you sink slightly less deeply into the snow. This method will help keep you above the small deviations and obstacles that you can no longer see. Regardless, continue landing quickly and carefully while remaining mentally engaged so that you can react quickly should you land in a less-than-ideal spot. You should still be able to see larger rocks and roots so that you can maneuver appropriately.

Running trails in the winter provides a completely new set of footing challenges. But practice makes perfect, and you'll soon get the hang of what snow feels like underfoot.

As the snow deepens, pay attention to how much the snow packs down. Dense snow, which may seem heavy or wet, better retains the shape of underlying objects and retains more of its original volume when compressed. This type of snow makes for easier travel because you're better able to see larger obstacles, and the snow quickly compacts to enough depth that you can simply run over smaller obstacles. As a bonus, heavier snow can compact on itself in a way that provides excellent traction.

Now, a foot (30 cm) of champagne powder? What is a gift to a skier can challenge the most adept trail runner. The light-as-air snow drifts with the wind and can easily obscure objects on the trail. It also compacts to next to nothing, such that a foot of snow can be less than an inch of snow after you've planted your foot on it. That means you can't see obstacles, and the snow doesn't do much to smooth out the underlying trail. This is a time to be cautious. If you know the trail and it's free of larger obstacles, you can run with a more-or-less normal stride. When larger obstacles are more likely,

Staying on Top: How to Avoid Postholing

At times, especially as winter nears spring and the snow goes through freeze and thaw cycles, a crust will develop on the snow. If you're fortunate, that crust will be thick enough that you can run over the snow as if it were solid ground—almost. You might be running along for 10 yards (m) or 10 miles (16 km) when, bam, your foot crashes through the crust and your leg sinks ankle, shin, knee, or even waist deep in the snow. Welcome to the "posthole," a funny and sometimes frustrating experience that most adventurous trail runners have at one time or another. If your foot hasn't sunk too deeply and the crust isn't too thick, you may be able to remove the sunken foot and accelerate it quickly enough to catch yourself with nothing more than an awkward stride or two. If you sink deeply or the crust is hard, you're likely to be stopped in your tracks with your torso lurching forward. The good news is that you're on snow, which should minimize the damage. If you've gone in really deep, have a good laugh and maybe snap a photo before extricating yourself.

The chances of postholing can be minimized by landing with your whole foot at once as well as by wearing shoes with larger outsole surface area to increase flotation marginally. It sounds silly, but every little bit helps. To be prepared for a posthole, keep your arms ready to react and consciously remind yourself to be ready to transfer weight quickly away from a foot that's postholing, as well as to accelerate that foot forward to help keep you moving. If the snow is deep enough that you might be postholing, wear high socks or long pants because the rough edges of crusty snow can make postholing painful for exposed skin.

One of the gifts of wintertime can be the smoothing out of uneven trails. In places where snow is copious and enough folks are willing to pack it down, the toughest of trails can become significantly easier and possibly faster in wintertime because snow temporarily eliminates obstacles that would normally need to be negotiated. Still, when running on what looks like densely packed snow, you should stay aware of the possibility of postholing. Staying to the center of the trail, where the snow is likely to be packed the densest, should also help lessen the risk of postholing.

slow your pace and shuffle your feet along the ground. Yes, you might kick the occasional rock, but that's far better than unpredictably landing on one.

The diehard trail runners and winter lovers out there might be tempted to hit the trail in a foot and a half to three feet (45 to 90 cm) of snow. In reality, a run in such conditions quickly turns into a hike. Whether you're boldly taking on such challenges or merely having a chance encounter with a snowdrift, adapt to what works best in the moment. In wet, heavy snow, you might need to high-step through the snow with foot lifts and footfalls that have a greatly exaggerated vertical component. You might find that you need to swing your leg out to the side over the snow, possibly even leaning your torso in the other direction to get enough lift to clear the snow. On the other hand, deep tracts of light, dry snow may warrant driving your legs straight forward with maybe a little extra lifting of your feet. In either case, you should drive your arms as needed to aid in propulsion.

Snowshoes can open up trail running terrain in the winter. You can even trail run in them, as long as the trail is well packed or you're on groomed snow such as a Nordic ski trail. (Check whether this is permitted on the trail you want to use first.) If you'll be on virgin powder or crusty snow, snowshoes can get you out there, but there's unlikely to be much running involved. The finer points of snowshoeing are beyond the scope of this book.

Ice Dancing

Wintry conditions also conjure images of slipping and falling. Besides dealing with the hazard provided by snow, you'll have to watch out for ice and mud. Ice can be found where snow has glazed over, where frozen rain has fallen, and where water has pooled and frozen. The inherent danger of running on ice should be obvious—it's slippery as anything. You can easily end up on your butt by irreverently running on ice. However, with good technique, some confidence, and some practice, you can run reasonably safely on ice.

As with any slippery situation, you want to minimize making sudden moves. This desire is greatly amplified on ice to the point that you want to eliminate rapid reactions. Aim for vertical footfalls, because any horizontal component to your footfall is likely to continue sliding outward. You'll want to make quick, light contact with the ground under your body with a rapid rebound. Long, committed foot plants are an invitation to slip and fall. You can also quicken your cadence, which will not only help to shorten your stride but also put you in a rhythm that allows you to take the next step even more quickly should your foot start to slide. Keep your body in rapid-reaction mode so that you can quickly take another step, throw your arms out for balance, or prepare for an imminent fall. Obviously, slowing down can reduce your chances of slipping.

If you're uncomfortable with running on ice or a particular stretch of it, don't! It's OK to walk, and traversing ice can be an entirely appropriate time to do so, especially when you have to ascend or descend on ice. Err on the side of caution here.

Although most ice on the trail will be readily apparent, you may occasionally encounter "brown ice," the trail equivalent to unseen "black ice" that you can come across on asphalt roads. Your best bets for spotting brown ice are to look for a glare or unexpected color change on the trail's surface. Run on it as you would on other ice.

A thin layer of mud on a frozen base can be as slippery and as treacherous as ice. This condition occurs during thaws when the surface layer is melting while the underlying ground remains frozen. Run on it as you would run on a layer of mud on hard-packed trails as described previously in "Getting Dirty: Muddy Trails."

Although the previous sections may have prepared you for individual wintry conditions, you're likely to have runs in which you encounter two or more flavors of frigid trail. Observe how they transition and interact so that you can prepare yourself as you move from one to the next. You can try a number of methods for improving traction in wintry conditions, from putting screws in the bottom of your shoes to wearing slip-on, over-shoe traction devices, which we'll discuss in chapter 5, "Trail Tools."

ZEGAMA-AIZKORRI MARATHON, BASQUE COUNTRY, SPAIN

Picture this: a trail coursing through beech forest and grassy meadows, up and over several peaks and ridges made of white rock exposed in uber-technical fashion, and wildflowers thickly lining the singletrack, along with a start and finish perched in the center of an idyllic mountain village. Sounds like a fair number of trail races, right?

Then, add in bad weather like heavy rain, high winds, and dense fog, which always seem to be the prevailing race-day conditions at this particular event. Yep, many races have bad weather, too.

Now, imagine thousands of fans lining the entire course, start to finish, even the highest, most exposed sections and even if the weather is terrible. And imagine those fans partying all afternoon and night after the race, often until the sun rises the next day. Trail racing is a niche sport, and the raging fan culture seen in sports like American and European football is almost entirely undeveloped in this one. Except in Spain's Basque Country each May at the Zegama-Aizkorri Marathon.

Indeed, racing the Zegama Marathon is, in part, about experiencing some of the highest mountains in northern Spain in a 26-mile (42 km) loop that boasts 9,000 feet (2,700 m) of climbing. More than anything, though, racing Zegama is about immersing yourself in this fan culture. It's about absolutely sprinting off the start line—as if you are in a 1-mile (1,500 m) race—because the town is vibrating with cheering fans. It's about pushing harder over each mountain summit because hundreds of people are there to urge you on. It's about taking that last descent back into town with your arms stretched wide to high-five the tunnel of fans through which you run. It's about clanging glasses of locally made cider in the restaurants and bars of town with everyone after the race, downing your serving of the sweet alcoholic treat, and filling your glass again and again.

Trail running is growing quickly in popularity, and some day, maybe a decade or two off, it will be so popular that many races will have sidelines lined with adulating fans. Consider a pilgrimage to Zegama sooner than later to see and join in the future of trail running.

Cruising sweet Swedish singletrack.

Chapter 4

Techniques to Match Terrain

Finding footing is only part of the challenge (and fun) of trail running. When you zoom out, the world is literally your playground. All those zigs, zags, ups, and downs on the trails are your roller coaster, skate park, and slalom course all rolled into one. Let the terrain turn you into a kid again!

Of course, knowing what you're doing out there can make things even more fun. In the following chapter, you'll learn techniques to help you tackle a wide variety of terrain.

Taking a Turn for the Best

Wherever you hit the trail, you'll come across twists and turns, and some-times those zigzags will be the defining feature of the trail.

Tangents Versus Wide Cornering

If you're running along at a moderate pace on a flat trail that weaves this way and that, choose the best line as dictated by the footing. If the trail is wide or you're on a dirt road, you can gradually make your way over to the inside of the turn. That is, you work on taking the tangent on wide trails while moderating that tangential line based on footing. But, if you're on relatively narrow singletrack and hit a sharp turn (think of a turn of 90 degrees or more within a few strides), consider heading toward the outside of the turn so that you can maintain better momentum.

When you're running at a faster pace, you'll need to exercise a bit more caution when taking a sharp turn. In particular, you need to take care that you have enough traction to take the turn without having your feet slide out from under you. Obviously, you can slip on mud or ice, but you should also be on the lookout for loose debris atop hard-packed trail. Moderating your speed before the turn is the surest way to stay safe in a potentially slide-inducing turn. While turning on loose footing, try to plant your feet on the most stable spots and generally avoid making sudden correc-tions. But if it looks like you have great footing for a step or two during a treacherous turn, take advantage of those islands of security to help carve

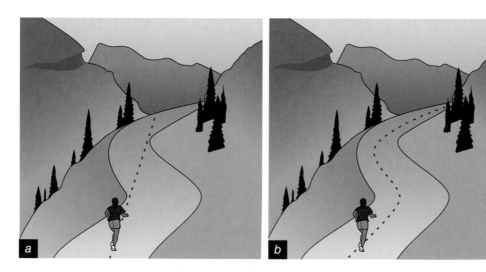

Cutting the tangent (a) can be shorter and faster, but take the natural line (b) if that feels more comfortable.

the corner. Regardless, you should choose a general line and commit to it throughout the turn.

Anna Frost, one of the world's best trail runners at all distances, suggests that personal preference should be your guide. "It's up to the individual as to what's going to be your tactic, what are you better at or more comfortable with. Some people might want to cut straight around the corner, and some people might want to bank around the outside of the corner. In the end, the time difference won't be big."

Quick Cornering

If you're rolling quickly though a turn with good footing, you might catch yourself leaning into the turn like a cyclist whipping around a bend. Go with it. But you don't want to lean excessively. Instead, trust your body's natural reaction, which should have you leaning from your ankles, like a cyclist who leans with both her bike and her body rather than just her body, so that you commit all your mass to the lean. This technique becomes great fun when you encounter a banked turn that allows you carry your speed around the turn while slanting your body into the turn and not having to lean actively. Although you'll encounter banked turns here and there, they're a prominent feature in trail systems developed with mountain biking in mind.

Blind Turns

You may encounter an occasional blind turn in which you can't see the trail on the other side of the turn. This sort of turn is especially common in forested areas. Changing topography and rock outcroppings can also hide the trail ahead. If you're moving fast or have recently encountered challenging conditions, consider moderating your pace when heading into the turn. Even if you don't slow down preemptively, be ready to slow or otherwise react as needed should you encounter a challenge in or after the bend.

When approaching a blind turn, you should also reengage your senses. Listen for any noises coming from the direction you're headed and see whether you can pick up any movement to give you a heads-up. Although four-legged animals are an occasional concern, you should be especially cautious about not running into another person. If you're in an area frequented by many outdoorsy folks, decide whether the conditions (traffic levels and degree of the turn's blindness) warrant slowing down. Regardless, you'll want to be able to stop in a hurry, so be ready put on the brakes. In heavily congested areas, making a bit of noise can give others a heads-up that you're coming. On singletrack, you'll also want to stay to the center or right side of the trail. In areas with lots of mountain biking, be prepared to step off the trail—just in case.

Going Up!

Want to get your heart pumping? Then head out and run uphill on trails. You will often find steeper climbs on trails than you would on pavement, and negotiating even small obstacles can add an energy-sapping challenge to your run.

Short Uphills

When you encounter a short, steep hill, you'll have to decide whether you want to run up it. If it's particularly steep, slick, or a makeshift obstacle course, good sense might dictate making a quick hike of it. But your mental approach will often dictate whether you walk or run up such a climb. Stevie Kremer, the 2014 Sierre-Zinal champion, embraces a mix of running and hiking, or "riking" as she calls it. So when does Stevie rike? Her answer: "When my shuffle of a run is very slow and my breathing is very heavy and I see there is still quite a ways to go on a hill or when I notice people riking around me are passing me and breathing less heavily than me."

Should you decide to walk up a steep slope, try hiking with small, frequent steps as opposed to taking monstrous strides outside your normal range of motion. On such climbs, trail runners have a tendency to bend too far over at the waist and hunch their torsos. This posture is counterproductive because it restricts airflow to your lungs. Bending forward when climbing is natural, but try to do so by leaning from your ankles. If you do bend farther than that, do so only slightly from the hips while keeping your torso straight, thereby maintaining your full lung capacity. On the steepest grades, some trail runners put their hands on their thighs and push down in sync with their footfalls. Again observing the immediately preceding words of wisdom, bend minimally from your hips, don't hunch over your torso, and be conscious of taking deep breaths to inflate your lungs fully. Says champion trail runner Kilian Jornet of his powerhiking, "I often go really low and push a lot with the hands on the legs to use all the upper body to climb. My back is low, but it's straight and I can look in front."

Jornet advises consciously switching climbing technique. "The more you use shorter steps with a higher cadence, the more you are working with your cardiovascular system. If you go with longer steps, you're working with the strength of the muscles. So if you start to feel your muscles tire, you can reduce the length of the step and increase the frequency. Like this, you will rest the muscles a bit while keeping a fast speed. If you are struggling cardiovascularly, you can take longer steps and work more on the muscular side."

Often times, running powerfully up a quick hill is more fun. Yes, the effort may leave you winded at the top, but the earned inner pride of leading a stiff charge is an ample reward. To get started, speed up before you hit the climb to build momentum. After you start ascending, drive your legs and arms forward and upward with more power than normal. Work hard to carry the

Use short but powerful steps, large arm swings, and an engaged core to run up short-but-steep climbs with good footing.

momentum you built heading into the hill. When running up a short hill, Kremer suggests, "take short, small steps, almost shuffles, while pumping the arms a lot. This is where a strong core and arms are important."

Bad footing can slow your steep ascent. If slick footing is the cause, you might shoot for building more momentum ahead of the climb and working even harder than usual to maintain it. Getting restarted will be tough. In addition, as discussed in chapter 3, try landing with your whole foot against the trail to maximize contact area. If that fails and you're wearing well-lugged shoes, you can try actively kicking your forefoot into the ground on each step in an attempt to find greater purchase. Also, look for little ledges with surer footing. These might come in the form of a root, rock, or a drier, flatter bit of trail. Multiple-time Skyrunning world champion (think "pro at running difficult terrain") Emelie Forsberg suggests, "when climbing on loose terrain find something that looks stuck in the ground and take normal steps but maybe with a bit more strength to keep the material planted in the ground."

If obstacles are impeding your uphill progress, choose the line that reduces the need to take oversized steps. Land with your feet underneath your body to minimize the dangerous horizontal motion that can cause you to slip. Western States 100-Mile Run podium finisher Dylan Bowman has this advice: "When running uphill on rocky sections of trail, it's especially important not to get frustrated and to be as efficient as possible. Oftentimes, these trails steal our momentum or force us out of our rhythm. It's easy to let this challenge affect our attitude, so the first step is to find the fun in the situation and embrace the circumstances underfoot. Though it may feel like a two-steps-forward, one-step-back scenario, chances are you're moving better than you think. If the rocks are small and spaced out enough, I do my best to find patches of dirt or rocks solidly fixed in the trail to plant my foot. It may not work for more than a couple steps, but it keeps my mind engaged and my attitude positive. If the rocky footing is particularly loose, don't be afraid to hike. It will be far more efficient and cost far less energy by the top of the hill."

Longer Uphills

Long climbs, be they a few minutes or a few hours, require a different approach. In general, shoot to maintain an even effort throughout and on par with your sustained effort on flat terrain. You want to run at the same effort at the top as you do at the bottom, as well as minimize the frequency and duration of spikes in effort along the way. Pushing too hard on climbs risks making the remainder of your run a less enjoyable slog. By nature, your pace will be slower when climbing than when running the flats. This disparity is a completely normal part of trail running.

This runner enjoys the sweet reward of topping out on a long climb at sunrise.

On shallower grades that are generally runnable, keep your effort such that you can keep running them. Staying efficient can help with this. Whereas a short, steep climb requires you to pump your arms and relax your shoulders and arms on longer climbs. Likewise, you don't need to drive your legs forward as you do on those quick bumps up. Instead, focus on maintaining the same cadence you run with on the flats while keeping your stride to a length that yields a sustainable effort. Your stride length on a sustained, runnable climb could be up to one-third shorter than the stride length you use when running at the same effort on the flats. The slower pace of a climb and the upward pitch of the hill mean that your gaze can be a bit closer to your feet than it is on even ground. On the other hand, the slower pace also means that when you per-

> If you're running up a hill at an effort that is becoming too difficult to maintain, switch to a strong powerhike before your legs or your lungs are totally tapped out.

ceive some smooth trail ahead, you've got a bit more time to take in your surroundings.

You'll have even more time to take in the sights if a longer climb requires walking. If you're out for a casual run, you would walk on any hill with a combined grade and length that would leave you speechless if you were to run it. If you experiment, you'll also find that you'll have particular grades at which you walk faster than you run given the same effort. For hills that require stretches of walking that last minutes at a time, focus on keeping your torso lengthened and avoid bending over too much from the hips so that you keep your lungs open.

Over time and with practice, you'll build a sense of which combinations of grade and duration call for you to walk and which don't. Many times, a climb of even just a few minutes calls for a mixture of walking and running. In such cases, work on smoothly transitioning between the two, carrying some of your momentum from running into walking and easing back into running. As you perfect these transitions, you may switch from one form of locomotion to the other for stretches as short as five or six strides. Brandy Erholtz, a U.S. Mountain Running champion and USATF Mountain Runner of the Year, still works on finding the right balance. "I used to think if I could run, I should. However, there have been many races in which 'powerhikers' have passed me. So, I've been working on my powerhiking when training on steep terrain and have actually found it to be more efficient at times. It also allows me to make bigger strides with a lower heart rate. I think this takes practice and experimentation."

Of course, sometimes you won't want to think about the length of a hill. Erholtz tries not to. Instead, she thinks, "for sure, I can get to the next tree." Then, when she's at that tree, she thinks, "I can make it to the next rock." And on she goes, climbing from one landmark to the next.

Aside from grade, obstacles, loose footing, and even tight turns can alter your approach when climbing for a prolonged period. The general goals are to maximize efficiency and maintain momentum, but each of these factors also increases the likelihood that you should walk a given grade. Trails with steep grades are more often rockier than the surrounding flat terrain, whether because of water runoff or the terrain itself. If you encounter small rocks, that is, rocks generally no taller than a foot (30 cm), head up the line with the fewest obstacles. If you encounter larger rocks (that don't require you to use hands for scaling), minimize the number of oversized steps you take. On loose footing, your first approach should be to maximize contact area between the tread of your shoe and the surface of the trail. If this method isn't providing traction, try kicking your forefeet into the ground as described previously.

If you're on a runnable climb and you encounter a tight turn, running along the middle of the trail often helps you maintain an even grade and therefore an even effort. Those already familiar with hiking or cycling in

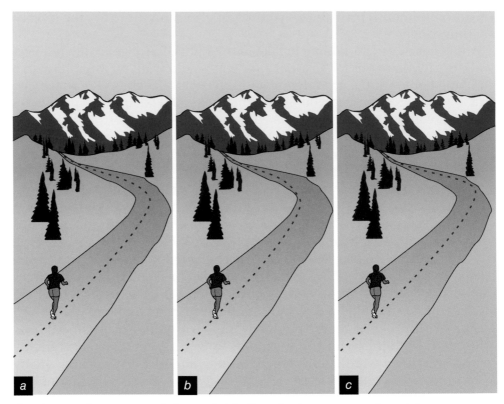

Staying to the center of the trail *(a)* often feels most comfortable on a switchback. Trying to keep to the inside of a curve *(b)* is only efficient in gentle turns or grades. Staying to the outside *(c)* can ease the effort on steep switchbacks.

the mountains may be familiar with switchbacks, an alternating series of near hairpin turns that provides a more mellow grade than a trail heading straight up a mountain. When you're fatigued, you may be tempted to run toward the inside of the turn, but the grade there is steeper than it is in the middle of the trail. If you're looking for a couple of easier strides to recover, take the outside of the switchback where the grade is shallowest.

Going Down!

Whereas the slower pace of climbing can lend itself to taking in breathtaking views, descending on trails is a thrill in and of itself. With gravity on your side, it's time to play.

A gradual descent on smooth trail is a great time to catch your breath and collect your thoughts. You may also want to use this time to take in water and food if you're on a long trail run, but we'll get to that in chapter 6. If you want to take it easy, settle into a comfortable effort, which will naturally be a bit faster pace than your pace on flat ground. Or, you can up the output a smidge and feel like a speedster. Either way, avoid overstriding, that is, landing with your feet far out in front of you. Instead, aim to have your feet land under your body or at least close to it. If you're landing far back on your heels while feeling a jolt with each impact, chances are you're overstriding. To avoid this, try picking up your cadence by up to 20 strides per minute. With the increased speed that comes with descending, adjust your gaze another couple of feet (1 to 2 m) down the trail. On corners, taking an outside line is often the best way to maintain your speed.

> From a momentum perspective, mountain biking and trail running are similar. As you pass around obstacles and up and down hills, look for the simplest, smoothest line to maintain your momentum.

Steep Descents

When you hit a steep descent, you need to be cautious. Steep descents can be a blast, but the consequences can be serious should you make a mistake. That said, remaining confident and relaxed are two of the most important things you can do when running down a steep hill. Keep a slight forward lean originating from your ankles and pick up your cadence. You'll have to read your running line quickly, while simultaneously picking up clues from farther down the trail than usual. If you need to slow down, do so gradually when you have good footing. Slamming on the brakes can get you in trouble. It's far better to maintain a slower, consistent rate of descent than to alter your speed rapidly. Keep your arms loose and reactive. Likewise, stay loose and reactive through your lower body. Locking out any of your leg joints, which is a common reaction to muscle fatigue on descents, can be painful and may cause injury. Hardrock 100-Mile Run champion Anna Frost recalls, "It took me a while to get confident going straight down the mountain. There was nothing I could change apart from just doing it and getting practiced at it. That was the only thing that made me more confident." She adds, "One of the biggest things that happened to me was getting a good pair of trail running shoes. The added traction gave me confidence to lean forward. Without that, one leans back, gets on his or her heels, skids out, and lands on his or her butt. . . In the end, you need to find what's best for you on the downhill. Some of the best descenders take massive steps, while others take tiny, tiny steps. Which one is better? Neither. You need to find which is best for you. That's part of the practice."

Kilian Jornet echoes Frost's call for practice, but with a twist. "To go down technical terrain fast, you cannot look to your feet because then you go too slowly. You need to look 10 feet (3 m) in front of you and maybe 5 feet (1.5 m) if it's very technical. For that, you need to memorize the terrain to know how you need to put your feet and have this coordination. You can practice with some exercises like trying to run with your eyes closed for three seconds. You memorize this terrain and for these three seconds you run and you know where you put your feet. I think that's good."

Steep and technical descents require quick feet and focus on each footfall.

If you have trouble relaxing on descents, here's what Jornet advises: "Go down as if you are dancing. Jump with the feet, with no tension in the body. Allow your body to stretch more when you go down. That's a nice thing. Go with good music. Try to dance and enjoy the downhill so that you relax more."

Descending With Obstacles or Poor Footing

Should you need to negotiate obstacles, especially on a steep descent, let your arms instinctively trend away from your torso. If the situation calls for rapid course corrections, your arms will flap around a bit. That is fine because they're acting as natural counterbalances to the equally rapid lateral motions of your lower body. All the while, you'll want to quicken your cadence to near its maximum, taking rapid-fire steps as you adjust course with each one. Try to follow the smoothest line down; you should factor in both the necessity of shifting from side to side as well as abrupt drop-offs. In other words, take the path that keeps your hips and torso on the smoothest path even if your legs and arms are going this way and that.

Descending a trail with poor footing can be one of the biggest challenges in trail running. If a hard-packed trail has just a bit of loose dust or debris, you only need to worry about that when you're cornering, braking, or descending the steepest bits of trail. The best way to brake or take tight turns in such cases is to ease off the speed ahead of time, gradually slowing over 5 or 10 strides. When cornering, make the speed adjustment before the turn. When she started mountain racing, Brandy Erholtz found she was too slow on the descents. "I knew if I wanted to be a serious mountain runner, I had to learn how to run the downhill fast. To get better and gain confidence on the downhill, I had to practice running fast over technical terrain. I know some mountain runners who run hard up the hills and easy back down, but even on my easy days I try to work on my downhill technique."

On a short technical descent, Jornet advises, "Lean forward and have your feet adapt to the terrain. Many times you just jump, and it's with your feet that you touch and realize how this surface is. You need to have a lot of perception in the ankles. You see a lot of rock and you go there with the foot, and it's when the foot touches the rocks that you say, "OK, I will stay like this," or "I will make it more strength on the right side or the left to keep the body in good position."

According to Jornet, technical descents are one area where experience with other sports can be a big plus. "I think all the sports of balance like slacklining or climbing or skiing or mountain biking are good. Skiing and mountain biking are good because you are used to looking forward, to having the knowledge of how the body quickly reacts, and to choosing the good line to go down. For perceiving terrain, slacklining and climbing are good for practicing how to place the feet and building strong ankles."

If you trail run enough you'll encounter a moderate to steep descent with poor traction because of mud, ice, or loose debris. At times, these descents might seem impossible, but that's rarely the case. For many trail runners, the best bet is to minimize speed going into such sections and aim to keep that speed quite low. Do not turn or brake rapidly. Have your arms slightly out to the side to help with balance and be ready to make rapid reactions should you need them. That might entail side stepping down the trail or grabbing branches, tree trunks, trailside rocks, or other fixed items to slow your speed and provide stability. Although you may have an instinctual reaction to lean back, avoid doing so because it will increase your chances of slipping and ending up on the seat of your pants. (Leaning back and landing on your bottom, however, can be a reasonably safe way to fall should you start going down. We'll get into that more in chapter 10.)

If, or rather when, you start sliding, point your feet in the direction of the slide and ride it out, so long as that option is safe. This scenario is not unlike hitting an icy patch as discussed in the previous chapter. In both cases, reacting by turning against the slide is a good way to end up on your butt. As experienced British fell racer Tom Owens explains, "some slipping is OK. Relax and go with the flow."

If you break out of the slide while treacherous footing persists, try to slow your speed over the next few strides, if that seems possible, or try running with very quick, short strides. Emelie Forsberg finds descending on loose terrain advantageous. "I think some of the best surfaces to run downhill on are the ones that slide, whether it is small rocks, grass and mud, or pine

Stephanie Howe dances downhill in California's Sierra Nevada.

needles and sticks. You just have to deal with it! To let go, don't think about anything else other than how fun it is to play with the ground, the ground that also helps you get a very fast pace. If the incline is not very steep, I can enjoy going really fast when I have control. If it's steeper, it demands more bravery to go faster."

On the other hand, there's something to be said for saving your own skin. Dylan Bowman takes a more cautious approach. "When running downhill on rocky terrain, I just try to remain safe while being guided by my instincts. Most of the biggest and most painful falls I've taken have happened in these situations, so it's important to have a feeling of self-preservation when descending particularly technical sections of trail. Once you feel you're at a controlled pace, relax as much as you can and use your instincts. I've found that looking five or six steps ahead really helps me maintain a rhythm as opposed to staring at each individual foot strike. Widening the scope of vision will give you a better feel for the entire environment and will allow you to move with more grace and confidence. Again, keeping a good attitude and embracing the challenge are important to improving these types of skills."

Prolonged Descents

Prolonged descents are a separate matter altogether. If you're in the mountains, you can easily find yourself descending a few thousand feet (many hundreds of meters) at a time. Here, efficiency becomes increasingly important. Your quads are powerful muscles and can handle some serious punishment, but if you overdo the eccentric muscle contractions that occur while descending, you might find yourself walking sideways down stairs two days later. To minimize the chances that this will occur, aim to run downhill smoothly and consistently. You do not want to be running out-of-control fast, nor do you want to be braking constantly with your quads. Finding the right balance can be tough, but it's important. Of course, if you feel like you've gone too hard, you can always take a break. Jornet suggests, "If you start to feel yourself going too fast and your quads are starting to work a lot, just stop for a second. Break the speed and start running again with slow, small steps to preserve your strength."

As you'll learn later in chapter 8, repeatedly running descents helps season your quads for future efforts.

Trees, Boulders, and Streams, Oh My!

As you may have recognized by now, the challenges of trail running are often its rewards. Figuring out how to negotiate obstructions on the trail and actually doing so can be a blast. Some folks pay $100 or more to participate in an obstacle-course race that's here today and gone tomorrow. Well, the same thing can happen any day on the trails. Fallen trees, boulders, water crossings—trail running has them and more.

Downed Trees

Toppled trees are a routine impediment for those who run forested trails. Wind, rain, snow, fire, and time can all lay logs across your desired path, leaving you with three choices: over, under, or around.

In most cases, your preferred option for dealing with a downed tree will be to go over it. If the log is small or lies below your knee, all you have to do is step over it. No big deal.

If the top of the log is between your knee and midthigh, you might be able to step carefully over it sideways, kicking one leg over before the other. Alternatively, you can place one foot on the log and step the other leg over. You can take a break with both feet on the log, if you prefer. If the log appears at all slick, take care to place your foot or feet on the log with a vertical motion to reduce your chances of slipping. When stepping off a potentially slippery log, lean forward and drop your leading foot toward the ground before picking your rear foot up. Trying to push off horizontally with your trailing foot can lead to perilous slippage.

If the top of the downed tree falls from midthigh to slightly above waist height, you can try swinging your legs over it in several ways. One option is to plant one hand on the log as you step over it, lean slightly toward that arm, using it for a little extra "hang-time" as you take the log in stride. As an alternative, you might be able to lift one foot on top, put your hands to both sides of that foot, and then pull the trailing foot through straight to the other side. In a final option, turn away from the log but put both hands on it. Lift yourself so that you sit on the log. Now, swing your legs, one at

If a log is low enough, planting one hand can get you over.

Planting both hands can offer stability when crossing a log.

a time or together, from one side of the log to the other before lowering yourself back down the other side.

If climbing over a tree won't work, try going under it. Going under a tree might be as simple as ducking. If the trunk is high enough, you might have success in crouching while running below the barrier. Chances are, however, that you'll have stopped in your tracks already. If that's the case, bend your knees and waist, hunch over, and walk slowly forward. Putting one hand on the log above you can give you a good sense of its location so that you're less likely to bump your head or, if you're wearing one, catch your hydration

When needed, you can sit on the log and swing your legs over.

pack. Although getting hung up is still annoying, you're far more likely to do the latter than the former. Depending on how far you're bent over, you can put a hand on the ground to balance. In some cases, crawling under the downed tree is the best option. Just remember to watch out for your head and pack.

Presumably, if you can go around a downed tree while staying on the trail, you don't really have much of an obstruction, do you? That being the case, you should go around a downed tree by leaving the established trail only if going over or under it is unreasonably dangerous, impossible, or would literally take minutes to crawl your way through the branches. With that said, if an apparent trail reroute goes around the downed tree, follow it. If a new trail has not been established, take the shortest easily negotiated path around the tree while taking care to minimize damaging vegetation. If you can easily open up a blocked trail by breaking branches off the downed tree, feel free to do so.

Big Rocks

In most cases, boulders and rock ledges on the trail offer one fewer option than downed trees do: You can go over or around them, but usually not under them. Because boulders and rock outcroppings tend to be fixed as opposed to transient impediments, trail builders are likely to have given you a route past the rocks. If you can stay on the trail and get around a rock that would otherwise require a tricky maneuver to overcome, go for it. Otherwise, adapt some of the techniques for overcoming logs when dealing with large rocks. Use your hands as needed and find a way to get safely up and down rocks. Don't rush yourself. Take your time and find a way to execute a move in a way that you're comfortable with, both physically and mentally. If a bunch of boulders block your way, Emelie Forsberg suggests this approach: "Try to find a way on top of the blocks and boulders. That is the most economical way, I believe. For sure, if it's only a few boulders you can always run in between them, but if the fastest line is on top, then go for it. It's so much fun jumping from rock to rock!"

Two-time USATF Trail 50-Mile champion Anton Krupicka notes, "when there are obstacles in the trail, I am constantly glancing a few yards up the trail so that I can pick the most efficient line. When picking a line, I would recommend stepping over—not on—small obstacles and either on or around large obstacles, depending on the situation. In order to be the most efficient and to save energy, when I am stepping up onto a large obstacle—be it a boulder, log, or large step in the trail—I find it easier to maintain a running cadence by stepping as close to the obstacle as I can before actually springing up onto the obstacle with my next step."

Heads Up! Head-Height Branches

Whenever you're running in forested or brushy areas, be alert for the possibility of branches overhanging the trail. True, you can brush some of these away in stride, but most experienced trail runners have unwittingly run headfirst into a limb or two in their day. Whether you should brush such a branch aside; run under it in stride by some combination of bending at your knees, folding at your waist, or crouching your torso and head; contort around the edge of the limb; or stop to negotiate carefully; the choice should be readily apparent. The key thing is to stay alert. It's easy to focus entirely on the trail below you or to bliss out on tame trail. That's all fine as long as you sneak a peek at head height along lengths of relevant trail.

Streams and Rivers

Running through a stream or shallow river can be a blast—and perhaps refreshing on a summer day—and plenty of trails incorporate such crossings in their established route.

Before we get to the how-to of crossing a moving body of water, let's get the safety warning out of the way. Water crossings can be dangerous. If a stream is flowing quickly enough, knee-deep water can knock you over. Waist-deep water can topple you that much more easily. Flowing, cold water can quickly numb lower limbs, making a water crossing even more dangerous. A slip and partial or full submersion into even warm water can lead to discomfort or hypothermia when the air is cool or will become so before you dry. Unless you have a great deal of experience and confidence in the situation (both in crossing successfully and being safe overall should you fall in), we generally recommend not crossing streams in freezing conditions. Do not cross a stream on an ice or snow bridge, a thick layer of snow over a stream that can unpredictably collapse, drop you into freezing water, and possibly trap you in the water below a solid snow layer. Turning back if you can't cross a stream safely is always perfectly fine. You should always have contingency plans in place for situations like this, as we'll discuss further in chapter 10.

Before crossing a body of water that is part of an established trail, check for signs of whether the water is flowing much higher than normal: Is terrestrial streamside vegetation submerged? Is there a ring of fresh flotsam at or near water level? Is the water muddy? Of course, recent heavy rains or snowmelt can give you a good heads-up for such conditions. If the water is higher than usual, you'll have to exercise additional caution in deciding whether to cross and in actually crossing the stream. If the water is flowing at what signs say is its customary level, go ahead and cross the stream.

Please note that if you come to a stream along a trail and signs indicate that a bridge has been washed out, the previous guidance obviously doesn't apply because the standard stream-crossing route is out of the picture. In that case, you'll have to make a full, independent assessment of whether, where, and how to cross the stream.

The most common streams most trail runners encounter are very shallow. You can clearly see that the stream is never more than a foot (30 cm) deep and you can see the footing the whole way across. When this is the case, you can go ahead and run or walk across, whichever is most comfortable.

When crossing a swift stream, move deliberately, face slightly upstream, and use trekking poles if you have them.

Just as with running on wet rock on land, use caution, a quick cadence, and minimal horizontal push off from your planted foot as you cross these shallow streams.

If someone has put stepping-stones across a stream or a natural path of stones leads across it, consider using them. Follow the advice in the previous chapter about treading on rocks. Any rock can be slippery, particularly wet ones. Because stepping-stones can unexpectedly wobble underfoot, we recommend walking across them.

When in doubt about the safety of rock hopping across a stream or when no such option is present, prepare to ford the stream if it doesn't appear too deep. Because appearances can be deceiving, proceed with caution. Unless the stream is clearly but a few inches (about 20 cm) deep, slowly edge out into the water one small step at a time. Feel around with your forward foot for firm footing. After you've found it, pick up your trailing foot and find a place for it. Try to keep one foot firmly planted at all times. Even if the footing seems relatively good, hold your arms a bit farther out for balance and let them drift higher should the footing deteriorate. If the stream bottom is rocky (which is often the case) and the visibility poor, keep your feet low in the water as you move them forward. They'll gently kick into rocks, letting you know their location. You can then feel your way to the next secure foot placement. Just remember to keep one foot firmly planted and move slowly enough to feel secure and balanced.

In swiftly flowing water, you'll have to brace against the current. Turning your torso partially upstream can help with this. When moving your feet and legs underwater, you'll also have to push actively upstream against the current. In this scenario, taking very small side steps will help keep you stable.

Always cross streams well upstream of any drop-offs. Should you accidentally fall into the water, this precaution will give you a chance to extricate yourself from the water before you plummet over a precipice.

Finding a Line

Anyone can choose a line down a trail. That line may differ from person to person, day to day, and season to season. Snow, sun, speed, and simple preference can change the approach. Without thinking, you might choose the same rocky uphill route step for step nearly every time you run it, but you might never take the same path down a wide trail with many low-risk roots and rocks.

Still, an experienced trail runner is more likely to find the more efficient or quicker line (depending on his or her desires) than a novice trail runner is. To be honest, many aspects of effective route finding are best learned by personal experience over years, given the disparate ranges of our personal anatomy, physiology, psychology, and running philosophy.

Nevertheless, one principle can guide your route finding as you tie together and implement all the lessons learned so far in this book: Flow like water.

Take that figuratively rather than literally. Water usually flows gently. Water doesn't correct course abruptly; it makes sweeping turns. With time, watercourses reflect obstacles found both upstream and downstream.

A few pointers can help you flow like water. Read the trail in front of you and make each step with the subsequent few steps in mind. When you're not moving in a straight line, aim to keep your hips and torso moving in close to a straight line with only gentle variations. In other words, avoid jarring movements unless they're unavoidable (and they rarely are).

Up and down, side to side in rhythmic cadence—trail running is your dance with nature. Your surroundings choose the songs, while the trail always leads. Just pick up the cues, follow the steps, and you'll star in a beautiful performance.

GRAND TETON NATIONAL PARK, WYOMING, UNITED STATES

Let's face it, as human civilization grows, fewer and fewer places are left in the world where we feel small, insignificant, and totally surrounded by the wild. Grand Teton National Park in western Wyoming is one such place. Here live several animal species that are higher than you are on the food chain. The Teton Mountains claw thousands of feet into the sky and overshadow everything around them. The roadless expanse is huge. In Grand Teton National Park, the power of nature is all encompassing.

Because this is an American national park, regulations prohibit trail races inside its boundaries. Therefore, all the trail running you do will be independent. The diverse trails of Grand Teton National Park offer opportunities for flat to rolling, easy runs to epics in excess of marathon distance. Any kind of trail running you do will offer up Teton mountain views and a chance to see elk, moose, bear, bison, and the park's other charismatic megafauna. Try running the trail around Jenny Lake; you can go around either the north or south side. When you reach the west side of the lake, make the short grunt of a climb past Hidden Falls to Inspiration Point for a panoramic view. You can either run back the way you came or take the boat shuttle across the lake for an interesting end to your run.

The park's 18-mile (29 km) Paintbrush and Cascade Canyons loop is an iconic route for hiking, backpacking, and trail running. Run it in a big day by heading up Paintbrush Canyon and down Cascade Canyon for a truly intimate encounter with the wild. You'll clock about 3,700 feet (1,100 m) of elevation gain up Paintbrush Canyon to Paintbrush Divide, the high point between the two canyons.

Before you head out, learn the proper safety practices for playing in big mountains and among big wildlife, especially summer thunderstorms, grizzly bears, and moose. You'll need to be 100 percent self-reliant when trail running here. Safety first!

Taking in the views high above Italy's Val d'Aosta.

Chapter 5

Trail Tools

Even the most minimalist of trail runners uses equipment to facilitate her or his singletrack sessions. From shoes to apparel and packs to lighting, having the right gear can make your time on the trails more enjoyable. That said, you don't need to become a gear geek as you become a trail runner—simplicity is one of the sport's defining characteristics and, we dare say, virtues. In this chapter you'll learn about the most common types of gear a trail runner uses, the options you might see within a gear category, and the best ways to use the gear.

Shoes

So, you want to dip your toes into trail running, but spending $100 or more on a new pair of shoes just to give it a try makes you hesitate? Well, the dirty little secret of trail running is that you can safely and enjoyably complete most trail runs in a pair of road running shoes. If you're already a road runner, just slip on your favorite pair of shoes and head out the door. Even if you're not a runner, there's a good chance that you have a pair of running shoes lying around somewhere that you can slip on for a couple runs. (A word of caution: If you give trail running a go with a pair of shoes you've been wearing casually for some time, please do yourself and your body a favor and pick up a new pair should you decide you enjoy trail running and plan to do more of it. Your old pair is broken in for casual wear and may be spent, as well.) Top trail runner Dylan Bowman echoes that sentiment, "a common misconception is that runners need a trail shoe in order to run effectively on trails. That usually means shelling out for a pair of shoes that are a bit heavier and more technically aggressive than your average road shoe. For people who come from a road running background or people who live where nontechnical trails are abundant, this may be an unnecessary expense when their tried-and-true road shoe of choice would perfectly suffice."

> One of the best parts of trail running is its simplicity. You don't need expensive gear to enjoy it. But if you make one trail running gear purchase, make it a pair of trail running shoes with a good grip on the soles and a little protection from the rocks.

Still, for reasons you'll learn in the text to come, you might want to skip hitting the rockiest, muddiest, and other superlative-warranting trails in road running shoes unless your personal experience has shown you that your combination of road shoes and running style are sufficient for those trails.

Why Trail Shoes?

Why wear trail running shoes at all? Well, the primary benefits of trail shoes are protection and traction.

Trail shoes can offer two types of additional protection over that offered by road shoes. First, they give underfoot protection in the form of a rock plate in the forefoot and, possibly, running the length of the shoe. This rock plate, which usually consists of either a piece of plastic a few millimeters thick or a dense woven fabric somewhere above the outsole and below your foot, is meant to prevent rocks, roots, or other obstacles from painfully impacting your foot from underneath upon footfall. This feature is sometimes known as push-through protection. With portions of outsole rubber increasingly removed from road running shoes to decrease weight, the full or nearly full coverage on the outsoles of most trail running shoes provides an additional layer of push-through protection. The thicker mid-

Well-lugged trail shoes can aid with traction.

soles (the foam bit between your feet and your shoe's outsole) found in some of today's oversized shoes can also add some underfoot protection.

Bowman points out, "Of course, there are some advantages to having a trail-specific footwear option in your quiver. First, trail shoes generally have more of a pronounced rubberized outsole to help with traction. Beyond the advantage of sure-footedness, extra rubber (and a rock plate in some cases) will also help with improving protection while increasing the shoe's durability. Because most road racing shoes have larger areas of exposed midsole foam, they often break down quicker and need to be replaced more often than their trail counterparts."

The upper of a trail shoe, the fabric and overlay materials that wrap over the foot, can also provide strategic protection. The most important aspect of this over-foot protection is the toe bumper. The toe bumper often consists of the outsole of the shoe bent up in front of the toes in combination with heavier fabric or a rubber horizontal wrap around the front of and, sometimes, the sides of the toes. Its purpose is to save you (and your toes) from a world of hurt when you inevitably kick a rock, root, or cactus. Trail shoes with uppers made from more robust fabrics or with more substantial fabric, plastic, or rubber overlays can help protect your feet should you brush a branch, cactus, or other pointy object. Although more subtle, the materials chosen for the upper of a trail shoe often reduce the entry of dust and sand.

Although trail running shoes a decade or two ago were the heavily constructed brethren of hiking shoes, the trend has been to streamline both underfoot and upper components to provide just enough protection while maximizing overall performance.

With the recent popularity of the minimalist and barefoot running movements, the term stability took quite the bashing when applied to running shoes. What was once an entire category of running shoes suddenly became antithetical to what running should be. Although some running shoes may indeed have been trying to do too much to control most runners' feet, stability shouldn't be seen as a dirty word when talking about trail shoes. One term that rose to prominence during the shunning of stability is lockdown. Quite simply, lockdown is the ability of the upper to secure your midfoot and heel and, as a result, lock your entire foot into your shoe. If someone says a trail shoe feels sloppy or loose, he or she could be talking about insufficient lockdown.

Trail shoes can offer an increased feeling of stability by flaring the outsole and midsole wider than your foot. In essence, this flare works in a similar manner to the outrigger on a canoe or training wheels on a bike; the wider platform reduces excessive movement in either direction.

The more obvious benefit of many trail shoes is the increased traction they provide. Before continuing, we must reiterate that good technique and some experience can go a long way in maximizing the traction inherent in any pair of running shoes. Nevertheless, adding deeper lugs to a shoe certainly makes it easier to find purchase amidst some slippery situations. If you compare the outsole of a road running shoe with a general-purpose trail shoe, you'll notice that the trail shoe has deeper, more widely spaced lugs.

Some trail shoes also have soles that are partly or fully made up of softer rubber. Although softer rubber wears down more quickly than the harder rubber found on road shoes and most trail shoes, the softer rubber is stickier, which helps when trying to find footing on rock. (The same concept applies to rock-climbing shoes.)

A final advantage of some trail shoes is additional durability of the upper. This increased durability can come from more robust meshes or material used in the body of the upper as well as strategic use of fabric, rubber, and plastic overlays. Even with a more durable mesh, if you find your shoes caked with mud or sand at the end of the run, a quick hose off can increase the life of the upper.

Yes, an extremely small subset of runners hits the trails in sandals or entirely barefoot. If this idea appeals to you, we suggest checking out the multitude of online resources or other texts.

As for an overall approach, Bowman says, "Many runners are looking for the footwear ideology that will allow them either to unlock some secret potential or simply to run injury free. My advice would be to choose a shoe that makes you feel good after you run rather than a shoe that makes you feel good during a run. Oftentimes, a minimal and agile road racing shoe is what feels best during a trail run, but it leaves us broken down the next day. Recovery and longevity factors should be considered along with performance when choosing our trail footwear."

Waterproof Shoes

All too often, the marketing and subsequent purchase of waterproof trail shoes centers on the waterproofing as an essential technical feature. In a small subset of conditions, a trail shoe with a waterproof membrane or other waterproofing technology is the best choice or, at least, a good one. For instance, a waterproof shoe can be great if you'll be running through a few inches (5 to 10 cm) of snow for an hour or two. Similarly, if it rained recently, and you're likely to run through small puddles. In really cold conditions a waterproof shoe might be effective. Other than that, leave membrane shoes at home. Running in waterproof shoes through a downpour or other conditions that are likely to direct significant amounts of water into your shoes from around the ankles will simply leave you running around in heavy, nondraining fishbowls.

Trail Threads

For the most part, running apparel is running apparel. Indeed, a great deal of athletic apparel translates well enough to the trails as well. Anyone who tells you otherwise is probably trying to sell you something.

Essential Ensemble

The essential trail running kit is in line with what you'd wear for most any sport: some bottoms, a top, a pair of socks, and applicable undergarments. Chances are you can go out for a trail run with something you already have at home. No matter what apparel piece you're looking to pick up, top international trail runner Anna Frost suggests, "We're all different, so the only way to find out whether a piece of clothing is for you is to try it. Even if I love this fabric and that fit, someone else who's the same size as me could think the same fabric is horrible."

Tops and Bottoms

Because running is a sport in which we engage in the same repetitive motion thousands of times, the friction of clothing against skin can lead to a significant and painful problem: chafing. You'll quickly learn what types of materials, fits, seams, and other features of a piece of clothing act as skin irritants when you run. It should go without saying to avoid those.

A good pair of athletic bottoms might be the most important part of the mix. If you have a pair of athletic bottoms that are breathable, offer a good range of motion, and are comfortable, they should work. Satisfactory choices might include your gym shorts, yoga pants, or board shorts. (But you might take a pass on padded cycling shorts.) If it's warm or hot, most trail runners opt for a pair of shorts, be they traditional running shorts, short tights, or a pair of general athletic shorts you might wear to the gym.

Whatever bottoms you wear, useful features include a secure pocket for a key as well as another pocket or four to stash additional items you might need. (More on that in a bit.) Dylan Bowman notes, "Shorts with an abundance of pockets are usually particularly expensive in comparison to the other simple necessities inherent to running. However, for me, the cost is a no brainer in exchange for the utility and convenience of having at least one pair of shorts capable of carrying a picnic."

Avoid excessively baggy shorts that might be prone to snagging on brush along the trail. Men, you'll also want to find bottoms with suitable support where you need it, whether that's from a built-in pair of briefs or some of your own.

More or less any T-shirt will do for trail running, although a breathable, wicking technical shirt made in the past 10 years will add comfort to your runs. If you don't already have one, you can find a basic version for less than $30 at any local running store, sporting goods shop, or outdoor retailer. Heck, head on down to your local thrift shop and try one out for just a couple bucks. High-end shirts do come with some nice add-on features, such as built-in pockets or a partial zip down the front. The pockets can carry a key, cell phone, music player, or snack, and the partial zip can help keep you cool.

Frost reminds new trail runners, "You don't need something super technical. You need something that's comfortable and that's going to do the job." She also suggests avoiding shirts with plastic-like printing or seams, which might promote chafing. Similarly, she says, "If you get chafing under your arms when you wear a tank top, wear a T-shirt."

Socks That Rock

Again, at their most basic, any pair of socks can get you out the door and on the trails. A step up would be a pair of athletic socks with some breathability. Any pair of running socks is yet another step up because they offer targeted breathability and cushioning as well as plenty of elastic to prevent the sock from wandering around your foot during aggressive maneuvers and descents. Some folks get away with low-cut or no-show socks on the trails. This choice comes at the expense of a bit more pain when you inevitably kick up a rock or stick that then hits your ankle. Although mostly benign, these ankle biters sure sting! A sock covering the ankle dampens the blow.

On the technical side, some trail socks feature PTFE (i.e., Teflon) fibers to reduce friction and the blisters it causes, whereas others, known as toe socks, individually wrap each toe in material to reduce the chance of blisters on toes caused by friction between them. In general, socks marketed as trail socks should have reasonable resistance to wear from trail grit.

Blocking the Sun

For most runners, a bit of sun shielding for the eyes also falls within the realm of essential kit. The combination of a cap or visor and sunglasses is

Summertime can mean less clothing and more freedom on the trails.

usually the solution. Any old hat or visor will do, but an inexpensive mesh running hat or visor with a sweat-wicking headband is even better. As long as they're UV protectant, a five dollar pair of gas-station sunglasses will work. A better choice might be a relatively inexpensive sporting model that grips your nose and hugs the sides of your face to keep your glasses on during sudden movements on the trail. Even photochromatic lenses that change their opacity based on apparent brightness can be had for a reasonable price. The biggest benefit to high-end sunglasses is often the scratch resistance and clarity of their lenses. Folks who lose things often might want to stick to the inexpensive end, whereas folks who keep things around for a decade might benefit from long-wearing but pricier brands.

Sports Bras

Sports bras are essential gear for women. If you're a road runner, whatever you run in on the roads will do equally well on the trails. For women who are transitioning to trail running from other active pursuits, make sure your sports bra is supportive for high-impact activity. In general, high-impact sports bras are of two kinds: compression bras that press and hold your breasts firmly against your rib cage and encapsulation bras that separate and encapsulate each of your breasts into unmoving cups. Some women can wear either kind, but others prefer one or the other. Women with larger cup sizes generally find that encapsulation bras provide the support they need. All sports bras are made with a wicking material. A few offer a wool lining, which is a little like heaven on a cold, winter day. Now, there are even sports bras made for nursing mothers, which have detachable cups to allow easy breastfeeding access.

Beat the Heat

Although we will address the topic in detail in chapter 7, "Conquering the Conditions," beating the heat is pretty easy. You will notice that wicking technical shirts are made of various weights. Seek out the lighter weight materials for hot days and, possibly, wear less of it. Lighter colored shirts can also make you feel cooler. In most instances, a thin, wicking, technical T-shirt is the best option.

A short-sleeve shirt is a must in the heat, unless you want to go with a tank top, sports bra, or, for men, no shirt at all.

Hot weather also counsels for the use of thin, breathable shorts and, to some degree, socks, although that can be more a matter of personal taste. Along the same lines, a pair of shoes with a thinner, more breathable upper can be more comfortable on a hot day.

Cool and Inclement Conditions

When heading out in the cold, dress so that you'll be a bit cold for the first 10 minutes. Running will quickly warm you, and you should be just the right temperature after that. Trust us, that's far better than setting off all toasty and then being a hot, sweaty mess for the rest of the run. That latter scenario is actually more dangerous, because an unexpected stop can leave you shivering in damp, sweaty clothes in no time.

Pants and Tights

Cool conditions call for wearing a pair of tights or running pants. As with shorts, choose a pair that is breathable and doesn't constrict your movement. You'll have to choose the coverage and warmth of the fabric based on personal preference, because many options are out there. Tights are available in full- and three-quarter (capri) lengths in thin, moderate, and heavy weights. Some tights have strategically placed windproof panels for additional protection from the cold, and options for warmer weather include mesh panels to shed warmth. Full-length pants have a similar range of options. Even more important than with shorts, avoid wearing excessively baggy pants, especially over your lower legs, because they are prone to catch on obstacles, collect mud, and all around get in the way. As with shorts, having a pocket or two in your pants or tights can be useful.

Warm Shirts

Cool weather can mean a switch to long-sleeve shirts. As with pants, you'll have to be the judge of how warm a shirt you'll want because they run the gamut from ultrathin and breathable to heavyweight fleeces. A long chest zipper (along with rolling up your sleeves) can make a long-sleeve shirt comfortable through a wide range of temperatures. Some folks are big fans of thumbholes in sleeves that allow the sleeves to provide some hand warmth should you need it, and a few shirts have tuck-away hand covers. Pockets are more common in long-sleeve running shirts than in their short-sleeve cousins.

Jackets

When a long-sleeve shirt isn't enough or a stiff wind is keeping you cold, throw on a windbreaker. A high-quality, lightweight, wind-resistant jacket can be had on the cheap these days. This jacket will get you through most dry conditions with ease. Many are highly compactable and can be folded into a self-contained pocket for easy storage if you're wearing a pack.

> If you plan to trail run in the rain, the trick is not to stay dry—you're going to get wet sooner than later—but to stay warm when you are wet. Plan your clothing to help maximize retention of your body heat.

A pocket or two are useful if you won't be wearing a pack, but others prefer the lighter weight and cleaner lines of a pocket-free jacket. Those looking for the lightest products on the market can now find plenty of options at three ounces (90 g) or less. Such jackets are light and compact enough that you can throw one in your running pack and not think of it until you need it. Some wind jackets come with a DWR (durable water-repellent) coating. This coating won't help you in a downpour or constant rain, but it sure is helpful in mist or falling snow.

For really rough weather, you'll want a fully waterproof jacket. The waterproof membrane excels in these conditions. A three-layer, seam-taped jacket with hood will keep you dry in a storm. Marketed for decades as waterproof–breathable jackets, the breathable part was a stretch; such jackets quickly became uncomfortable from the inside out. (Try running for 10 or 20 minutes in a traditional rain jacket.) But the current iterations of membrane jackets are more breathable, less annoyingly crinkly sounding, much lighter, and better designed with good use of venting appropriate for running. Keep the venting part in mind if you buy a waterproof jacket because it's a key feature in a sport like trail running that involves high energy output and relatively low forward speed. Many waterproof jackets are made with zippers in or below the armpit that you can unzip to allow ventilation in a protected fashion. Some jackets also offer permanent vents in the back, with overlapping material that promotes airflow. Remember, though, that these vents can also allow water in if you're running in a storm accompanied by high wind. Although somewhat pricy, the lightest of these jackets now fits in as a viable alternative to a wind jacket, negating the need to own two jackets.

Layering Is Your Friend

The secret weapon for cold-weather running is layering. If the temperature is near freezing, a wind jacket over a lightweight or midweight long-sleeve shirt is much more versatile than one thicker shirt. Aside from fully wearing

Dressed in a rain jacket, layers, and gloves, this runner is ready for inclement weather.

both layers, you can partially or fully unzip the jacket or take it off entirely. Layering provides an exception to the rule to start out a little cold. If you can quickly and easily make your outfit cooler, you have no reason to start out cold. On calm days, a second shirt, whether short- or long-sleeve, on top of a long-sleeve shirt can also work well. Indeed, layering possibilities are endless. Don't hesitate to add even more layers as temperatures fall.

Layering works on your legs, too. You can slip a pair of running pants over some shorts and then take the pants off when you get too warm. The same goes for throwing running pants over tights in very cold conditions. The saying is that there's no such thing as bad weather, only bad clothing choices.

Accessories for Appendages

You'll also want to keep your extremities warm in the cold. Any variety of winter hats and gloves or mittens should work at the outset. Avoid wearing too warm a hat. Also, aim for breathable head and hand covers lest the sweat turn a source of warmth into a sapper of it. Multiple hand-covering layers might be necessary when the temperature is significantly below freezing. In conditions like those, we recommend a thin fleece glove with an overmitten, which can be wind resistant, waterproof, or insulated depending on conditions.

Arm sleeves and Buffs are two accessories that you may be unfamiliar with, but they can be great in cool weather. Arm sleeves are essentially a pair of detached long sleeves you wear along with a short-sleeve shirt. Then, when you warm up, you just slip them off over your wrists or leave them scrunched down over your wrists. You can slip them back on in seconds should your arms get chilly. And then there's the Buff and Buff-like products. A Buff can be used in so many ways that we cannot highlight them all here, but these tubes of highly elasticized fabric are most often used as hats, neck warmers, and face covers, occasionally all at the same time. A face cover, be it a Buff or a balaclava (or maybe a beard), is a necessary tool for running in extremely cold temperatures. We'll address running in severe conditions more fully in chapter 7.

Carrying the Essentials

From time to time (or, perhaps, all the time), you might want to bring along something more than your shoes and apparel on a run. What then? Well, you have a multitude of options.

The first option, which we'll get back to later, is to leave it at home. Really, running is simple. Embrace it!

If you still think you need to bring along some additional gear or a bit of food, improvise. Will a couple of energy gels or your key fit in your shorts pocket? Can you tuck your pair of gloves in the waistband of your pants or the pocket of your windbreaker? A light jacket or an extra long-sleeve shirt is easily twirled into a roll and then tied around your waist. Although it's a tad risky if you're carrying a phone or camera, holding something in your hand also works. Handheld hydration bottle systems work that way, more or less, by using an adjustable strap to hold a water bottle against your hand. These simple systems often include a small pocket with space for a key, a couple bits to eat, or another small item.

If you still need extra carrying capacity, a waist belt or backpack can greatly add to what you're able to bring along with you on the trail.

Waist Belts

For a simple and light solution for carrying a limited amount of gear, consider a waist belt. Yes, such a pack may remind you of a grandparent on vacation, but they can work quite well out on the trail. They range from a step-in fabric tube (it lays flat and almost unnoticeable around your waist) with openings into which you can shove items, to a small pack with a rear pocket that clips together in front of your waist, to the same concept with a place to slide in a water bottle behind you, to large systems that hold two 26-ounce (750 ml) water bottles with many pockets to boot. For runs with long stretches without drinkable water, you might pair a handheld bottle with a waist belt, swapping out the bottle that you're carrying in your hand with one from the pack as needed.

But not everyone is a fan of waist packs, including Dylan Bowman: "In the case that I need to carry a bit of extra food, water, or clothing, I much prefer a stripped-down backpack to a waist pack. I've experimented heavily with both options and find that waist packs upset my stomach after a few hours from all the jostling that occurs around my midsection."

A hydration pack can help make your runs safer or longer.

Backpacks

To carry more gear or get things off your waist, slip on a backpack. Running packs are typically called hydration packs because almost all are intended to carry fluids in some manner. They have improved a great deal over the past decade, and significant changes have been made in the past few years. These days, hydration packs are lighter, more breathable, and altogether better designed. Packs start at little more than a mesh sleeve in the rear designed to carry up to a two-liter hydration bladder with a few small, easily accessible pockets on the front straps.

The sweet spot for a new trail runner would be a hydration pack with approximately five liters of storage space in the main, rear compartment. That's enough storage space to carry a few liters of water and some extra gear for your longer adventures while still being light and compact enough to use if you want to jump into a race with it. With ultramarathons and fastpacking taking off, running packs are available with 10, 20, 30, or more liters of rear storage space and a slew of side and front pockets.

Some amazing running-specific backpacks are on the market these days. As you're getting started, however, don't hesitate to throw on the 10-year-old Camelbak you used to hike with or a mountain-biking hydration system. Yes, the 10-year-old pack will be heavier than the latest and greatest, and the cycling pack won't have ideal ergonomics, but you'll be trail running.

Less Is More

As mentioned throughout this book, one of the great joys of trail running is its simplicity. There are no chains to oil, tires to pump, kayaks to stow, or skis to wax. Ah, but there's a ton of helpful running gear you could buy and might end up collecting over time. You may be tempted to throw it all in your pack when you go out for your next run. After all, you might need it. Think again. Take time to consider whether you really need all the gear and food that you're taking with you. Consider each piece of gear individually. Ask yourself these questions:

- Do I need this item to run safely today?
- Will this item make me considerably more comfortable today?
- Is there another item I'm carrying that can fill the same role today?

When you see how enjoyable it is to run with less stuff, you'll naturally shift to carrying less over time under the same conditions. In paring down your pack, take care not to go too far. Going fast and light is wonderful, but safety is paramount. Don't forget to read chapter 10, "Trail Safety and Stewardship," and heed its cautions about going into the wilds.

Lighting the Night

Whether you're headed out the door before the sun peeks over the horizon or you're tempted to stay out after the sun sets, a lighting system makes trails accessible around the clock.

Trail runners have two main options on the lighting front: headlamps and flashlights. Of the two, headlamps are the more popular because they leave your hands free to run with a natural motion, scramble over obstacles, and manipulate any other items that you're carrying. In addition, they automatically track wherever you're looking.

Handheld flashlights have their advantages. For one, they're great at pinpointing objects, whether it's a rock on the trail, a distant trail marker, or an animal in the woods. Held at waist level, the lower angle of a flashlight is better for casting shadows of low-to-the-ground obstacles, such as rocks. These shadows enhance your depth perception and therefore enable you to react appropriately instead of running overcautiously on uneven terrain.

Some trail runners like to wear a light around their waist or on their chest. For many years, folks made this happen by stepping into or pulling down a headlamp with an elastic strap. Some runners still do that, but commercial products on the market now integrate a light into the front of a waist pack or the chest strap of a hydration pack. This solution allows hands-free running while enhancing beneficial shadows on trail obstacles.

Runners climb a steep hill during a night race.

Night owls and early birds who often hit the trail under cover of night, as well as those looking for a little extra help at night, should consider running with both a headlamp and a flashlight. This setup provides great overall light with a head-synced light source along with a shadow-casting, spotlighting source.

Just as with hydration packs, don't let a lack of up-to-date gear stop you from experimenting on the trails. That said, updating from your 10-year-old headlamp will make a world of difference when night running. For starters, the current generation of LED-based lights are a couple of times brighter and last a great deal longer on a single set of batteries, or a single charge for rechargeable models, than those made five years ago. Some of the high-end headlamps are programmable through a USB cord and your computer. In just a minute or two, you can optimize light intensity versus burn time (i.e., duration of a charge or set of batteries) depending on your needs for a particular run or set of runs. From a safety perspective, the biggest enhancement is the replacement of filament bulbs with LEDs, negating the need to bring spare bulbs. Yes, you can render a modern headlamp or flashlight inoperable, but you really have to try.

Don't discount the value in having a light source so that you can be seen. Whether you have to run a few miles of road before hitting the trail or need to cross a road, you want to let the drivers know you're there. If this might be a frequent scenario for you, consider a headlamp or flashlight with a rear-facing, blinking red light that you can turn off. Such a light could be annoying on the trail if you can't shut it off, but it's a nice safety bonus on the roads.

Navigation Equipment

You might often be running trails that you're quite familiar with or running with folks who know the route well, but you may also venture into new terrain. A useful tool for such adventures is a map, whether a fancy plastic map from the outdoor store or a quick printout from a website (adequately protected from your sweat as well as potential precipitation and water crossings). If you're in an area with tons of natural space, your map should extend beyond your planned route in case you take a wrong turn or need to bail. If you're not well acquainted with the broad geography of the area or can't reliably read nature's clues on cardinal directions, take a compass with you. Even a tiny compass with only five degrees of accuracy can help sort things out if you're on trail and have a map.

It's been more than a decade since wrist-top GPS units first hit the market. They're now much smaller and more reliable. Some have a helpful back-to-start function that plots your course to that point in case you need to backtrack your way out of going off course. You should also be able to preload GPS waypoints or even entire routes to keep you on the right track.

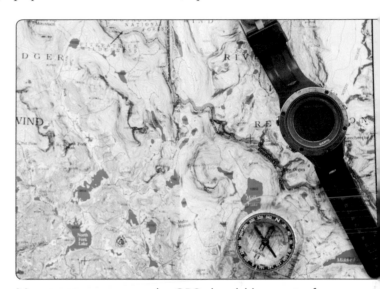

Maps, compasses, and a GPS should be part of a trail runner's navigational tool kit.

Smartphones are another navigational tool. Whatever phone and operating system you have, map apps can plot your current position. If you might be using your phone to navigate and there's a chance that you'll enter areas without cell service, try to find an application that preloads map data so that you're not stuck staring at a blank screen when you need it most. As with wrist-top GPS devices, some map applications allow you to preload waypoints and entire routes.

A word of caution: If you're relying on an electronic device as a navigation aid, be sure to top off the charge before heading out. Turning off unused features, such as putting a phone in airplane mode until you need it or disabling the heart-rate function on a fancy GPS watch, can extend the battery life. But consider yourself warned: The usefulness of these devices is negated completely when the end of their battery life is reached. Even if you plan to navigate with an electronic device, carry a map as a backup.

You'll learn a great deal more about the ins and outs of trail navigation in chapter 10, "Trail Safety and Stewardship."

Scenario-Specific Gear

So far in this chapter, we've looked at the gear most commonly used by trail runners, the real bread and butter stuff. In this section, you'll learn about equipment more suited to specific conditions or gear used because of personal preference.

Gaiters

A prime example of the role of personal preference in choosing trail running equipment is gaiters. Gaiters are pieces of fabric that attach to your shoe and cover some or the entire upper of your shoe and ankle. When trail running, the primary purpose of gaiters is to keep debris out of your shoes by covering the shoe openings at the tongue and ankle as well as to provide an extra barrier over the mesh portions of the uppers. Gaiters can be effective in keeping loose dust and dirt as well as small debris (pebbles, pine needles, bits of twigs, and so on) out of your shoe. So, the more of that stuff you'll see on the trail, the better the case is for gaiters. On the other hand, gaiters can trap heat, leading to damp, sweaty feet, and they can keep shoes from draining or drying should they get wet. Gaiters also make adjusting your shoelaces more difficult. Despite their possible usefulness, many trail runners forgo wearing them because they'd rather deal with some occasional grit in their shoes than the downsides of gaiters.

Perhaps the two strongest cases for using gaiters are sand and snow. A full-coverage, breathable gaiter can eliminate the need to stop frequently to remove sand from your shoes if you'll be running in long stretches of it. Waterproof gaiters worn with waterproof shoes can be quite effective when running through snow.

Trekking Poles

The use of trekking poles is one of the major differences between trail running in the United States and continental Europe. In Europe, runners use them in trail races of all sorts, and you're bound to see runners with them on the most popular Alpine trails. In the United States, you have to head to the highest and steepest of races to find runners with poles. Even then, the proportion of runners with poles will be much smaller than that seen in Europe. That difference may largely reflect the difference in terrain. The heart of Europe, where a huge number of the continent's trail runners train or race, is full of long, steep climbs, whereas most trails in the United States, even in the mountains, are at shallow grades that reduce the usefulness of trekking poles.

Sustained, steep trails are where trekking poles are most useful. If you already have them with you, they can provide a boost on shallow climbs and even a bit more pace on flat ground when your legs are fatigued. They can also be useful as a third or fourth point of contact when crossing a stream with uncertain footing or swift water. (A couple of streamside sticks

Give yourself a boost with trekking poles on long or steep climbs.

can serve the same purpose in a pinch.) Finally, they can be used to take some strain off your quads on prolonged descents.

Many general-use trekking poles are on the market, so what should you look for in a pair? Well, light weight is a bonus because most trekking poles are designed with hikers in mind. Even more desirable are collapsible poles. These will be either telescoping poles or accordion-style poles, both of which lock into place. Some poles have an additional adjustment that lets you fine-tune their height. Be sure to check whether the poles you're buying are sized in addition to being adjustable. Unless you intend to use trekking poles on snow, look for poles with only tiny baskets above the tips to lessen the chance that they'll get caught on low brush.

Gaining Traction

Should you encounter wintry conditions, you might welcome a little extra traction. One way to gain that advantage is to slip a set of traction devices over your trail shoes. A multitude of manufacturers have now entered the market and offer a range of designs. Two designs stand out: the Yaktrax Pro and Kahtoola MICROspikes. Of these, the Yaktrax Pro are lighter, less expensive, and the best all-around option. If you'll be running on much ice, the MICROspikes offer a little more bite.

The cheapest way to add traction is to "screw your shoes." Aside from providing a good chuckle over the phrase, inserting 8 to 20 sheet-metal screws into the outsoles of a worn pair of running shoes (most folks convert a previously used pair and dedicate them to this use) can add a great deal of traction. A number of similar commercial products are on the market, but 3/8-inch or 1/2-inch (10 or 12 mm) #8 hex-head sheet-metal screws from the hardware store work just fine. Make sure to insert the screws into deeper lugs so that they don't poke through into your foot. Use an electric screwdriver with a 1/4-inch (6 mm) socket to keep yourself from going crazy trying to hand crank screws into dense rubber. The head of each embedded screw thus offers bite into snow or ice. You can find full instructions on how to make a screw shoe online.

A few shoe brands offer models with carbide tips embedded in the outsole. At the moment, these brands include Icebug, Inov-8, and Salomon. The tips don't do much on soft snow, but they can provide extra traction on ice.

Safety Items

A number of safety-related items that we'll discuss further in chapter 10 should be carried on some trail runs. These include water-purification systems, fire starters, signaling devices such as a mirror or whistle, and first-aid supplies.

Screw shoes ready for winter exploration.

Outfitting yourself for the trail isn't rocket science. Wear clothes that keep you comfortable. Bring the food, drink, and auxiliary gear you'll need to stay happy, as well as a way to carry it. Remember, you don't need much. One of the allures of trail running is that often all you need to do is throw on some shoes and clothes and head out the door. Now, get out there!

One Last Thing

So you're out for your awesome trail run when, uh-oh, you have to take care of some urgent business! Did you remember to bring some toilet paper or some paper towels (they work better if you're sweaty or otherwise wet) in a pair of Ziploc baggies? We hope so. The usefulness of the paper is self-explanatory and one of the bags is obviously for keeping the paper dry, so what's the other bag for? Carrying out that used paper consistent with the Leave No Trace principles discussed later in chapter 10. No one likes to see used toilet paper blowing around the trails. Refer to the instructions in chapter 10 on how to poop effectively and ethically in the woods.

MONT BLANC REGION, THE ALPS OF FRANCE, ITALY, AND SWITZERLAND

Approach Mont Blanc from any direction—its north and west sides in France, its east side in Switzerland, or its south side in Italy—and it becomes immediately apparent why it's named the White Mountain. Draped with a cloak of snowfields and glaciers, the 15,782-foot (4,810 m) behemoth is the Alps' tallest mountain. With its first-known ascent in 1786, the mountain has long been an icon for mountaineers, skiers, hikers, and now, trail runners.

The French town of Chamonix and the Italian town of Courmayeur sit on the mountains' respective north and south shoulders, and they serve as year-round recreation gateways to the mountain. If the mountain itself is an icon, so, too, are Chamonix and Courmayeur. A saunter through either town will have you sharing sidewalks with dedicated mountain athletes of many disciplines. In the past decade, these towns have become hubs of both trail running and racing. Indeed, they make superior vacation destinations for the singletrack inclined.

The UTMB® is the region's most famous trail race. Each year some 2,000-plus runners make the race's 105-mile (169 km) circumnavigation of the big mountain. If 100 miles is not your cup of tea, don't worry; a passel of other races of all distances start or finish in Chamonix or Courmayeur, such as September's Trail des Aiguilles Rouges in Chamonix, which offers distances as short as 9 miles (15 km). Arrancabirra is an 11-mile (18 km), well, let's call it event, taking place from Courmayeur each fall. Along the path of Arrancabirra are several beer aid stations.

(continued)

Mont Blanc Region *(continued)*

If you would prefer a trail running vacation that doesn't include a race, take heart in the knowledge that hundreds of miles of trails snake away from both Chamonix and Courmayeur, a lifetime's worth of exploration. Buyer beware: This is the land of great vertical, and every trail run here will involve going up and down big hills. But the distractions are grand, from the hulking Mont Blanc to the rest of the Alps spanning in every direction, not to mention the wine, cheese, pizza, and gelato awaiting you back in town. You don't necessarily have to wait until your run ends to enjoy such indulgences, either; mountain refuges all over the Alps offer drinks, sandwiches, multi-course meals, and more.

Chapter 6

Hydration and Fueling

Often enough, because of the challenges of a trail, you'll need more time than you might expect to cover a given distance. Further, a more relaxed approach while trail running facilitates long outings. Therefore, adequate hydration and fueling can come into play out in the wilds. Learn here about what to ingest to stay happy and healthy on the trail.

Before diving into specifics, you should know that most of your trail runs won't require hydration and fueling. They will be short enough that you can rely on your body's own water- and fuel-storage capabilities. That's right. We're telling you that much of the information in this chapter is irrelevant to most of your trail running. But when the water, electrolytes, or fuel needed for a run exceeds your body's natural storage capacity, you will need to take in more of that item to have a healthy and enjoyable experience. This chapter covers those situations.

Many new approaches to hydration and nutrition have recently been developed. Some are based on emergent science, but others are simply gimmicks. Those based on emergent science need more time for repeated research before they become accepted by the endurance-sports community. With that in mind, this chapter focuses on the tried and true theories on hydration and fueling immediately before, during, and after your running.

Finally, hydration and fueling are an experiment of one. Your body has unique and variable hydration and fueling requirements based on the weather, your fitness, and your body's specific needs and tolerances. You should repeatedly test various approaches in differing conditions to see how they apply to you. The good news is that such testing involves running and is loads of fun!

Hydration

Water and electrolytes are crucial parts of the hydration equation, and the right quantities of each are required by your body's systems, organs, and cells. Almost every part of your body needs water to operate, and water makes up well over half of your body's weight. Your blood needs sufficient water to transmit oxygen and nutrients around the body. Your muscles need it to perform their continued contractions. Your kidneys require water to excrete waste products from your body. And on it goes.

Electrolytes, particularly sodium, as well as potassium, calcium, magnesium, and others, are also crucial to the body's health. The role of electrolytes is even more complex than that of water. These electrolytes do two things—help maintain appropriate water balance both inside and outside our body's cell walls and incite miniscule electrical currents that cause certain cells, like those of a muscle or nerve, to behave as they should. You need to regulate both your water and electrolyte intake to maintain the right ratio for all of your body's functions.

When you run, you lose water and electrolytes through sweat and waste elimination while you lose water through respiration. You should replace whatever water and electrolytes you lose. You don't always need to do that during your trail run, so much as over the course of a day through adequate hydration and refueling.

The human body can healthfully lose about two percent of its body weight in water before it is dehydrated and before the previously described bodily functions begin to function inefficiently. In some athletes, however, this shortfall leads to performance decline. But scientific research has shown that some human bodies can perform just as well at this and even higher states of dehydration. Although we don't advocate undergoing significant water and electrolyte loss while running, you don't necessarily need to take water and electrolytes during shorter trail runs in pleasant conditions.

In the balance of this section, you'll see how to hydrate immediately before, during, and after trail running. You'll then learn the reasons behind these basic principles. In this sense, you're getting the sum of the equation first, followed by descriptions of its parts.

The Quick and Dirty on Trail Running Hydration

Magda Boulet is an Olympic marathoner who converted to competitive trail running in 2013. She works in research at Gu Energy and has a master's in exercise physiology. Magda says that you need to maintain proper hydration on a daily basis, not just when you're running, including taking in water and electrolytes. All-day hydration is where it's at, says Boulet: "A key aspect of maximizing performance is arriving at the start of a workout or race well hydrated. Many, if not most, athletes cannot consume enough fluid during exercise to match rates of loss, which has been documented by many studies. Therefore, prehydration before starting exercise can help ensure that athletes start the event or exercise bout in a hydrated state and can improve performance."

How can you do this? Drink when you're thirsty, and stop when you aren't anymore—in life, when running, anytime. It's just that simple.

> Staying hydrated in life and running is simple: Drink to thirst.

Here are a few more hydration basics:

- Continue to monitor changes in your thirst and resulting fluid intake in variable environmental conditions such as cold weather, high heat, high humidity, and an average day of running in your hometown. Track your sweat rate to compare your thirst and fluid intake with your fluid expenditures. This record should give you a good idea of your body's fluid needs during exercise in various environmental conditions. (The "Sweat-Rate Test" sidebar explains how to do this.) As mentioned earlier, in many circumstances you don't need to hydrate during a run. You may find that you develop thirst in the later stages of these types of runs. If that is the case, drink to thirst as soon as your run ends.

- Use extra care and attention to monitor your thirst and hydration in high heat when your sweat rate can be extremely high and dehydration can occur more rapidly. Research has shown that some people have depressed thirst cues in extremely hot environments, so in those conditions you may need to rely more on your understanding of your fluid needs than your thirst cues.

- You consume electrolytes naturally through the food you eat. If you need to supplement your natural electrolyte intake during a long run, use a food product or supplement at a rate that agrees with your body.

- Lastly, safety should always trump the body's ability to operate in low-level dehydration. If you're headed to a remote place or if it's a hot day, carry water, even if you don't think you'll need it. If the run takes you longer than you think or you take a wrong turn, you'll be glad you have that water!

Sweat-Rate Test

Because hydration is linked to overall health and performance during running, we encourage you to take a scientific approach toward understanding your water expenditure. Magda Boulet explains, "Weighing in before and after exercise can help athletes figure out the right amount of liquids to consume during exercise."

First, weigh yourself naked before a run. Then, run for one hour without eating or drinking anything and without using the bathroom. Weigh yourself naked immediately afterward and record the weight difference. One fluid ounce of water weighs 0.065 pounds, so 10 fluid ounces of water weighs 0.65 pounds (1,000 ml of water is 1 kg.) Do the math to see how much water you lost. That number represents your sweat rate, the amount of water you lose per hour of running in those conditions.

Keep in mind that your sweat rate will vary according to temperature, humidity, your attire, your fitness level, and more. For this reason, you should repeat this test in various conditions so that you can collect a series of data points representing your sweat-rate range.

Thirst Cues and Drinking to Thirst

The human body has thirst cues, such as the feelings of parched lips, a dry mouth, or a raspy throat. These are responses to water loss. Scientists believe that people who listen to their thirst cues by drinking when they feel thirsty and stopping when those feelings disappear, during daily life and exercise, hydrate adequately.

As recently as a decade ago, doctors were categorically recommending that we drink eight 8-ounce (240 ml) glasses of water per day, whatever our body size, our daily exertion, or the weather. Dr. Timothy Noakes, author of *Waterlogged: The Serious Problem of Overhydration in Endurance Sports*, points to another culturally pervasive issue, at least in our running culture—the historical recommendation to drink to excess during sports be it through water or sports drinks. But overhydration can be a serious medical issue, which is addressed later in this chapter. In response, Noakes began promoting the drink-to-thirst principle as a way to encourage people to drink the proper amount of water in daily life and during exercise.

Although thirst cues are now believed to be a solid guide to deciphering how much water each of us should drink daily, scientists also know that human bodies' thirst cues occur at different times. Some bodies won't produce a thirst cue until a person is approaching dehydration, whereas others produce thirst cues much earlier. But research shows that, in the end, thirst cues usually lead to proper hydration when they are heeded. For instance, people who have a late thirst cue may remain thirsty longer as they drink. The feeling of thirst disappears more slowly, which allows them to take in more water to recover their water loss.

When drinking to thirst, some runners find that they feel better when they sip small amounts frequently, whereas others like to guzzle at irregular intervals. The water you drink goes to your gastrointestinal tract, and it's then transferred elsewhere in your body. The stomach has an average maximum processing capacity of about one liter of water per hour during aerobic exercise, an amount that will vary depending on how hard you're running, the climate in which you're exercising, and how much liquid and material containing calories is in your stomach. Drinking a beverage containing calories can also slow the emptying rate of your stomach. If you exceed that emptying ability, water will begin to pool in your stomach, which can lead to the sensations of bloating, sloshing, and even nausea. Of course, this is uncomfortable when it happens. With practice, you will learn your body's preferred rate of water consumption.

We encourage you to test the drink-to-thirst concept to learn how it works for you. Spend a day following your thirst cues, including before, during, and after your trail run. Monitor the color of your urine throughout the day. If your urine is light yellow, you're likely adequately hydrated. Any lighter- or any darker-colored urine could mean that you're overhydrated or dehydrated, respectively. You may find that it takes a little while to identify your thirst cues because people in Western cultures often drink for purposes other than quenching thirst.

Dangers of Extreme Overhydration and Underhydration

As noted earlier, water and electrolytes are the two components of hydration, and hyponatremia is defined as a state of inadequate sodium. This condition typically manifests in athletes when they ingest too much water and not enough sodium, resulting in dilutional hyponatremia.

Acute hyponatremia is serious and can lead to coma or death because of brain swelling following nausea, headache, confusion, and possibly, seizures. Occasionally, runners are hospitalized or die because of hyponatremia, most commonly after a race. Use drinking to thirst to avoid this dangerous condition.

On the other hand, extreme dehydration causes your body's cells, organs, and systems to malfunction because of insufficient water. The initial symptoms of acute dehydration include lightheadedness, dizziness, and extreme thirst. Left untreated, acute dehydration can lead to death from heart failure or brain swelling. Extreme dehydration is rare because reaching this condition takes a while, and the body gives off numerous thirst cues along the way to stop you from getting there. Generally, people who experience a medical event because of extreme dehydration are in an exceptionally hot environment, which speeds the dehydration process, is often lacking in water access, and is thought to suppress thirst cues in some populations.

Staying hydrated in the heat is important for both your basic health and athletic performance.

Electrolyte Intake

How and when do we actually take in electrolytes while trail running? Generally, you'll need to supplement electrolytes only on outings of several hours, or, rarely, during shorter runs in extreme environments, like high heat. But unlike achieving adequate hydration by simply drinking to thirst, getting electrolyte supplementation right is a challenge because the rate at which you lose electrolytes through sweating varies depending on your fitness, the amount of electrolytes you consume, the ambient temperature, your acclimation to the environmental conditions, and more. Every long trail run can require a different electrolyte intake.

Numerous electrolyte supplements, as well as food and drinks containing electrolytes, are on the market. Test them one at a time, using each for a couple of long runs, to see how your body responds. If you're trying a supplement, follow the recommended dosing. Start at the low end of the dosing recommendation and adjust up or down on the basis of your body's response. The onset of nausea immediately after taking electrolytes often suggests that you're taking too high a dosage or not drinking enough water when taking the supplements. Electrolyte ingestion should not have negative side effects, and you should feel like your normal self when you are running.

Pre-Dehydration

As mentioned earlier, dehydration is scientifically defined as a water loss of more than two percent of your body weight. Scientific research often shows that performance during aerobic sports begins to lapse when an athlete becomes dehydrated.

Still, the body can perform well in a state of pre-dehydration, before hitting that point of two percent body-weight loss, and some athletes perform well in a state of moderate, true dehydration. Some scientific studies have shown that very fit endurance athletes can tolerate a loss of at least six to eight percent of their body weight before performance starts to drop off. In fact, the fastest finishers at a marathon or Ironman triathlon often have the greatest body-weight loss among those in the front of the pack.

What all this tells us is that dehydration and the performance loss that results from it, as well as the serious health issues that can arise from moderate to severe dehydration, are all a study of one. Treat yourself as an experiment, because that's exactly what you are. We don't recommend regularly operating in a state of dehydration, even if you feel good during it, because every single part of the body requires water, it's clearly one of the most crucial parts of our lives. Water your body!

Fueling

Stephanie Howe has a master's in exercise physiology and a PhD in nutrition and exercise physiology, and she was the winner of the revered Western States 100-Mile Run in 2014. She explains the basics of energy sources in the human body: "Carbohydrate, fat, and protein are the macronutrients (energy-yielding nutrients) that provide our bodies with energy. We need all three nutrients to survive and to optimize performance. For an endurance athlete, an ideal nutrient profile includes 55 to 65 percent carbohydrate, 20 to 30 percent fat, and 10 to 30 percent protein. The exact amounts required depend on the individual (gender, training level, fitness, genetics, and so on), but the basic framework remains the same."

Our bodies can tap carbohydrate reservoirs as well as fat dispersed throughout the body as fuel for endurance exercise. (The body consumes a small amount of muscle protein as a fuel source during endurance exercise, but because the rate is extremely low, let's leave it out of our fueling equation for the moment. The "Amino Acid Supplementation" sidebar in this chapter addresses this.) Explains Howe, "First, we have stores of carbohydrate—glycogen—in the muscles and the liver. When we start activity, the body begins to use this stored glycogen for energy. Around 90 minutes or so, the amount of stored glycogen begins to dwindle, and the body turns to another source, blood glucose, to supply energy to the working muscles. This strategy works only for some time because the amount of glucose we're using is not replenished fast enough (by gluconeogenesis in the liver) to prevent a decline in blood glucose. Blood glucose is closely monitored by the brain and maintained in a narrow physiologic range, and fatigue sets in after it starts to decline. Low blood glucose is a sign to the body that there's not enough fuel available and subsequently fatigue sets in."

The body can convert massive amounts of fat for endurance exercise, and even runners with very low body-fat percentages have many thousands of calories of usable fat. Because our bodies differ, the amount of carbohydrate and fat that your body stores and is able to convert varies.

In running, the average human body calls on those energy stores at a rate of about 100 calories per mile (60 calories per km). At moderate to high heart rates, the body draws significantly on its glycogen stores and more minimally on fat. At lower heart rates, the body uses smaller amounts of glycogen and a lot of fat. You can run at higher heart rates until you deplete your accessible glycogen. Unless you are consuming carbohydrate-based running fuel, you will have to slow to a lower heart rate, but you will still be able to run using your fat stores. This phenomenon—running out of internal glycogen and not putting in more fuel—is sometimes called "hitting the wall" or "bonking" because it makes you feel weak and forces you to slow down. To prevent that, we take in fuel during prolonged exercise.

In the following sections, you'll learn the basic principles of fueling immediately before, during, and after your trail runs, as well as how you will need to adapt those ideas to the specific needs of your body. The information is presented as the main concepts of fueling first, followed by larger explanations of those principles.

The Quick and Dirty on Fueling While Trail Running

Here are a few fundamental concepts for fueling before, during, and immediately after trail running.

- Properly fuel on a daily basis, not just when you're running. Make sure that your calorie intake roughly matches your calorie expenditures. Eat a variety of whole, unprocessed foods as much as possible.

- Eat a small meal containing foods you know you can digest two to three hours before a long trail run. Consume 100 calories of a carbohydrate-based, easily digestible food source 15 to 30 minutes before beginning a long trail run. This food could be a fuel designed for consumption during aerobic exercise, like a gel.

- As mentioned earlier, in many circumstances you don't need to fuel during a run, such as a two-hour run during which you can rely entirely on your body's energy stores. You may find that you have hunger cues during such runs. In this case, you can consume a small amount of fuel to quell those cues until your run is over.

- Consume 200 to 300 calories per hour of fuel designed for consumption during aerobic exercise, which includes glucose through maltodextrin and fructose at a ratio of 2 to 1. Avoid consuming much more than 100 calories at once and try to space those calories over the entire hour. Howe says, "Fueling should begin within the first 60 minutes and continue at regular intervals throughout exercise. Normally a feeding schedule of every 20 to 30 minutes is ideal to supply a steady stream of energy and prevent stomach distress (by maintaining blood flow to the gut, rather than a large bolus of fueling with long periods in between)."

- Consume 150 to 300 calories of your preferred recovery fuel in the first 30 minutes after ending a long trail run or at the end of a shorter, intense run.

- Safety should always trump the body's ability to operate well without fuel while trail running. If you're headed to a remote place or if the weather is particularly bad, bring a bit of food with you. What will happen if you become lost or stuck out there? Although the human body can survive for days without food, eating food can help keep your body warm and energized, as well as keep your spirits up.

Fueling Before Running

If you've eaten a regular meal within 12 hours or so of a run without having exercised much, your muscle glycogen stores will be full. But the glycogen stores in your liver vary from hour to hour. Thus, the purpose of a prerun meal is to restore the glycogen in your liver to its maximum capacity. The general recommendation is to eat a meal containing 100 grams (400 calories) of carbohydrate two to three hours before your run. This interval is enough time for your stomach to absorb the food and convert it to liver glycogen. This should also be enough time for any insulin-level changes to occur and return to normal, which affects how fast you burn through that liver glycogen. Many experts also recommend a very small dose of glucose in the 15 to 30 minutes immediately before starting a run. This fuel may come from a sports nutrition product.

Fueling While Running

As noted, you don't need to put energy into your body before or during your run unless you're planning to burn through your body's accessible glycogen stores. And even after that, you could keep going much farther at a slower pace using your body's fat stores.

But if you are planning to run long and fast enough to expend your accessible glycogen stores and you would like to keep running at that pace, you will need to fuel. You are limited, however, by what your stomach can process. Shoot for up to 300 calories per hour if you are running at an easy or moderate effort. If you're pushing hard, you might be limited to processing 200 or even 150 calories per hour because blood flow shifts from your stomach to the muscles you're using to run. Most of your calories should come from easily digested, high-carbohydrate foods.

For maximum performance, Howe says that we should consume multiple carbohydrate sources, namely glucose through maltodextrin and fructose at a ratio of 2 to 1. If you are consuming maltodextrin, your body can process

Sports gels are an easy, portable way to fuel during longer trail runs.

about 60 grams (240 calories) of it per hour. But if you consume fructose along with maltodextrin, notes Howe, your total carbohydrate absorption rate increases to 75 grams (300 calories) per hour. She emphasizes, however, that more is not better in this scenario. The 2-to-1 ratio of maltodextrin to fructose is best in terms of what your body can process. When you combine carbohydrate sources, such as by simultaneously ingesting both maltodextrin and fructose in that ratio, says Howe, the rate of absorption will increase and you will have the lowest risk of stomach distress.

> On long trail runs, take in 200 to 300 calories of running fuel, like gels, blocks, or sports drinks, per hour to maintain your energy level. On short trail runs, you won't need to eat until afterward.

Many fueling sources are available, from sports gels and blocks to cookies, from carbohydrate-laden sports drinks to fruit juice, and others. Test a number of products to see how they make your energy level and stomach feel as you run. Runners who have sensitive stomachs or plan to fuel while running at a decent effort may find that their stomachs tolerate run-specific fuels better.

Running fueling is an experiment of one. Your stomach will tell you what it likes and what it can process per unit of time. Its ability to process foods while running varies according to how fast you're running, what the weather is, how well you're accustomed to eating while running, and more. For instance, many people would never be able to consume 300 calories per hour while running. For others, fueling on the run comes easy, and their stomachs are flexible to both the kinds

Amino Acid Supplementation for Very Long Bouts of Endurance Exercise

The human body uses a very small amount of its own protein as fuel during endurance exercise. In most cases, protein represents around 6 percent of the body's fuel consumption, but this number can inflate to 12 percent under endurance exercise duress or if carbohydrate consumption during very long endurance exercise is not adequate, such as during high-mileage training or a run of ultramarathon distance.

Says Magda Boulet, "If you are planning to run in these circumstances, branched chain amino acids (BCAAs) play a significant role in inhibiting central fatigue during exercise as well as promoting recovery post exercise." Boulet continues, "As important as carbohydrate is in sustaining endurance activity, BCAAs are equally important in the ability to recover and perform optimally the next day. Studies have shown that BCAAs may reduce muscle damage associated with endurance exercise and delay fatigue. As exercise intensity and duration increases, the importance of BCAAs in muscle tissue repair increases." Some running and recovery fuels already contain these amino acids. A number of BCAA supplements are on the market.

and number of calories they consume. Other people have to experiment with fuel sources and volumes in varying conditions until they find a set of consumption parameters that works for them.

Recovery and Other Postrun Fueling

You've gone for a run using some of your body's glycogen, some of its fat, and a bit of its protein stores to fuel yourself. "Nutrition in the postexercise period is also critical for recovery," begins Magda Boulet. "Your recovery meal should include quality protein to maximize protein synthesis rates, speed recovery, and promote muscle repair. As important, the consumption of carbohydrate will maximize glycogen synthesis to prepare for the next workout."

To elaborate, your body has an increased capacity for synthesizing carbohydrate back into your muscles and liver in the 30 to 60 minutes immediately after exercise. If you've gone on a run during which you've depleted a significant amount of your body's glycogen stores, use this window to replenish. Make sure that your recovery fueling also includes some protein to help repair muscle tissues stressed by your exercise and to replace the small amount of protein you burned as fuel. Today, many recovery products are available, typically powders of easily digestible carbohydrate and protein that you mix into water before drinking. But many people refuel with readily available food and drink that are rich in carbohydrate and contain a modest amount of protein. Pick what tastes good and what your body responds to best.

Although a detailed discussion of daily nutrition is beyond the scope of this book, check out *Racing Weight: How to Get Lean for Peak Performance* by Matt Fitzgerald for its deep discussion of full-spectrum fueling and nutrition for endurance athletes.

Metabolic Efficiency and Crossover Training

The body uses its internal carbohydrate and fat stores to fuel exercise. Stephanie Howe says, "If we examine the distribution of energy coming from fat and carbohydrate at varying intensities, there is an increase on the reliance of carbohydrate as intensity increases. There is a point, referred to as the crossover point, where the amount of carbohydrate becomes greater than the amount of fat being used for energy. This usually occurs around 60 percent of $\dot{V}O_2$max."

We'll talk in detail about $\dot{V}O_2$max in chapter 8, "Training for the Trail," but for now you should know that your $\dot{V}O_2$max is the amount of oxygen your body can absorb during a minute of the fastest running you can possibly tolerate. Envision running at your $\dot{V}O_2$max as running as fast as you can.

Howe continues, "Training can help shift the crossover point, meaning that fat can be used at a higher percentage of $\dot{V}O_2$max to fuel activity. But the important thing to note is that both carbohydrate and fat contribute at any given intensity. At rest, we rely primarily on fat, but as exercise intensity increases, even to 25 percent of $\dot{V}O_2$max, we rely on both nutrients. Even though fat may be the primary fuel at a lower intensity, we never rely solely on fat."

This crossover point is not fixed. It can vary over a person's training cycles and running career. The way you train and fuel can change it. You will benefit by increasing that crossover point, by training your body to burn additional fat at higher running intensities.

Moving that crossover point and thereby increasing your metabolic efficiency requires you to modify your training and fueling. While training, spend the beginning of a training cycle running below your crossover point, which you can determine by an exercise test conducted by sports medicine professionals. When fueling and not running, decrease your intake of carbohydrate that is not fruit based or vegetable based. For fueling while running, when you are training below your crossover point early in your training schedule, don't fuel. Later in your training, when you are running at speeds above your crossover point, supplement with traditional carbohydrate-based running fuel. But if you've increased your crossover point, you'll find that you should need much less than the standard intake of running fuel.

The benefit of all this is to make you more fuel efficient when running, in all of these respects.

To learn more about metabolic efficiency and implementing its concepts into your running, read *Metabolic Efficiency Training: Teaching the Body to Burn More Fat* by Bob Seebohar.

Troubleshooting Hydration and Fueling Problems

No matter how hard you try, you're going to mess up your hydration or fueling at some point in your trail running career. More likely, it's going to happen many times. Sometimes you're going to feel awful as a result, so you need to troubleshoot those circumstances, get back to feeling good again, and add that experience to your knowledge base so that you can avoid or minimize similar problems in the future.

Here are some of the more common problem scenarios you might encounter and ways that you can cope with them.

Symptom

Sudden fatigue (especially if you've run more than three hours)

Potential Cause

Glycogen depletion

Correction

If you go from energetic to feeling weak or seeing your pace slow significantly over a short time, you're likely experiencing glycogen depletion. Consume about 100 calories of a running-fuel product every 15 to 20 minutes. Stephanie Howe explains, "The best choice is simple carbohydrate, in either liquid, gel, or energy block consistency. I think a soda, like Coke, works well in this situation. It's easy to get down and quickly enters the bloodstream. Drinking something for a quick pick-me-up is the first step. Then, to prevent a relapse, you need to get back on a schedule of frequent fueling—every 20 minutes. Keep the calories coming in. You may have to slow your intensity for a little bit until your body can recover." You're likely to start feeling better within 30 to 60 minutes.

Symptom

Bloated or sloshing stomach

Potential Cause

Overhydration, electrolyte deficiency, or overfueling

Correction

If your stomach begins to feel or look noticeably bloated (in contrast to swelling in your hands or feet), or if you can hear or feel your stomach sloshing, you have a buildup of unprocessed food or liquids in your stomach. In this case, either you've consumed too much material too quickly for your stomach to process or you've consumed too much material and not enough electrolytes. Howe suggests that the right ratio of water and electrolytes is necessary for the processing of materials in your stomach. In this situation, you may be able to decipher the cause by recalling what you've most recently consumed.

Did you take in a whole bunch of water quickly because you felt thirsty? If so, give your stomach some time to catch up by not putting anything into it, either food or water, for 30 minutes. In addition, think about slowing your pace so that your body can divert oxygen being used in your muscles to your stomach for increased absorption capability.

Have you been drinking water normally but not consuming electrolytes? If so, take some electrolytes and wait for at least 30 minutes to see whether the bloating and sloshing start to disappear. If they do, return to your normal electrolyte schedule, if you have and need one. If they don't, take another dose.

Symptom

Swollen fingers, feet, or other body parts

Potential Cause
Electrolyte deficiency

Correction
The occurrence of swollen fingers, feet, or other body parts during trail running can be the result of consuming too few electrolytes for the amount of water inside your body. If this is the case, your body will siphon those electrolytes (along with adequate water) to the place it needs it the most for the aerobic exercise, the bloodstream. Excess water, if it has already been absorbed by your gastrointestinal tract and is among your body's systems, will be shuttled to extracellular spaces. The result is noticeable swelling, which concentrates in the hands and feet of some people and causes general body swelling in others. Correcting this issue should be simple: Give yourself a dose of electrolytes along with a bit of water so that they can be absorbed by the stomach, and then return to proper electrolyte (according to your personal experiments with electrolytes) and water intake about 30 minutes later. The swelling should begin to recede within an hour.

Be aware that appendages can also swell in cold weather, at high altitude, or when you've been walking for long periods.

Symptom

Cramping

Potential Cause
Muscle fatigue or electrolyte deficiency

Correction

Cramping of your major running muscle groups, such as your quadriceps, hamstrings, and calves, can occur because of simple muscle fatigue. Fortunately, if you call it a day when this happens, the cramping will stop. A short walking break can cure those cramps, as can drinking or even swishing an electrolyte beverage around your mouth. Although it's not a cure, some light stretching of the affected muscle can also feel good.

The cramping of random muscles, such as those of your hands, forearms, or neck, along with your major running muscles can result from electrolyte deficiency. If electrolyte deficiency is likely the cause, consume electrolytes along with appropriate water. If the conditions haven't abated in 30 minutes, take another dose. This should correct the issue. Maintain a proper electrolyte intake afterward, if you take electrolytes.

Symptom

Nausea (which can progress to vomiting)

Potential Cause

Presence of undigested food in the stomach, not enough water for food to digest, overhydration, or too many electrolytes

Correction

Phew! Nausea is the most complicated condition to troubleshoot because it can result from many causes. The best way to start troubleshooting nausea is to think about what you've been eating and drinking to see whether you've taken too few or too many electrolytes or something else. If you suspect that you have undigested food in your stomach, you'll probably need to slow down a bit so that oxygen can divert from your muscles to your stomach to aid digestion. If you feel nauseous in addition to the sensation of a bloated or sloshing stomach, you may have overhydrated or you may not have enough electrolytes in your stomach. In this case, take electrolytes and give it a little time to see whether the nausea (and stomach sloshing) abates. Finally, you may have too little water in your stomach for the amount of food or electrolytes that are there and waiting to be digested. If you suspect this could be the case, you'll need to consume enough water to get the job done. Sip water slowly, however, so that you don't further inundate your already taxed stomach. In this complex scenario, what you do may not fix your stomach and you will have to try something else. Don't forget that slowing down or stopping your run will probably help, too. If worse comes to worst and you do vomit, this unpleasant emptying might reset your stomach and give you a clean slate with which to work.

TORRES DEL PAINE NATIONAL PARK, CHILE

Way down in the southern tip of South America in Chile's Patagonia region, not far from where the land yields to the meeting of the Pacific and Atlantic Oceans, lies Torres del Paine National Park. Although the park's namesakes, the insanely photogenic Torres del Paine—three rock fingers sticking vertically into the sky—have helped the park become a household name around the world, the park gets relatively few visitors and not many people arrive knowing much about the park beyond those impossible rock towers.

When they do arrive, tourists find glacier-carved mountains, glaciers, rivers, lakes, forests, and steppes, as well as robust wildlife populations including guanacos, pumas, birds, and more. They'll also find a national park, although it was first established in 1959 and has expanded multiple times since then, the park is still in the throes of recovery from pre-national-park farming and grazing. Throughout, visitors will find a climate of extremes; wind and rain are almost everyday occurrences.

Finally, trails await, of course. The O and W Circuits are the most popular trails of the national park, named because of the shape they make on a map. The W Circuit is an abbreviated version of the O Circuit, which is a full-monty loop of the Paine Massif including a couple of out-and-backs into side valleys. Trail runners can plan anything from a daylong out-and-back on these circuits to a multiday running tour supported by overnights in the refuges of the park. Beyond these popular routes, the park has many other hiking trails that you can run, as well.

If racing is your thing, you'll be happy to know that the racing scene of the Patagonia region of Chile, including Torres del Paine National Park, is rapidly expanding. Every year for the last couple of years, new trail races of varying distances have been established. Should you decide to participate in a trail race here, do your research and be prepared for a more remote, less-supported trail racing scene than you may be accustomed to in other parts of the world.

Challenging conditions empower a runner atop Pritchett Canyon outside Moab, Utah.

Chapter **7**

Conquering the Conditions

The world can throw some pretty nasty conditions our way, from blistering heat to frigid cold and much in between. Although such conditions might send some folks inside to the treadmill or the sofa, the good news is that you can trail run in almost any condition so long as you are adequately prepared and equipped.

That said, heading out into treacherous conditions underprepared or ill equipped is a major no-no. In doing so, you risk not only your own well-being but also that of anyone sent out to aid you or search for you.

With that in mind, three steps can greatly increase your safety and the safety of others when you tackle extremes while trail running:

1. **Plan**. The first step to being safe in any extreme trail running situation is to assess both the likely and long-shot dangerous aspects for the run and develop a plan to minimize danger to yourself by your route, fuel and hydration, and equipment selection.

A twilight run can be captivating, not to mention cooler.

2. **Share**. Share that plan, including a preferred route and one or more bailout options, with someone not on the run in case something does go wrong. Counsel them about how much time cushion they should allow after your planned return before they take action. The more extreme the conditions are, the shorter the time cushion should be. And the more personal experience you have in those conditions and the more equipment you carry, the longer the time cushion may be.

3. **Play it safe**. Finally, whatever your plan and safety backup, you still need to take care of yourself out there. Ultimately, you are responsible for your well-being, so err on the side of caution. The 110-degree Fahrenheit (43-degree Celsius) day likely isn't the best day to check out that stone spire on the other side of an unknown canyon. Likewise, you shouldn't test your rock-hopping skills across a stream when it's minus 10 degrees Fahrenheit (minus 23 degrees Celsius) or practice your alpinism 10 miles (16 km) from home with a storm blowing in.

With that in mind, let's look at exactly how you can maximize your enjoyment and safety when running in extreme heat and extreme cold, how to brush off the elements in heavy rain or snow, how to avoid getting burned by the sun or lost in the dark, and what to do in the thin air at high altitude.

Extreme Heat

Extreme heat is extremely detrimental to performance. Even moderate heat can slow you down. In a study of road marathoners, runners slowed from 1.6 to 3 percent for every 10 degrees over 55 degrees Fahrenheit (every 6 degrees over 13 degrees Celsius). This performance decline occurs because your blood supply is shifted from the leg muscles to the blood vessels near the skin in an attempt to prevent overheating.

Heat-Related Health Issues

Aside from decreased performance, heat can lead to a host of minor and major medical issues. On the minor side, nausea can quickly creep into the picture, especially if you're eating or drinking, as blood is moved from your gut to your skin and muscles.

Heat exhaustion and heatstroke are more serious. Heat exhaustion can include the following symptoms: heavy sweating, rapid pulse, nausea, vomiting, fatigue, cool skin with goosebumps, headache, and dizziness. At this point, the solution is to stop running, move to a cool place, drink cool water or sports drink, and, if possible, use cooling methods like a cool shower, a fan, towels with ice, and more. If your condition doesn't improve within an hour, seek medical attention.

If untreated, heat exhaustion can progress to heatstroke, an extremely urgent and serious medical condition in which the body temperature rises to 104 degrees Fahrenheit (40 degrees Celsius) or higher. Heatstroke requires immediate emergency medical treatment because it can quickly damage the heart, brain, kidneys, and muscles. If untreated, heatstroke can lead to coma and death. Symptoms can include

On a hot day, the shade of a rock offers a runner respite.

altered mental states or behavior (reduced level of consciousness, confusion, agitation, slurring of speech, delirium, seizures), alternation between sweating and not, nausea, vomiting, diarrhea, flushed skin, rapid breathing, rapid heartbeat, and headache. While awaiting emergency medical treatment, a suspected heatstroke victim should be moved to a cool place, have excess clothing removed, and be actively cooled (but do not place the person in an ice bath).

Avoid the Heat

Perhaps the best way to deal with extreme heat is to avoid it altogether. Finding shade is often a good way to stay cool. In a forest, the shade and plant-respiration-based cooling can often make the environment noticeably cooler than open space. Likewise, a run in the shadows of mountains or hillsides can be cooler than running on ridges. One key caveat for seeking out shade is that narrow, rocky canyons that receive midday sun can be much warmer in late-afternoon shade or even the following morning as the rocks bake and then radiate heat long after the sun is gone.

If you can't find a locally cool environment for a midday run, try running early in the morning or at night. On average, days are at their coolest right at dawn, so the early bird certainly has an advantage here. Although it's noticeably hotter at sunset than at sunrise, the environment cools down after the sun goes down. The longer you wait after sundown, the cooler things should be, so night owls have an advantage here. To avoid the worst heat, avoid running in mid- to late afternoon when temperatures are usually at their highest.

If you run enough in the same area, you may notice that some locations simply tend to be cooler than others. Obviously, seeking out such places on hot days can be beneficial. Some spots to look for your local microclimate icebox are higher elevations; along cool bodies of water such as a river, lake, or ocean; or a vegetated valley into which the night's cooler air might settle.

Get Naked, Get Wet

Should running in extreme heat be unavoidable, you have a couple of options for keeping yourself cooler.

To start, you can often wear less clothing that is lighter in weight and lighter in color. When running in full sunlight in the very hottest environments, however, you may want to opt for full-coverage clothing that is light colored, lightweight, and loose fitting to keep you cooler by reducing the amount of sunlight absorbed directly by your skin. Likewise, wearing less clothing on hot days needs to be weighed against exposure to the sun's ultraviolet light, which you can read about later in this chapter.

Pam Smith, who won the Western States 100-Mile Run in a blazing hot year suggests, "When getting dressed for a hot run it may seem like a good idea to wear as little as possible, but your clothing can actually assist you in combatting the heat by keeping the sun's rays from directly warming your body. Either a hat or a visor will keep the sun off your face, but I always choose a hat because I can get it wet or put ice in it to cool my head. Some hats have attachments to keep the sun off your neck. Light-colored clothing is preferred because it reflects sunlight away from your body. I like a short-sleeve shirt to keep the sun off my back and shoulders, but others wear full sleeves to protect the arms, too. I cover all my exposed skin with a thick layer of sunscreen. This will not only prevent a nasty sunburn, but also block ultraviolet rays (and their energy), which will keep you cooler. Many sports-specific sunscreens are available now that don't feel sticky when you run."

In drier conditions, you can dowse yourself in water that you're carrying or with water that you find along the way. That water will evaporate and cool your body the same way your sweat does. In rare circumstances when you'll be running for a long time in hot, dry conditions and have ready access to water, you may choose a light- or moderate-weight cotton T-shirt to absorb water for prolonged evaporative cooling, like a swamp cooler in a desert environment.

So long as all signs point to safety, immersing yourself partially or fully in a body of water also cools you quickly. In particular, submersing your core, neck, and hands can quickly lower your body temperature, so jump into that lake or lie down in that shallow stream on a scalding day.

When running from home, you can throw some ice in a water bottle you carry (great for quick cooling through your hands too) or in your hydration pack for internal cooling whenever you drink. Although a much rarer find on the trail, natural ice and snow also provide respite from the heat. Tucking some snow in a cap can keep you cool for longer than you think. You can also throw some clean-looking snow or ice in your hydration system.

Speaking of hydration, you want to be even more vigilant than normal in hydrating in extreme heat. You can read up on proper hydration in chapter 6.

A stream can provide an excellent cool-off spot during a hot trail race.

Staying Healthy in the Heat

Finally, each person reacts differently to extreme heat. In effect, we all have different heat tolerances. Our individual tolerances vary with our fitness levels and our acclimation to the heat in the preceding weeks and months. A lack of acclimation and its accompanying physiological changes is why a 70-degree Fahrenheit (21-degree Celsius) day in early spring can feel and be debilitating, whereas the same conditions would be welcomed during the heat of summer. Allowing yourself 10 to 14 days to adjust to warmer conditions before a particularly strenuous run in heat can leave you more comfortable and safer.

Smith, also a medical doctor, advises, "On your run, start conservatively. Because your heart has to do extra work pumping blood to the skin, all of your normal paces will require more effort. If you are racing, you will likely need to adjust your goal pace. If you do find yourself overheated, stop running! Even if you are in a race, remember that your health and well-being are more important than any finish time. Douse yourself with water to try to bring your body temperature down. If you feel OK, you can continue walking, but if you are lightheaded, having vision trouble, or throwing up uncontrollably, you should find a shady place to sit or lie down. Find help if you can. Otherwise, wait until you are feeling better and daytime temperatures have dropped before beginning to walk again."

Extreme Cold

To some degree, dealing with extreme cold is simpler than dealing with extreme heat. Although you can take off only so many clothes in the heat, you can keep putting them on when it gets colder. Just as in cool and moderately cold conditions, layering is the key. You'll want to be able to add layers quickly should your progress slow or conditions worsen. Just as important, you'll want to be able to shed layers as temperatures warm or as you increase your aerobic output. Zippered apparel and tops with sleeves you can push up add the option for fine-tuning along the way. Basic options for cold-weather apparel are discussed in the section "Cool and Inclement Conditions" in chapter 5. Also, don't forget your hat and gloves.

Hot Foot

Keeping your feet warm can be a bit trickier. Geoff Roes, an Alaska resident and the 2010 Western States 100-Mile Run champion notes, "The number one thing to be aware of in regard to keeping feet warm is circulation. It's not primarily the amount of insulation that you wrap around your feet that will keep them warm, but rather your circulation in conjunction with this insulation. In most cases, increased insulation leads to decreased circulation, and this will always cause your feet to be colder rather than warmer.

In this sense, anytime you start to add insulation, it's important to take measures to avoid decreased circulation."

Roes wears "a medium-weight, over-calf-length sock (keeping the lower legs warm will help keep the feet warm) with a pair of shoes that are at least a half-size larger than normal sizing." If it's also windy, Roes suggests "a water- or wind-resistant shoe."

Cold-Related Health Issues

Extreme cold is no reason to shy away from trail running, including on Colorado's Mount Elbert.

Although the basic method for dealing with extreme cold may be simple, cold can quickly lead to injury, loss of an appendage, and even death. In some cases, we're talking minutes rather than hours for frostnip or frostbite to occur when temperatures fall well below freezing, especially if it's windy. Generally, hypothermia settles in over longer periods as your core temperature slowly falls. It can happen quite quickly if you become wet, particularly if you're immersed in water. Hypothermia can occur even if you're moving.

Frostbite is the freezing of skin. It's characterized by skin that first turns very cold and red before becoming numb, hard, and pale. Frostbite is most common on the fingers, toes, nose, ears, and other exposed facial skin. Minor frostbite, such as its first stage—frostnip—can be self-treated with gentle rewarming of the skin. Seek emergency medical attention for significant frostbite, indicated by skin that is pale or white, skin that remains numb, or skin that blisters within a day or two of rewarming.

Hypothermia is the dangerous lowering of the body temperature below 95 degrees Fahrenheit (35 degrees Celsius). Mild hypothermia includes symptoms such as shivering, dizziness, hunger, nausea, rapid breathing or rapid heart rate, trouble speaking, or slight confusion. As hypothermia progresses to its moderate or severe stages, symptoms include increased shivering or inappropriate cessation of shivering, lack of coordination, slurred speech, confusion or poor decision making, drowsiness, decreased consciousness, weak pulse, or slow, shallow breathing. Seek immediate medical treatment for anyone who exhibits symptoms of hypothermia.

Eating Icicles: Fueling and Hydrating in the Cold

One nonintuitive consideration for very cold days is hydration and fueling. Although your hydration needs may be slightly lower on colder days, longer runs will still require some drinking. The problem is that darned tendency for water to freeze! For shorter runs, you can heat up some water before heading out, which will give you a bit more time until it freezes. Using an insulated water bottle, water-bottle holder (whether handheld or waist pack), or hydration bladder sleeve can also add time before freezing occurs. Still, the nipple on the water bottle and the nipple and hose of the bladder system are the items most likely to freeze. Keeping the bottle or hydration system (hose and nipple included) under a jacket and closer to your body can help keep the fluid flowing. Smaller, more frequent sips can also help keep the smaller, more susceptible pieces of your hydration system from freezing. Blowing water out of the nipple and hose and back into the bladder after each time you drink also prevents water from freezing in the nipple and hose.

On the fueling front, gels, chews, and bars can get rock hard in the cold. If you put your food against your body for 10 minutes before you want to eat, you'll have a much more manageable meal. Try placing the item against your palm inside a glove or mitten, in an interior hip pocket, in the band of your running bottoms, or, for women, in your sports bra.

Avoid the Cold

Just as you do on hot days, you can adjust when and where you run in cold weather for a more comfortable experience. Running in mid- to late afternoon usually means maximizing the day's warmth, whereas an early morning run will assure that you're running in the deep freeze. Choosing a time and route that keeps you in the sun will also keep you warmer. On the other hand, you'll want to stay out of any strong, sustained winds. On a windy day, a leafless deciduous forest can be a good wintertime solution for running in the sun with reduced wind.

Dry Body, Warm Clothes

The quickest way to fall victim to hypothermia is to get wet. This can happen by being rained on, sweating heavily, or being immersed in water, partially or fully. As such, you should take great care to stay dry in cold conditions. You need to be even more cautious than normal around bodies of water and to take greater care to stay dry when it's cool and raining. More on that soon.

In terms of mere comfort, Roes notes, "Warming up your head is one of the easiest ways to warm up your entire body, so often times it's worth adding an extra layer on your head, even if that's not where you are feeling cold. I have had dozens of times in which I've had a chilled-to-the-bone feeling when running in the cold and had it disappear within minutes of adding an extra layer to my head."

Carrying spare clothes is good insurance if you underestimated the cold or some of your apparel becomes wet. Gloves and mittens have a tendency to get wet, so carrying an extra pair can be well worth the marginal weight. Make sure you have a way of keeping the apparel you carry dry from sweat, precipitation, and possible submersion.

Two additional items you might want on your coldest trail runs are something to keep your face warm—be it a mask, balaclava, or Buff—and chemical hand warmers, which can be used to keep just about any body part warm.

Rainy Days

If you want to hit the trails most days, you'll get a little wet at times. In some climates, you might be rained on during most runs for months on end. Either way, you'll want to be prepared. How you prepare depends on the apparent temperature, which includes the effects of wind. What feels cool varies significantly from person to person, so the advice here is subjective. Besides, preparation represents a continuum of measures. You'll want to experiment (while being cautiously overprepared) with the rain setup you use in various conditions. Let's work our way from coldest to warmest, shall we?

Anton Krupicka motors through driving rain at the 2014 UTMB®.

Cold Rain

On cool to cold days, you need to stay dry as well as warm. After you're wet, the cold can make life miserable in a hurry. Therefore, you'll want to run in a waterproof membrane jacket. These jackets, along with their options and features, are discussed in full in the section "Cool and Inclement Conditions" in chapter 5. Here, your goal is to keep out all water. You'll want a jacket with a hood to keep water from rolling off your head, down your neck, and on to your otherwise dry torso.

Unless you're out for a very long run (more than a couple hours), it's a matter of personal preference whether you wear waterproof pants to complement your jacket. Some people prefer to stick with running shorts, tights, or maybe light windpants over shorts. The same sort of personal preference goes along with whether to wear waterproof gloves or mittens.

Temperate Rain

In milder conditions, staying dry in a passing shower is nice, but ultimately, your goal is to stay warm enough. Doing this can mean getting a bit wetter. Indeed, if you run in a zipped-up waterproof hooded jacket for long in warm conditions, you're likely to get wet from the inside out as you sweat. Therefore, you might consider a waterproof jacket with additional zipped vents or even always-open covered venting. Unless the rain will be pouring for hours or you'll be running into colder conditions, you might opt for going without a hood. In light rain or sporadic rain showers, a jacket coated with durable water repellent (DWR) may be more than enough. In such conditions, a long-sleeve half-zip shirt can be a valuable tool in fine-tuning your warmth.

It is often said that there is no truly bad weather in outdoor pursuits, only bad gear choices. For a long trail run, always bring a little more—whether it is water, food, warm clothing, or other items—than you think you'll need.

Another option in mild conditions where you're aiming to stay warm, not dry, might be a light fleece jacket or vest over either a midweight wool or synthetic long-sleeve shirt. The key here is in material choice and thickness: You want layers that offer enough insulation even when wet to help hold in your body heat and keep you warm. Getting the right thickness of these layers can be a challenge, so make sure to test gear in a benign situation first.

Hot Rain

On hot days, embrace the rain! Rain can be a welcome break from a sweltering day. Do keep in mind, however, that rain, especially rain from a thunderstorm or at high elevations, can be a great deal colder than the ambient temperature. So if you're out for a long run or in a remote area, consider carrying an emergency backup layer if cold rain is likely.

General Considerations on Rainy Days

Of course, rain itself isn't the only thing you need to deal with on a rainy day. You'll likely have to deal with mud. Look at the section in chapter 3, "Getting Dirty: Muddy Trails," to learn about various techniques for finding additional traction on mud. Heavily lugged shoes can also help you find more traction. Sometimes, however, the right call is to skip running on muddy trails altogether. Read "Dirty Politics: The Ethics of Muddy Trails" in chapter 3, which will give you the tools to decide when and where you should seek out drier trails.

In any wet conditions, from cold through warm, you'll want to have a full change of dry clothes to change into when you finish your run. Otherwise, after you lose the warmth produced by running, you can become cold quite quickly.

Finally, if you'll be carrying nonwaterproof electronics, such as a mobile phone or camera, make sure to place them in a resealable plastic bag or a small waterproof stuff sack. If you're on a run long enough to warrant extra clothes, you'll want to keep them dry in a plastic bag or stuff sack, too.

Snow Day!

As discussed in the section "Winter Wonderland: Wintry Trails" in chapter 3, running in and on snow can be a blast. A short trail run in light snow might not call for an alteration of your normal routine. Throw on your shoes and some cold-weather clothes and get out there!

Colorado resident Anton Krupicka uses winters as a chance to change up his trail running. "In general, I use the winter weather and trail conditions as a good excuse to slow down and take a less-intense approach to my running. I know I'm not going to be setting any PRs on my local climbs when there's a foot (30 cm) of fresh powder, but for me the winter trails provide an experience that I find extremely rewarding in other ways. With fresh snow covering everything, the scenery completely changes, providing some of the most beautiful surroundings that I encounter all year. The snow muffles sounds, too, offering a very calm, peaceful environment. All of this combined with the challenging footing means that in the winter I focus on just maintaining the ritual of getting out there every day and enjoying my surroundings, not necessarily being concerned with maintaining a certain pace, heart rate, or intensity of effort. Most of my uphill efforts end up being no more than a hike, because of the footing. After the snow melts in the spring, however, I'm often surprised at how simply focusing on consistency and not intensity through the snowy months has laid a solid foundation of basic fitness for the spring and summer."

Snow Comfortable

The same cautions and appropriate reactions laid out in the previous two sections apply to running in the snow, but staying dry is often much easier than when running in the rain. If it's more than a few degrees below freezing, snow will routinely bounce off your apparel without sticking. If it's close to or slightly above freezing and sloppy snow is falling, you might want a waterproof jacket. In between, a jacket with a DWR treatment can be the answer. Just be aware that the DWR properties fade with use and washings, although after-market products can reinvigorate the DWR coating.

You'll also stay drier (and warmer) if you stay on your feet. If you skipped over it, go back to the section "Winter Wonderland: Wintry Trails" in chapter 3 for an extensive discussion on staying upright on snowy or icy trails.

Anton Krupicka amongst Colorado's Flatirons after a snowstorm.

Navigating in the Snow

Aside from staying upright on snowy trails, you might occasionally be in a situation where navigation issues arise from the snow. This issue will rarely come up when you're running on familiar trails, but use caution when exploring new trails in heavy snow. First, your ability to visually navigate by landmarks and topography can diminish or vanish in heavy snow. Second, trails and even your reassuring footprints can quickly be erased in heavily falling or blowing snow. In other words, you might consider forgoing an exploratory trail run on a snowy day and instead enjoy your favorite trails with a twist.

Although the topic is largely beyond the scope of this book, you should be aware that snow, whether fresh or weeks old, can present avalanche danger on some slopes. If you'll be running through steep, mountainous terrain, do your due diligence to see whether, when, and where your trail running might put you in avalanche danger. If that's a possibility, avoid the danger or continue your learning to mitigate your risk. A good first stop is the American Avalanche Association's website (www.avalanche.org).

Sunny Days Are Here Again

Although feeling the sun on the skin can energize like few other things, too much of a good thing isn't all that good. Sun is particularly troublesome the closer you get to the summer solstice, when the sun is at its highest angle and the earth's protective atmosphere between the sun and your skin is at a minimum.

Sun Exposure

Obviously, brilliantly clear skies maximize exposure to harmful ultraviolet (UV) rays, but you can sunburn even on an overcast day. The arid air of the desert can result in a stronger sun. Snow cover can reflect massive amounts of UV radiation and cause wicked burns (as well as temporary sun blindness). Higher elevations also expose you to higher levels of UV light, which can be made all the worse by lingering snowpack. If you're light skinned, red-haired, or freckled, you probably know that you're particularly susceptible to sun overexposure.

Anna Frost and friends running in the sun high in Montana's Beartooth Mountains.

Avoiding the Sun

So what can you do to keep from being sunburned while out on the trails? Well, for starters you can avoid the worst of the sun. One way to do this is to minimize exposure between 10 a.m. and 4 p.m. (The sun is at its strongest at midday, but this range is centered one hour later to acknowledge that many locations apply daylight savings time during the summer.) As with avoiding heat, you can seek out shade whether from a forest canopy, canyon wall, or another source.

Blocking the Sun

Whether or not you can avoid the worst of the sun, additional protection might be in order. As anyone with a farmer's tan can testify, clothing makes a good sunblock. For skin that you leave exposed—particularly on your head, hands, arms, and torso, apply a broad-spectrum sunblock of SPF 30 or higher. Look for a sports-specific or sweat-resistant sunblock.

On its own, a brimmed cap can provide moderate protection for your face and a second layer of protection when you use sunscreen. A cap is paramount for men who might not be as lusciously locked as they once were. Prolonged exposure to extreme solar radiation may mean wearing a hat with a rear cape or 360-degree brim.

One final piece of protection you'll want for those sunny days is sunglasses. Sunglasses make trail running much more comfortable in bright light, and a pair with broad-spectrum UV protection significantly shields your eyes in both the short and long term.

Into the Night

Trail running at night is magic. The world is quieter. The sun's harsh shadows are replaced with soft moon shadows or even star shadows. (Yes, the light of the stars and planets can be strong enough to cast shadows on the darkest and clearest of nights.) The world feels smaller and more intimate. The distractions of the day seem to fade away. In short, the solace many seek by trail running is amplified come nightfall.

Rory Bosio has twice run through the night to win the prestigious UTMB® in the European Alps, and she loves it. "Instead of ogling the gorgeous scenery, running at night forces us to focus more intently on the body, on the actual act of running. I love the intense mind–body connection that comes with running in the dark. The stillness in the air at night makes running feel spiritual, like one is seeing the world during a time when humans aren't supposed to. I don't feel scared or uneasy being in the woods at night. Instead, I feel adventurous. I feel like I'm getting a sneak peek at a part of the world that usually goes unnoticed by most people. Everything changes in the darkness. The entire vibe of the natural world at night feels more peaceful, more soothing than it does in the harsh light of day. I love how time passes differently at night, as well. It's like the world has hit the pause button. Mother Earth gets a respite from the turmoil and hustle and bustle of the daylight. I love experiencing this quietness. It somehow seeps into my body and makes me feel at peace. Running at night, whether it's under the stars or in the glow of the moonlight, is as close to going to church as I get. It provides a spiritual sensation that connects my mind and body to the natural world around me like nothing else can."

Runners congregate before a night run.

If you decide to take on the trails at night, you'll usually want to run with supplemental lighting. Various lighting options are discussed in full in chapter 5.

For a bit of adventure, if you find yourself out on a night with a bright moon (or a cloudy night with manmade light reflected off the clouds), you might want to turn off your light and keep moving by the ambient light. As your eyes adjust, you'll be amazed at how well you can proceed.

> A headlamp is one of the best tools for running, on the road or trail. Using one opens up extra hours in your day for running.

Navigating at Night

As long as you have a functioning light, your toughest challenge at night might be navigation. Now, if you know the trails well or they're well signed and you have a map, navigating at night poses no added challenge. But if you're on less familiar or poorly signed trails, you won't necessarily have the visual assistance of landmarks or topographical features to help you navigate.

Although it can be fun to try on occasion, you don't particularly want to get caught on the trails at night without a light. Even if you plan to be home well before dark on a late-day run, you might want to bring an emergency light source, perhaps a small penlight or even a fully charged smartphone, in case your run goes longer than expected.

If you are caught off guard and find yourself on the trails after dark without a light because you didn't bring one or your battery dies, err on the side of caution. Go slow. Follow the established trail. (Don't try a shortcut through the bush!) To the degree needed, use the techniques described for running when the trail tread is obscured outlined in "Hidden Obstacles" in chapter 3.

Into Thin Air

The high mountains have always drawn humans. They are revered by our species, and those who venture into them are celebrated. After we start our way up a mountain, we are called onward by the sirens of the summit.

As we ascend, our spirits soar, and the amount of oxygen in the air plummets. The less oxygen that is in the air, the greater the reduction is in your cardiovascular performance. In other words, expect to move slower on high-altitude runs and prepare accordingly. Above 5,000 feet (1,500 m), performance decreases by roughly three percent for every additional 1,000 feet (300 m) of elevation gained.

Altitude-Related Health Issues

Aside from leaving you huffing and puffing, the lower oxygen levels at higher elevations can also make you feel acutely awful. Beginning at

Finding freedom high in the Himalayas of Nepal.

around 6,500 feet (2,000 meters), people can begin experiencing acute mountain sickness (AMS). Above that height, the likelihood of developing AMS increases as altitude does. The constellation of unpleasant symptoms of AMS can include headache, fatigue, nausea, dizziness, and poor sleep. (It's kind of like a mountain hangover.) Symptoms can come on within 6 to 10 hours of arrival at high elevation. They rarely last longer than a couple days. AMS affects people quite differently and can affect the same person quite differently on different occasions.

You can avoid the effects of AMS by not going high, but that's probably not the answer you're looking for. The good news is that short outings into the mountains shouldn't result in AMS. More commonly, AMS becomes an issue when you travel somewhere to run high in the mountains for a few days. In that case, try hydrating better than usual throughout the day, suck down some extra carbohydrate in your meals, and take some over-the-counter remedies to lessen the symptoms should you encounter the effects of AMS.

Even relatively short trips to very high elevations can result in the much more serious, but quite rare, high-altitude pulmonary edema (HAPE). HAPE is fluid in the lungs, and it can occur at an altitude as low as 8,000 feet (2,400 m) in healthy people. Signs and symptoms of HAPE can include difficulty in breathing at rest, coughing, chest congestion or tightness, wheezing, a blue tinge to the skin, rapid shallow breathing, and a rapid heartbeat. The initial treatment for HAPE is to descend to lower altitude as quickly as possible. After that, a doctor's visit along with rest, oxygen, and possibly common prescription drugs will get you back to normal.

Much rarer is high-altitude cerebral edema (HACE), which starts to become an issue above 13,000 feet (4,000 meters) and is nearly exclusive to high-altitude mountaineers. Therefore, we have little need to delve into it here. Should you be venturing to the high Himalaya or the like, you can learn more at the Institute for Altitude Medicine website (www.altitude medicine.org).

As George Herbert Palmer wrote, "Neither snow nor rain nor heat nor gloom of night" prevents the trail runner from hitting singletrack. A little forethought and some simple gear can have you ready to run in the gnarliest conditions. Braving such conditions can enhance your sense of accomplishment as well as the adventure quotient of your runs.

KEPLER TRACK, SOUTH ISLAND, NEW ZEALAND

New Zealand's South Island is known for its untrammeled terrain. Fiordland National Park, in the southwest corner of the island, is perhaps its most wild part. Here, in Fiordland, as it's colloquially called, land rises abruptly from fiords—valleys once carved by glaciers and now submerged in water—and lakes through thick, green forests before giving way to alpine terrain and jagged, snow-capped mountains. From the town of Te Anau on the east side of the park, the Kepler Track climbs from the shores of the town's namesake lake and makes a 37.3-mile (60 km) loop through the high mountains.

Highlights of the Kepler Track include taking in pretty much all the views above tree line, gaining the 360-degree perspective from the track's Mount Luxmore high point at 4,829 feet (1,472 m), staying overnight in one or more of the huts along the route, examining Luxmore Cave by flashlight, climbing the steep limestone bluffs that guard the alpine terrain from the low-country valleys, enjoying the thick beech forests at lower altitudes, and meeting the spirited trampers, as hikers are called in New Zealand, with whom you will share the trail.

If you're keen to tramp the entire Kepler Track trail running style, consider taking either two or three days to do so, to split the mileage into reasonable chunks and allow time to enjoy side trips, picnics, and the vistas. The Kepler Track is one of New Zealand's most popular trails, and the huts offer limited bed space, so you'll have to book your bunk well in advance. Also, bring your own food because it isn't offered at the huts.

If you don't have time to take on the whole track, make a long day trip out of an out-and-back run from the Kepler Track car park to the top of Mount Luxmore and back. This run of right around 20 miles (32 km) roundtrip will offer you huge bang for your buck in experiencing much of what the Kepler Track offers. Take note that the weather in New Zealand's alpine zones can become severe quickly, so watch weather forecasts and plan accordingly, no matter how long or short your run is.

Max King runs strong midway through the Western States 100-Mile Run.

Chapter 8

Training for the Trail

Because you're still reading this book, chances are you're interested not only in being a trail runner but also in being a better, stronger, more comfortable trail runner. This chapter will help you make that happen, whether you're looking to run your heart out in a trail race after following a structured training program or you're a recreational trail runner looking for ways to improve part of your trail running game.

This chapter starts by sharing five basic types of workouts used by runners of all kinds: easy runs, recovery runs, long runs, speed work, and hill workouts. Those tools can make any runner better, and each has a distinct purpose. Read on to see which might appeal to you and how each type can be applied to trail running. The chapter also includes sections on drills and cross-training that you can use to make yourself a stronger and more agile trail runner.

Easy runs can take place on trails as long as you can control your effort based on the conditions.

Trail Run Training Components

A standard running training program consists of five types of runs: easy runs, recovery runs, long runs, speed work, and hill work. Keep reading to learn the how and why of each so that you can effectively use them in your own training.

Easy Runs

Easy runs are the bread and butter of a trail runner's training, making up from 70 to 80 percent of it. Their purpose is to build your foundational aerobic capacity and fitness. Max King, who was a Division I All-American steeplechaser and has won road and trail races ranging from 5 to 100 kilometers in length, advises, "The bulk of your training should be done at a low heart rate between 120 and 150 beats per minute, what's called the aerobic endurance zone. This is important for fat metabolism, capillary development, oxygen utilization, and so on."

Easy runs are also just plain enjoyable! We don't need to overcomplicate what an easy run is: It's a run that feels easy, in both pace and distance. You should recover from an easy run almost immediately, feeling about the same 15 or 30 minutes after the run as you did before it.

With personal and terrain variations, the pace of an easy run might range from 7 to 12 minutes per mile (4 1/2 to 7 1/2 minutes per kilometer). Regardless of pace, easy runs should always remain conversational; your effort should allow you to talk easily throughout the run. While trail running, your heart rate can occasionally rise on short hills, but it's best to scale back your effort on longer hills to keep your heart rate from spiking for more than a minute or two. King notes, "Keeping your heart rate low is what is important and it may require walking to keep it there, especially on a trail run." His recommendation is to keep your heart rate below 75 percent of its maximum. This is a perfectly legitimate reason to walk a steep or long hill.

The distance of your easy runs varies based on your running history and current goals. It may range from 2 to 10 miles (3 to 16 km). In general, an easy run should not exceed 90 minutes, whatever distance you cover. Vary the time or distance from day to day by making some easy runs shorter and others longer.

Easy runs can take place on any surface, including roads or trails, or some of both in the same run. If you decide to tackle a trail with significant elevation change, be sure to regulate your effort so that the run still feels easy. You'll also find that trail conditions will dictate your effort. Fresh snow, mud, sand, and rocks, for example, will require more effort than clear, dry trail. When you encounter these conditions, control your effort to keep the run in the easy category.

Understanding Heart Rate

The big muscle beating in your chest is an incredible piece of machinery. Twenty-four hours a day, the heart pumps blood—which is filled with oxygen, minerals, and other nutrients—that body tissues need to function. When you run, your heart pumps blood faster to keep the supply chain operating. But, like any muscle, your heart has a maximal capacity, something in the hypothetical range of 220 beats per minute at birth. As you (and your heart) age, the heart's maximal frequency decreases. A good rule of thumb to estimate your heart-rate maximum as the following:

220 − your age = your maximum heart rate

In this chapter, you'll notice that target heart rates are offered for several types of runs and that those targets are shown as percentages of heart-rate maximum, which you can easily calculate from your estimated max heart rate.

Keep in mind that everyone's heart is a little different. Some people have maximum heart rates that defy their age and their estimated maximum, whereas the hearts of others beat close to the hypothetical drum.

One of the most common mistakes endurance runners make in their training is running their easy runs at too hard an effort. You might make this mistake for many reasons: You're running with friends and their pace is faster than your easy-run pace, you feel as if you should be running faster than you are, you encounter bad trail conditions and push through them trying to maintain an even pace, or you just get excited while enjoying a run. Occasionally running your easy runs too fast is OK, but if you do this often enough, you are likely to find that your body performs more poorly during your speed work and long runs and generally becomes run down, as well. Instead, revel in the fact that your fitness allows your runs to feel easy, and appreciate that you could go much faster. You should feel no shame in running easy.

Recovery Runs

Recovery runs are easy runs taken one step further. That is, they're one, or sometimes two, gears easier. Although the purpose of an easy run is to have an easy aerobic workout, the purpose of a recovery workout is to increase blood flow into your body's soft tissues to help them recover from previous runs, including the longer or faster runs described later. Those runs have the effect of fatiguing, tightening, and causing microscopic damage to the body's soft tissues. The recovery run actively aids the body in returning to a healthy status quo.

Like an easy run, a recovery run can vary in pace and distance, but the pacing is slower than that of an easy run. It's probably slow enough to call it jogging, and that's alright. When you begin a recovery run, perhaps after a fast run or a race in recent days, your legs may feel sore or heavy. Your goal for a recovery run is to create an experience that allows your body to feel better at the end of the run than it did at the beginning. Perhaps you can channel the thought of "gentle" on your recovery runs. Most experts recommend recovery runs shorter than one hour, usually in the 20- to 30-minute range.

You can do recovery runs on any surface. The soft surfaces of trails are especially helpful for recovery because the soft terrain absorbs some of the impact of your footfalls so that your muscles and joints don't have to. Some people find that benign, rolling trails make better grounds for a recovery run than trails that are more technical or that have significant elevation change because the latter two types of trails require greater effort to negotiate. Steep climbs and descents can also cause discomfort in sore muscles. A trail on such terrain might be too taxing for a recovery run.

There's also nothing wrong with taking days entirely off from running. An aching muscle or flagging energy can make such a rest day more useful than an easy run or even a recovery run. On rest days, you can rest completely or, perhaps, do some light cross-training, which is discussed later in this chapter.

Long Runs

Few things are better than enjoying a long run on the trails. Although it can be challenging, a long run—a run substantially longer than most you complete on a weekly or biweekly basis—is a wonderful opportunity to travel a significant distance through a beautiful natural environment. A long run can end up feeling a lot more like play than work. Beyond these mental benefits, long runs increase your aerobic fitness, strengthen particular muscles, and generally prepare your body to run farther.

You can define your long run either by the distance you cover or the time you are out running. A long run can vary from one to five or perhaps more hours in duration, and the length could vary from 10 to 20 miles (15 to 30 km) or more.

As with an easy run, shoot for conversational pacing. If you go on a long run with friends, you should be able to talk your way through the entire run. A long run differs from an easy run in that the length or duration of the long run is often enough to fatigue your muscles significantly or otherwise exhaust you. In the later stages of a long run, you might find that although your heart and breathing rates still allow talking, the accumulating fatigue in your muscles might distract you from lengthy conversations. For the more technically minded (or the gear geek), aim to keep your heart rate at roughly 65 to 70 percent of its maximum.

If you pace your long runs correctly, they will feel very easy for the first half or more. As your muscles fatigue in the second half, you will have to concentrate on continuing to run despite the discomfort. A common mistake among trail runners is to start long runs too fast or to work too hard when climbing or navigating obstacles, which forces them to slow significantly toward the end of the run. A well-executed long run allows you to run very close to the same pace at the end as you did at the beginning. Because of accumulating fatigue, you may find that your heart rate increases for an identical effort toward the end of a long run. This phenomenon, called cardiac drift, is one of the reasons that running a given pace at the end of a long run feels more difficult than it did at the beginning. With this in mind, it's OK to run through that sense of accumulating fatigue or to let your heart rate increase a few percentage points above the recommended 70 percent of maximum, but you should avoid running at this increased effort for more than the final 20 or 30 minutes of your long run.

If you want to add a little spice to your long run occasionally, try a progressive long run during which you intentionally increase your effort during the second half of the run. Progressive long runs garner all the benefits of the long run while forcing you to work on maintaining a strong effort when fatigue makes doing so a physical and mental challenge. Avoid taking your progression to the extreme, or it will take quite some time to recover from the effort. It shouldn't feel as if you're doing speed work; it should be a steady, challenging push at the high end of conversational effort. For those interested in heart rate, don't exceed 80 percent of your maximum heart rate at the end of a progressive long run.

A progressive long run has many looks. For example, you can gently increase your effort starting at about the halfway point and then gently increase it again when you have about a quarter of the run left. In another example, you can complete almost the entire run at a steady effort and then significantly increase your pace for the final 3 to 5 miles (5 to 8 km).

A final recommendation on progressive long runs is to be a bit more mindful of difficult trails than you are on a standard long run so that you can keep your effort within the preceding recommendations. Keep your effort in line with your intentions as you progress, even if mud or a hill requires you to slow your pace a bit.

Speed Work

Getting out on the trails and putting the pedal to the metal is not only a blast but also will make you a better trail runner. Although speed work should make up only a small portion of the running you do, it can improve all of your running, no matter the speed. With speed work, you attempt to increase your lactate threshold (the running speed at which lactate begins to accumulate in your muscles and bloodstream and therefore affects your running), your $\dot{V}O_2max$ (the amount of oxygen your body can absorb during a minute of the fastest running you can possibly tolerate), and your running economy (the physiological and biomechanical efficiency of your running stride). These gains transfer to your slower running. For example, an increase in your running economy makes your slower running more

Use speed work to jumpstart your trail running.

efficient, as well. The balance of this section introduces various breeds of speed work, the effects that each has on the body, and ways to implement them on the trails.

Measurements in meters, such as 100 or 400 meters, are used to explain and prescribe some forms of speed work in this section. This is how distance is measured on a modern, 400-meter (at least around the inner, first lane) track. Yes, even trail runners can do speed work on tracks because they provide a perfectly uniform place to monitor the distance you've run and the improvements you make from workout to workout. Just in case you are still living only in the imperial-units age, a meter equals 1.09 yards, 400 meters is a little under a quarter mile, and 1,600 meters is a bit less than a mile.

Fartleks

Fartlek is a funny-sounding word (at least to us English speakers) that means "speed play" in Swedish. Unlike the more structured types of speed work described later, the basis of fartlek runs is their unstructured nature. The entire concept is that you play with speed over the course of a fartlek run. What this means is open to interpretation and, perhaps more important, your interest. Fartlek workouts are superb workouts for runners who are new to speed work or who aren't interested in more structured kinds of speed training. With fartleks, you'll reap the benefits of running fast, but you'll do so in an unregimented, creative way.

To prepare for a fartlek, warm up by logging 20 or 30 minutes at an easy effort. Then jump into the speed play. By its nature, your speed play will vary, but it should include time running faster followed by time running slower, at the effort of a recovery run, to recover. You repeat this faster and then slower combination a number of times. The speed and duration of your faster running can vary among one fartlek run. For example, you could run hard for 2 minutes, easy for 3 minutes, even harder for 45 seconds, easy for 3 minutes, and so forth. Many possibilities are feasible here, but make sure to regulate the length of your faster running and include enough recovery running in between so that you can do each bit of faster running feeling nearly as good as you did during the previous one.

After your fartlek, make sure to do a cooldown wherein you run at an easy, conversational effort for at least 15 minutes. The total length or time of your fartlek run, including the warmup, speed play, and cooldown, will vary depending on your conditioning and goals, but keep the total distance of your faster running to no more than 2 miles (3 km) if you are new to fartleks or 6 miles (10 km) if your body is more acclimated to speed work.

Although technical or steep terrain is detrimental to some speed work, such terrain can enhance a fartlek. For example, you could use a meadow that separates two stands of trees or a shorter uphill to define the length of your fast running. You could then accentuate your recovery period with a section of flat or gentle downhill terrain. Indeed, defining the hard and easy sections of your fartlek using your natural surroundings is one of the joyful aspects of fartleks. The sky is truly the limit with the diversity of fartleks you can run. Have fun and get fast at the same time.

Steady-State Runs

As suggested previously, various types of speed work target different aspects of your running physiology. Steady-state runs work on your lactate threshold, the speed you run when more lactate, a by-product of running, is produced than your body can utilize and it begins to accumulate in your body's muscles and bloodstream. At slower running speeds, the body uses lactate as quickly as it is produced. But as your running speed increases, so does lactate production, and your body reaches a point where it is unable to clear the lactate as fast as it is produced. This point is your lactate threshold. You cannot run for very long at speeds above your lactate threshold because your body tolerates the buildup of only so much lactate before you must slow down and wait for your body to process it.

Lactate threshold varies from runner to runner, but for all runners, it ultimately limits the length of time you can run at faster speeds. You can increase your lactate threshold by running just below it for short periods, which can help train the body to efficiently clear lactate.

Greg McMillan is a renowned running coach and owner of the McMillan Running Company. The McMillan Running Company website is a go-to tool for all distance runners looking to improve their running ability. On his website, McMillan recommends running steady-state runs at an effort you would race at for races lasting from 75 minutes to 2 1/2 hours, which equates to about 83 to 87 percent of your maximum heart rate, and which should be just under you lactate threshold. You will find that running at a steady-state pace feels like an easy challenge when you first begin. You will be putting some effort into it, but you might wonder if you are possibly going too slowly. Stick with the pace and soldier on because maintaining the pace will get harder. In the end, you should be able to maintain the same pace, but doing so will require focus and concentration, and it definitely won't be easy.

Like a fartlek run, a steady-state run should begin with a warmup and end with a cooldown. A 20- to 30-minute warmup should feel like an easy run, and the 15- to 20-minute cooldown should be like a recovery run. Between the warmup and cooldown is when the steady-state running takes place. Like all speed work, the length of your steady-state sessions will vary. Runners new to speed work might try a run in which the steady-state portion lasts 20 minutes, whereas those who are more experienced could build up to an hour of running in the steady-state zone.

You can easily run a steady-state workout on trails, roads, or a mix of both. If you run on a trail, monitor your effort when the trail pitches up or down so that you don't overdo or underdo it. Doing steady-state runs or any of the faster speed work described in the following sections on technical trails is not recommended. The technicality can distract you from monitoring your effort, and the navigation of rocks and roots can slow your speed to the point that you are no longer working at the intended effort level. The best sort of trail for steady-state runs or faster speed work is one with a relatively even surface over flat to rolling terrain.

Tempo Runs

A tempo run is another type of lactate-threshold run in which you run the fast part faster and for less time than you do in a steady-state run. The fast part of a tempo run is generally run at your lactate-threshold effort, such that you are accumulating significant lactate in your body as you run, explains Olympic marathoner turned trail runner Magda Boulet. Herein is the challenge of a tempo run: pushing through that accumulating lactate, which makes your legs feel like they are burning or weighed down with lead. This kind of challenge can be a fun one. Boulet says, "This pace should feel comfortably hard. This pace is a little faster than marathon pace, but slower than the pace you can maintain for 30 minutes."

Greg McMillan recommends doing tempo runs at an effort you could race at for 40 to 75 minutes, which equates to 85 to 90 percent of your maximum heart rate. After an adequate warmup and before your cooldown, run at tempo effort for 15 to 30 minutes. When you start doing these runs, you will find that 15 minutes is a challenging amount of time at tempo effort. But as your body adapts, you will find that you can increase the amount of time you run at this effort without an increase in deleterious effects that make you slow down. This adaptation process is precisely what you're shooting for. "These runs are my bread and butter," says Boulet. "I aim for a total of 30 to 60 minutes of running at threshold pace each week." If you plan to run a tempo run on the trail, choose a benign one.

$\dot{V}O_2$max Intervals

If you want to run fast and get even faster on the trails, you should think about logging some $\dot{V}O_2$max intervals. These $\dot{V}O_2$max intervals approach the fastest speed work we do, and they are meant to be conducted just below or at $\dot{V}O_2$max. Your $\dot{V}O_2$max is the amount of oxygen your body can absorb during a minute of the fastest running you can possibly tolerate. Basically, your $\dot{V}O_2$max is a measurement of the fitness of your aerobic system. Like lactate threshold, it varies naturally among humans over the course of a lifetime and over the course of training cycles. The good news is that if you run near or at your $\dot{V}O_2$max, you can increase it.

If you've ever had to sprint a couple blocks for the bus or pushed a middle-distance run in gym class, you know that running near or at your $\dot{V}O_2$max is extremely difficult. You can do it for only a very short time before your body automatically slows. For that reason, $\dot{V}O_2$max workouts are run as intervals. In these intervals, you run for a short time at or just below your $\dot{V}O_2$max effort and then slow to a jog to recover for the same amount of time. You repeat this sequence anywhere from 4 to 12 or more times. Interval lengths can range from 400 meters to 1 mile (1,600 m). The McMillan Running Company website says to run the intervals at an effort you could sustain for a race lasting from 5 to 25 minutes. The shorter the intervals you do, the faster you can go, and the longer the intervals you do, the slower you go. Max King recommends that you run these $\dot{V}O_2$max intervals at between 90 and 95 percent of your maximum heart rate. To find the appropriate pace if you are trying $\dot{V}O_2$max intervals for the first time, sprint as hard as you can and then tone things down by one or more clicks, depending on the length of your intervals.

Your recovery between intervals is as important as the fast running. Because running at the extreme end of your aerobic capacity is extremely taxing, you need to give your body adequate recovery. To do so, your recovery periods of slow jogging should be the same duration as your intervals. Obviously, you will cover much less distance, but the time at recovery effort is crucial.

As with all speed work, you'll want to warm up and cool down. Before you begin $\dot{V}O_2$max intervals, do several strides, described later in the drills section of this chapter, to help warm up your body for the fast running. The strides can be integrated into or done just after your warmup.

One of the beauties of $\dot{V}O_2$max intervals is their diversity. You can use hundreds of combinations of intervals to create a solid $\dot{V}O_2$max interval workout. Here are a couple examples:

- 15- to 30-minute warmup, 4 × 400 meters (or 60 to 80 seconds, if you want to measure by time rather than distance) with equal recovery time, 20-minute cooldown
- 15- to 30-minute warmup, 6 × 1 mile (1,600 m) (or 4 minutes and 30 seconds to 8 minutes) with equal recovery time, 20-minute cooldown
- 15- to 30-minute warmup, 2 × 400 meters (or 60 to 80 seconds), 2 × 1,000 meters (or 2 minutes and 45 seconds to 4 minutes), 2 × 400 meters (or 60 to 80 seconds) with equal recovery time, 20-minute cooldown

In trying a $\dot{V}O_2$max workout for the first time, run just a couple of shorter intervals. You've run enough when you're unable to maintain the same pace as when you started the workout. After you start getting comfortable with the pace, try running up to 1.5 miles (2.4 km) at $\dot{V}O_2$max effort over the course of your whole workout. Runners experienced in speed work can tackle up to 4 miles (6.4 km) at $\dot{V}O_2$max pace, and up to 8 miles (13 km) at a bit below $\dot{V}O_2$max pace.

You should run $\dot{V}O_2$max workouts on a track, pavement, or only the most manicured of trails. Because you need to run quite fast to reach your $\dot{V}O_2$max, you need focus to reach and maintain that speed. Distractions on the trail are likely to slow you and sap your concentration. If you want to do such a workout on a trail, seek out a flat, wide, dirt stretch such as a Rails to-Trails path.

Anaerobic Intervals

Anaerobic intervals are intervals run at faster than $\dot{V}O_2$max pace, at a pace you can tolerate for only a short time. According to Max King, your heart rate will be in excess of 95 percent of its maximum during these very short, fast intervals. In fact, the human body can withstand an anaerobic effort for only about two minutes. A trail runner runs anaerobic intervals primarily to improve running economy. The intervals also have some positive effect on your aerobic capacity. In addition, you sharpen your mental fortitude when you push through the intense discomfort of anaerobic running.

After a warmup and some strides, you'll run intervals of between 100 and 400 meters. In between, the recovery periods will be longer than those of $\dot{V}O_2$max workouts. In fact, they should be up to five times the interval duration. Because anaerobic workouts are extremely taxing, they should be brief and include just a few intervals so that you can get the most out of each of them.

Here are a couple examples of anaerobic interval workouts:

- 20-minute warmup, 6 × 200 meters (or 20 to 30 seconds) with recovery jogging for five times the duration of the interval, 20-minute cooldown
- 20-minute warmup, 4 × 400 meters (or 50 to 70 seconds) with recovery jogging for five times the duration of the interval, 20-minute cooldown

Anaerobic workouts are best run on a track or the easiest of trails, like a bike path or rail trail. In other words, do these workouts on a surface where you can focus 100 percent on the effort rather than worry about what is underfoot.

Hill Workouts

A trail runner looking to build strength quickly while improving aerobic capacity needs to look no further than the nearest hill. By varying the grades and lengths of the hills you charge up, as well the speed at which you run them, you can imitate every type of speed work described previously. Says Magda Boulet, "I love incorporating long and short hill sessions into my training program. I like to balance hill workouts with speed workouts since both provide similar benefits of improving strength and economy, which is something that all runners can improve." As a trail runner, hill workouts kill two birds with one stone because you're preparing specifically for the literal ups and downs you'll face on the trail. With stronger legs and an improved cardiovascular system, your ability to run hills can make your daily trail

> If you want to be fast running uphill and downhill on the trail, practice to gain the aerobic ability, strength, and coordination you'll need to do so.

Build strength by hitting hills of all kinds, including shallow and steep grades.

runs even more enjoyable. On the flip side, hills can be a real drag if you're underprepared.

Although you may instinctively think of training to run uphill, do you need to train to run downhill? Guess what? It's important, too. If you're aiming to be a smooth and sturdy descender, a few types of workouts can help get you there.

Keep reading for ideas about workouts to get you ready for the hills. If you want a reminder about effective body position and mental approaches to running uphill and downhill, look back at chapters 2 and 4, respectively.

Hill Fartleks

As with the speed play on flatter terrain discussed earlier in this chapter, you can head out for some hill-focused fartleks, too. If you're brand new to trail running or you aren't interested in more structured hill intervals, hill fartleks might be right for you.

Hill fartleks are made for the trails. Almost any trail, as long as it has some hills, is appropriate for this type of run. Carry out a hill fartlek as you would a regular fartlek run, except do the speed play on the uphills and the downhills of the trail and recover from those efforts on the flatter sections. Alternatively, you could focus your speed play solely on either the ascents or descents—whatever strikes your fancy.

Note that you may need to curtail the length of your intervals if a hill is quite long. Don't be afraid to roll back the effort a bit if the trail is really technical.

Structured Uphill Workouts

Uphill workouts are made to be run on the trails. Seek trails with the appropriate gradient and degree of technicality for what you are trying to achieve with your workout. In general, the faster your uphill workout gets, the more you'll appreciate smoother trails so that you can focus on the effort, not the terrain. Choosing steeper hills for shorter intervals is a great way to develop strength and power. On the other hand, you're likely better off finding a more gradual slope for workouts during which you'll be pushing for stretches of 10 minutes or longer. One easy way to recover during hill intervals is to jog or walk back down to where you began your previous climb. If you jog down, do so at a recovery-run effort, no harder. Always warm up before and cool down on calm terrain after your hard efforts. Read on to find out how to tweak each of the four types of speed work to the hills.

- **Uphill steady-state runs.** Run your uphill steady-state run up a long, continuous, mostly gentle uphill.
- **Uphill tempo runs.** For an uphill tempo run, find an uphill that's long enough to accommodate the length of your tempo session. Adjust your pace to the steepness of the hill, so that your effort is at your lactate-threshold level.
- **Uphill $\dot{V}O_2$max intervals.** Again, the steepness of the hill defines your pace. Although you don't necessarily need to run a steep hill to achieve $\dot{V}O_2$max effort, doing so will help you get into that zone quickly.
- **Uphill anaerobic intervals.** As with $\dot{V}O_2$max intervals, use steeper trail terrain to help you get anaerobic more easily.

Downhill Repeats

When you see a trail runner flying down a technical trail, you'll see that his or her torso is steady and leaning forward slightly, the head is tilted down to look at the ground ahead, the legs are cycling quickly underneath the runner, the feet are landing underneath the center of gravity, and the arms are flailing to counteract the small changes in balance that occur when landing on uneven ground. Strong downhill trail runners are a sight to behold, and nothing can stop you from becoming one of them—you just need to learn and practice. On the learning side, you can read more about downhill technique in chapter 4.

The purpose of running downhill repeats is quite different from that of running uphill intervals. Here, your goals are not to get an aerobic workout, although your heart rate may increase when negotiating a tough downhill. Instead, you're looking to train the muscles of your core, hips, and legs as well as your nervous system to be fast, efficient, and durable when running downhill.

Strong downhill running is achieved through practice.

"Muscle Seasoning" Downhill Repeats   When you run hard downhill, you're asking some of the muscles of your lower body to do a difficult thing: to be in a lengthened state while absorbing the impact of your body weight and the extra force created by your body's mass descending. It's like asking someone whose arms are extended and carrying a large load to manage another bag or two. When exposed to such work, untrained muscles fatigue and fail quickly. Some trail runners say that muscles need to be "seasoned" to the act of running downhill, but it's more accurate to say that the muscles need to be strengthened by repeated exposure to and recovery from the extra work of downhill running so that they can do it without soreness and muscle failure. The quadriceps' four muscles are the main muscles that need to be strengthened for downhill running because those muscles are significantly lengthened in the downhill-running motion.

The best place to run muscle-seasoning repeats is on descents of decent steepness and light to moderate technicality. Doing them is simple: Run downhill. Hike or run easily back uphill as the terrain dictates. (Remember that working the climb isn't the focus of this workout.) Repeat until your quadriceps start feeling fatigued. Don't worry; you'll really feel the workout a day or two later when delayed-onset muscle soreness (DOMS) kicks in. As you continue to season your legs for downhill running, once leg-crushing workouts will quickly become easy. That's when you know you can increase your downhill workload. See "Ouch! The Scoop on Sore Muscles" for more information on DOMS.

How long should each downhill interval be? For those trying this workout for the first time, the downhill intervals should last no longer than five minutes each, and they can be repeated a couple times. As your muscles

Ouch! The Scoop on Sore Muscles

Acute muscle soreness is the immediate pain felt by doing a significant amount of work with a muscle. In contrast, delayed-onset muscle soreness (DOMS) is the soreness you develop belatedly—usually 24 to 72 hours afterward. Muscles doing work are contracting either concentrically, shortening while being loaded, or eccentrically, lengthening while doing work. Scientists aren't exactly sure why it occurs, but they do know that repeated eccentric contractions cause more DOMS than concentric contractions do.

As we run across relatively flat ground, various muscles of our body contract concentrically or eccentrically to support those actions. One muscle group that contracts eccentrically while running is the quadriceps. When we run downhill, our quadriceps undergo significantly increased eccentric contractions, which exposes them to significant opportunities for DOMS development.

If you wake up quite sore a day or two after a run with lots of downhill, don't fret. This is normal. Although scientists tell us that exercising when we have DOMS is OK because the act of light exercise doesn't further damage muscles, you'll still need to allow your muscles recovery time to repair and rebuild. The cool thing is that if you repeat this process a couple times, soon your quadriceps muscles won't get sore at all.

become seasoned, you can increase the length and number of intervals. Some long-distance trail runners do their intervals at ski resorts that are open for summer activities. These runners descend a ski hill, take a chairlift back up, and repeat. Other seasoned trail runners opt for logging a long run with a great deal of elevation change during which they push the descents in lieu of running organized repeats.

You should run these workouts on trails to accustom your body to the steeper grades found only on trails. But you shouldn't regularly run these workouts on trails so steep that you can't maintain good running form.

Coordination Improvement Downhill Repeats   If you want to become a gravity-defying descender, you'll need to work on your motor coordination. In trail running, a few key items contribute to our coordination:

1. Muscles and joints of the feet communicate with the brain through the body's central nervous system about what is under them and what is needed to negotiate it.

2. With information collected visually, the brain analyzes a section of trail and decides what actions will be needed by what body parts to travel through it. The brain then uses the nervous system to command those movements by the body.

3. Muscle groups communicate with each other through the nervous system about how much of the load each is going to take to perform a motion.

Your coordination is important whenever you're trail running, but it's especially important while descending because you're moving faster with greater forces and have less time to react. The good news is that improving your downhill coordination is easy and fun, even if occasionally harrowing. Throughout these workouts, you'll want to focus on good downhill technique.

Ideally, you should run downhill coordination improvement workouts on moderate or steep technical descents. In these places, the terrain requires your full attention and all of your body parts must work in synergy with each other. Your comfort level is important in choosing a spot for these workouts. Sometimes you'll want to choose trails that are technically within your wheelhouse on which you can practice pushing your speed. At other times, you'll want to push up to and perhaps beyond your technical comfort zone to work on becoming more comfortable (and skilled) on such terrain.

Both muscle and nervous-system fatigue will occur when doing these intervals. For example, proprioception, which in trail running is the way that the muscles and joints of the feet communicate to the brain and rest of the body what they are encountering and how to react, lapses during fatigue. When you find it becoming mentally or physically challenging to negotiate the obstacles on the trail, that's a sure sign to stop practicing them to avoid a dangerous fall.

Your overall approach to the volume of your downhill intervals should be similar to how you approach the muscle-seasoning downhill intervals in that you should start with small intervals, build up, and not overdo it until your mind and body adapt. In addition, you don't need to do formal intervals if you care to incorporate meaningful and mindful descents into some of your training runs. Use care not to overdo downhill running practice on easy runs.

Trail Running Drills

In the previous section you learned that including highly specific kinds of running in your training can make you a better all-around trail runner. Using drills, you can similarly break down the components of your stride and repeatedly engage them in a highly focused manner. The goals of drills are to strengthen muscles needed for running and improve motor coordination. Although you can do dozens of drills, this section outlines a few that can help take your trail running to the next level.

Strides

If this book were a trail running infomercial, at this point we'd pitch you the incredible returns that will result from just five minutes of exercise three times a week. Strides are the simplest drill a trail runner can do, yet they're incredibly effective. In essence, strides are 75- to 100-meter (or 10- to 20-second) sprints in which you gradually build up your speed for half the distance before cruising along for the remainder at a notch or two below full speed. The goal is to improve your running economy by running fast briefly without taxing your aerobic system. You should do strides at the end of an easy run or ahead of very fast speed work. Run five or six strides with a full-minute break after each (no need for a watch, though). You can jog, walk, or stand around between strides.

Practice strides to gain running economy.

Fast Feet

Trail runners must be quick on their feet; the brain and body should be "talking" to each other constantly. The fast feet drill works to develop motor coordination in a safe, obstacle-free environment. The goal here is to lift and lower each foot as fast as possible while maintaining good form.

To practice fast feet, find a grassy, flat surface with 20 meters of open space and get into the runner's ready position discussed in chapter 2. That is, lean forward slightly from the ankles and keep the legs and trunk in a straight, slightly forward-leaning line. Your core muscles should be engaged but not rigid. Swing your arms and lift your knees, but lift the knees much less than you do with the typical running stride. Your feet should lift only 3 or 4 inches (7.5 to 10 cm) off the ground with each step, and you should land on your midfoot. Let the arm swing come naturally to reinforce this leg lifting. Repeat this drill five times for 30 seconds each and rest for 30 seconds after each repetition. You can do the drill by staying in one place or by slowly moving forward, whichever you prefer.

You may find that when you first practice fast feet you'll be tired at the end of the final repetition, and you'll struggle to keep your feet lifting and falling as fast as they did when you began. This deterioration won't occur because you're breathing hard or because your legs are fatigued, but because you're reaching the limits of your motor coordination. Focus and concentrate.

This fast feet drill encourages speedy, coordinated feet.

High Knees

To run trails well, you need a stable core and a strong, hip-flexor-based leg lift. The high knees drill helps make this happen. Practice this drill on a flat, grassy surface with at least 75 meters of open space. Put yourself into the runner's ready position and then lift one knee up until your upper leg is roughly parallel to the ground.

This knee lift should be a powerful, exaggerated one. Bam! Lift hard and fast. After you drive the knee up, let the leg naturally return to the ground, making certain you land gently on your midfoot. Repeat with the other leg, speeding up the drill as much as you can while maintaining good form. Your arms should swing to act in opposition to each leg lift, just like in the running stride. The leg lift and arm swing propel you forward, but not as far as in a typical running stride.

Gain core and hip-flexor strength with the high knees drill.

A common error is to lean your torso back, past vertical. You need significant core strength to keep the torso leaning forward ever so slightly. If you feel your torso slipping back, you don't yet have the core strength to do this drill properly. Don't worry; this is normal and why we practice.

Be conservative when you add high knees to your routine. Start with five times for 12 seconds with 30 seconds of rest between repetitions. Over time you can work up to five 30-second iterations.

Push Backs

When one of your legs is driving forward, the other is pushing off behind you. That push off is key to generating speed and power, and the push back drill will help you develop it.

For push backs, find 75 meters on a flat, grassy surface and get into the runner's ready position. Essentially, you're bounding during this drill, except that your forward motion comes from the back leg pushing back rather than the front leg driving forward. Lift one leg and swing the arms in natural counter-reaction, as you would to run normally. With force and gusto, push backward with the leg that is still on the ground, which will propel your whole body forward, and let that foot naturally lift off when the time is right. When the forward leg lands, use it to push back and then

Push backs help develop strength and stability in the push-off element of the running stride.

off, continuing to propel your body forward. Although the movement should look like bounding, it might take practice to get to that point. Repeat push backs five times for 20 seconds and rest for 30 seconds after each repetition.

The challenge of this drill is to exaggerate the push back while balancing on one leg, so you might find yourself going slowly at first to get the action right. That's OK; your goal is not speed, but rather that push-back action. You will find that as you develop the strength and coordination to push back and balance yourself at the same time, the motion will speed up.

Arm Swings

Try running, especially trail running, with your arms tucked motionless against your torso. Yeah, it doesn't work too well, does it? Developing powerful arms to assist in driving forward will make you a better trail runner.

Unlike the other drills in this section, you can do arm swings anywhere you can find a pair of 5- to 8-pound (2 to 4 kg) weights (rocks work) and enough room to swing your arms in a running motion. To get going, pick up a weight in each hand, get into the runner's ready position, and begin swinging your arms as fast as you can in a running motion while standing still. Although your arms should be moving quickly, maintain good form throughout the drill. The angle between your upper and lower arms should be 80 to 90 degrees, and your arm should swing nearly straight front to back and parallel to your body.

Powerful and efficient arm motion will improve your running stride.

As with high knees, you may tend to tip your torso backward, past the vertical plane. Use core strength to keep your torso in the correct position, leaning a few degrees forward of the vertical plane. Your shoulders will naturally rise with tension as you tire, and you may find yourself tensing the muscles of your neck and face. Stay relaxed and keep your shoulders down, letting the effort come in your arm swing and core engagement.

Do this drill to exhaustion or until you can no longer maintain proper form, whichever comes first. That may mean from 30 to 50 swings of each arm. Rest completely for a minute and do it again. Repeat no more than three times the first time you try this and build up to five to-exhaustion sets.

Cross-Training

You can do plenty to make yourself a better trail runner even when you're not out cruising singletrack. Such cross-training can purposely accentuate your trail running fitness or simply be an activity you love that happens to complement your trail running. Cross-training also provides a good physical and mental outlet if you are injured or taking a break from running. The greatest benefit of cross-training, other than the pure enjoyment, is engaging muscles that are neglected or used differently while running.

This activity results in a more balanced musculature, which helps us avoid running overuse injuries.

Although you don't necessarily need to have a purpose or plan for your cross-training, breaking it up into categories, such as aerobic, strength, and flexibility, can be helpful. Yes, some activities certainly overlap between these designations, but let's roll with them for now.

Other aerobic activities are a natural supplement to your trail running. All will help build your aerobic engine, and most will work at least some of your major trail running muscles. For example, hopping on a bike, whether it's a mountain bike, a road bike, or even a spin bike in the gym, will get your heart pumping and your leg muscles working. Activities like Nordic skiing and snowshoeing imitate running, and their benefits are even greater. Of course, you can participate in a slew of other enjoyable aerobic activities including swimming, soccer, canoeing, skinning on skis, using cardio equipment in the gym, and backpacking, to name a few.

Aerobic cross-training provides a workout similar to running with at least some and often much deviation from the running motion. This activity can give your muscles and other soft tissues a chance to rest if you're tired or injured. Many trail runners more or less play around with their cross-training, but you can usually mimic any one of the five major components of running training—easy runs, recovery runs, long runs, speed work, and hill workouts—with another aerobic activity. For example, you can go on a long road bike ride that aerobically mimics a long run, carry out $\dot{V}O_2$max intervals on an elliptical machine, or sneak in a steady-state workout while snowshoeing.

You've probably gotten the sense that trail running takes more than just a strong heart and big set of lungs. Agility, strength, flexibility, and more come into play out on the trails.

If you're looking to enhance your strength, you can go the traditional strength-training route by weightlifting or using your own body weight to strength train. Other sports, such as downhill skiing (moguls anyone?), cycling, climbing, and others can help you tone up.

The words flexibility and runner aren't often found together except in negative association. So why are runners so notoriously inflexible? The reason is that runners engage in a highly repetitive weight-bearing exercise within a limited range of motion. Runners perform the same stride thousands of times in each run and maybe millions of times a year. Their muscles become incredibly efficient at the running motion but little else.

Some research has shown that too much flexibility can be detrimental for endurance runners, because it decreases running economy and possibly makes runners more susceptible to overuse injuries. That said, too little flexibility does precisely the same thing. Flexibility work, such as yoga or Pilates, dynamic stretching, or active isolated stretching, should be a twice-weekly part of your running routine.

Trail Run Training Cheat Sheet

Here you'll find the various kinds of trail run training you can do in one, simplified cheat sheet.

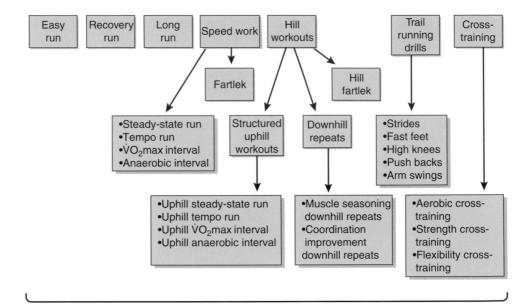

Consider this chapter a gigantic buffet of trail run training opportunities. Among all these kinds of runs, drills, and cross-training, you'll find an abundance of opportunities not only to improve your running but also to have fun in the process. Of course, now that you know about the diversity of specific trail run training you can do to improve, flip over to chapter 9, where you'll learn how to put it all together into an effective and healthy training plan. Read on!

PIKES PEAK ASCENT AND MARATHON, COLORADO, UNITED STATES

Participating in the Pikes Peak Ascent or Marathon is about racing hard, sure, but it's also about experiencing history in the American West. Pikes Peak is a mammoth mountain with a unique coral-pink color that stands a staggering 14,115 feet (4,302 m) tall. It protrudes separately and starkly from the rest of Colorado's Front Range, the range of mountains that makes the eastern front of America's great Rocky Mountain chain. The mountain itself has long been an American icon. A paved road, a cog railway, and a network of trails facilitate tourist journeys to its top.

Manitou Springs, a small mountain village perched at 6,400 feet (1,950 m), some 7,700 feet (2,350 m) below the summit on the east side of the mountain, has been a Pikes Peak jumping-off point since the 1800s. In earlier days, Manitou harbored mineral prospectors, and tourists used the town as their adventure base camp. Manitou Springs and the top of Pikes Peak are linked for foot travel by the historic Barr Trail, completed in 1918 and originally used to carry tourists on burros up and down the mountain. Today, the Barr Trail has become one of America's most popular hiking trails.

Every year since 1956 (and even once in the 1930s before that), a group of hardy runners has participated in races of various kinds on Pikes Peak. Although the format and starting line changed in the early years of the race, the Pikes Peak Ascent and Marathon has grown to nearly 2,000 annual participants. The weekend's races have long been among the most competitive mountain races in North America.

(continued)

Pikes Peak Ascent *(continued)*

The Pikes Peak Ascent is a one-way half-marathon race from downtown Manitou Springs up to the summit. These days, the Ascent is run on Saturday. Then, Sunday morning dawns with the Pikes Peak Marathon, the round-trip voyage from town to the mountaintop and back again. Both races use the Barr Trail, and competitors must contend with the continuous 8,000-foot (2,450 m) climb (and descent if they're running the marathon), the thin air of the high-altitude summit, and sometimes awful race-day weather up high, which can include snow. No matter the challenge, the races and Pikes Peak itself represent all things American West.

Hal Koerner and Stephanie Howe training hard.

Chapter 9

Creating a Training Plan

This chapter provides you with the tools to make a structured and well-thought-out training plan. For instance, you'll learn about the 10 percent rule, periodized training cycles, the components of a training plan, and more. Your health on and off the trails affects your experience on them, so this chapter closes with considerations of overall health issues like overtraining, sleep, and stress, as well as a discussion about balancing running with the rest of life. Even if you wish to keep your trail running entirely free and unstructured, the casual application of the principles in this chapter to your life will help you maintain a sustainable and long-lasting relationship with running.

Building a Training Plan

Some trail runners run off in search of fun without any real structure to their training. Heck, most trail runners probably don't think of what they're doing as training at all; they see their running as a simple act of moving through beautiful places. But for trail runners who want to add a framework to their trail running, a structured training plan—containing a balanced combination of running, cross-training, and rest—can be as fun as it is rewarding. Building and following through with a training plan can maximize your fitness, increase your speed and strength, build your confidence as you complete tough workouts, reinforce your goals, show your commitment to a long-term process, give you the edge in trail races, help prevent overuse injuries, and more. This section is a how-to for creating a training plan for those runners who desire one.

Note that structured training and the freedom of trail running are far from mutually exclusive. Even with a training plan, you choose your own routes, run with friends, take in the sights, and ditch the plan and embrace spontaneity when you desire.

Periodization Primer

As much as there is to love about trail running, you must recognize that the sport is mentally and physically taxing. You need to rest and occasionally take time away from it to stay healthy. Periodization is the organization of your running on yearly, monthly, and even-smaller scales that balance periods of focused training with necessary rest.

> Train hard and rest harder! It is on your rest days that your body absorbs the hard work you do.

Although the concept of periodization is most often applied to runners seeking strong race performances, all trail runners should periodize their training to some extent so that they have some down time. First, let's consider the periodization of short time frames. Max King, the 2011 World Mountain Running champion, who has had success running on the track, roads, and trails, recommends that we organize our training into four-week blocks. "Studies have found that the body responds best to three weeks of increasing training followed by a week of decreased volume. I like to stack three weeks together increasing volume or intensity by 5 to 10 percent per week followed by a week of decreased volume and intensity that is equal to the first week of the block, or about 70 percent of the maximum week. This four-week training block allows people to increase volume slowly while working on each physiological system and specific workouts targeted to their goals."

In addition, the weeks of decreased volume that King describes allow your body to assimilate the hard work you've been doing, give little aches and pains a chance to heal, and offer reprieve for your mind. With that understanding, if you find that three weeks of hard work and one week of recovery is a bit too much for your body to sustain, shorten the work part of this periodization to two weeks and follow that with a recovery week.

About longer-scale periodization, King explains, "Many athletes periodize their training into three- to six-month blocks depending on their seasons and races planned. These longer periods of buildup allow athletes to reach closer to their potential but also limit the timeframe they can race at or near peak fitness."

Your running cycles may be defined by the seasons if your off-season running aligns with your participation in winter sports. Maybe your running takes a downturn when your work, family, or social schedule gets busy. Or perhaps you simply schedule some intentional time off from running.

If you're looking to crush some big trail races or take on a major new challenge—we're talking about anything from a 10K to a trail marathon here—it's best to stick to three or fewer major outings per year. These are the races or runs you care most about, the places to which you want to take your A game. If you have any more big events on your calendar, you may not be able to train specifically enough for them or your body may not be able to recover fully from them. You can still run other races as part of training for your goal events, but you probably won't be at your fittest for them. When building toward a big goal, divide your training block into four parts: base building, peaking, sharpening, and recovery. Depending on the length of the goal event and how specifically you want to train for it, these blocks can last anywhere from 15 to 26 weeks long.

Base-Building Phase

In the base-building phase of your training block, you build aerobic fitness by running most of your runs at an easy pace. During this time, your muscles grow, you develop more efficient channels for blood flow into those muscles, and your skeleton and soft tissues adapt to the stresses of running. Nearly as important, you establish a positive routine and become accustomed to the sometimes-challenging nature of running. An average base-building phase lasts 8 to 12 weeks, but it could be longer for runners who are training for longer trail races.

Peaking Phase

After base building, you move on to the peaking phase, during which you continue your easy running while adding speed work and hill workouts that are applicable to the type of event for which you're training. These workouts, explained in chapter 8, build on your aerobic base to make you faster and stronger. This phase is normally 6 to 10 weeks long.

Sharpening Phase

Sharpening serves up your body's final preparations for your goal event. During sharpening, you cut a significant part of your easy running and maintain most of your goal-appropriate speed work and hill workouts.

Smooth trails can make for speedy training.

Aside from keeping your mind and body sharp, this period allows your body to recover physically from the tolls of hard training. But this period isn't about rest, because fitness can be lost if you do too much of that for too long. Sharpening should last from seven days to three weeks.

Recovery Phase

Taking time off after your goal event is often a good idea. Time off can mean 100 percent rest, cross-training, or disorganized running. You do this to give your mind a break and your body's various systems a chance to recover fully from the stresses of running. For shorter goal races, like a 5K or 10K distance, this phase might be a couple days long, but longer goals like half marathons or marathons may require two to three weeks of recovery.

Additional Periodization Considerations

Suppose that you really want to run two races that are only four weeks apart. You can perform well and enjoy both of them, but you'll have to exert special care in the weeks between races so that you are as ready for the second as you were the first. After the first race, your immediate goal should be recovery. After your body has bounced back, you'll reenter the sharpening phase. Depending on the length of the first race and the time between the two races, you may have to restart sharpening before you're 100 percent recovered. This second sharpening phase should emphasize even more the reduction of easy running while retaining speed work and hill workouts.

Tracking Your Training

Most people track their workouts on a weekly basis, such as from Monday to Sunday or from Sunday to Saturday. Rarely, an unusual work arrangement or personal preference will cause someone to choose a 10-day, biweekly, or some other schedule. The exact length of your training period doesn't matter, but you should keep it a uniform length for significant spans so that you can compare your running from period to period.

If you build a training plan, you may want to keep tabs on how much you run so that you don't do too much too soon, which can open you up to injury. Some people track their running by the distance they run, whereas others track their time spent running. Either is fine.

Organizing Your Training Schedule

Whether or not you develop a training plan, you should vaguely aim to include an easy run, recovery run, or rest day every other day or at least every third day. After you get into the heart of your training program, your weeks might be a roughly even mix of hard days—long runs, speed work, or hill workouts—and easier days.

Although the focus here is organizing your running schedule, don't forget that you can add in cross-training. Just make sure not to do a hard cross-training workout on a day you are supposed to be recovering from a hard running workout. Give your body the rest it needs.

You'll also want to make sure that you don't increase your training too quickly at any one time. You should follow the 10 percent rule, meaning that you shouldn't increase your training volume, measured by either distance or time, by more than 10 percent from week to week. More experienced runners can use this as more of a guideline than a rule, but you should still avoid massive increases of 20 percent or more. Your body needs time to adapt, and you may be only a couple of weeks from injury if you increase your training volume too fast.

> Consider tracking the patterns and progress of your training with an online tool like Strava, in a Microsoft Excel file, or in a hand-written notebook.

Schedule for the Base-Building Phase

When you are in the base-building phase of your running, your weekly running schedule should be composed of easy runs, one long run or shortened long run, and one recovery run the day after your long run. From time to time, it's OK to infuse a little extra effort into your running, but keep in mind that your goal with base building is to create a strong base of aerobic fitness to use in later phases of training. Also, don't be afraid to replace easy runs, recovery runs, and cross-training with a rest day when you need one. Many top athletes take one full day of rest for every week of training. This sample base-building weekly schedule (see the base-building phase table) is one example of how you can build your own schedule.

Schedule for the Peaking Phase

In the peaking phase of training, a typical weekly schedule includes the easy, long, and recovery runs of the base-building phase and at least one speed work session or hill workout added and possibly two workouts if your body can tolerate it. The most challenging part of designing a weekly plan in your peaking phase is deciding what speed work and hill workouts you should do. Keep in mind the type of race you are training for and consider workouts that mimic it. For example, if you're training for a half marathon, consider steady-state workouts an important part of your plan, wherein you're training at half-marathon effort. Especially important for trail running is to practice running fast on the kind of terrain you'll face in the race. If you are training for a very hilly 10-mile (16 km) trail race, then hill workouts would be of enormous benefit. Still, your body's aerobic system should be worked at all speeds, so you should cycle in a diversity of speed work and hill workouts.

As mentioned previously, alternate hard and easy days. Although you must do hard work to grow stronger, it's during recovery that your body absorbs and incorporates that hard work. We'll say it again and again: Fear not the rest day! Sometimes a day of rest can help heal an aching muscle or restore your energy much faster than an easy or recovery run.

The following sample weekly schedules (see the peaking phase table) from the peaking phase demonstrate two of the many ways to compose a training schedule that offers freedom and diversity but will also help you improve your running.

Schedule for the Sharpening Phase

In the sharpening phase, remove much of your easy and long running but keep speed work and hill workouts in the schedule. The sharpening phase is when it's most important to tailor your speed work and hill workouts specifically to your goal race. You can also practice a bit of your high-end running here, such as anaerobic intervals, to help solidify your running economy for game day. The sharpening phase table provides an example of a weekly schedule in this training phase, which includes more rest and shorter easy and long runs than you'll have in the schedules for the other phases.

Schedule for the Recovery Phase

Don't forget to take time off after your goal event. This section doesn't prescribe a recovery schedule, because you shouldn't have one. Your running should be dictated by how your body is feeling, not by instructions on a piece of paper.

Sample Base-Building Phase Weekly Schedule

DAY	TRAINING TYPE
Monday	Recovery run
Tuesday	Easy run
Wednesday	Rest or cross-training
Thursday	Easy run
Friday	Easy run
Saturday	Easy run or cross-training
Sunday	Long run or shortened long run

Sample Peaking Phase Weekly Schedules

DAY	SAMPLE 1 TRAINING TYPE	SAMPLE 2 TRAINING TYPE
Monday	Hill workout	Rest
Tuesday	Easy run	Easy run
Wednesday	Speed work	Speed work
Thursday	Recovery run	Recovery run
Friday	Easy run	Speed work
Saturday	Long run	Easy run
Sunday	Recovery run	Long run

Sample Sharpening Phase Weekly Schedule

DAY	TRAINING TYPE
Monday	Rest
Tuesday	Short, easy run
Wednesday	Speed work
Thursday	Rest
Friday	Speed work
Saturday	Easy run
Sunday	Shortened long run

Your training can inspire those around you.

Running Healthy

No matter how easy it is to focus on your trail running and how tempting it can be to run as hard and as fast as you want, whenever you want, your body is only so resilient and your running is but one small factor affecting it.

Nonrunning stress can set back your running more than any workout or training block can move it forward. Work, family, school, and more can cause boundless stress. If left unmitigated, stress changes the body's hormone production, which can leave you feeling physically and psychologically drained. Life stress can destroy your desire to work out, physically hamper your ability to run, and combine with the (beneficial) stress of running to leave you burned out.

You cannot eliminate all of life's stress, but you can minimize and mitigate it as it happens, before it negatively affects your well-being. Running is an incredible stress-reduction tool, but only if it's a healthy part of your life. Reading, yoga, meditation, cooking, writing in a journal, walking your dog, and taking a weekend camping trip can all be effective stress-reduction tools. Choose the tools that interest and work for you, practice them enough to counter everyday stress, and employ them when irregular stress happens.

To be a strong trail runner—and a good, contributing, sustainable member of society—you need to take care of your health outside running. Adequate sleep is probably the most underutilized health tool in Western culture. Sleep experts say that people generally need seven to nine hours of sleep per night. You may find, however, that you need increased sleep when you are training hard for or recovering from a goal race. Get enough sleep!

Should you start feeling tired when you first set out for your runs, lack motivation to head out the door to run, need far more sleep than normal, or wake up tired, you should start thinking about if you're not fully recovering from your runs and the other stresses of life. If these symptoms have just appeared, a few recovery or rest days, a few good nights of sleep, and a reduction in stress can turn you around.

But if those or similar symptoms—such as sleeplessness, increased irritability or a set of nonchronic grumbles—lasts for more than a week (and you'll often only notice them in hindsight), you may be heading toward overreaching in your training. Another sign of overreaching is that you're training hard but encounter a period of several weeks to perhaps a month in which your running fitness is not progressing or appears to take a step back. Overreaching is most common in trail runners who run a significant amount (generally, 10 or more hours per week) or who have significantly increased their running in a short period. Overreaching affects runners whether or not they have an organized training plan. After they identify the problem, most runners recover from overreaching with a couple weeks of rest or near rest.

Overtraining syndrome is the big, bad brother of overreaching. You experience the same symptoms as you do in overreaching, but with great intensity and duration. Overtraining syndrome can be crippling and, sadly, can take months or a year or more to overcome.

But it's heartening to know that overreaching and overtraining syndrome are preventable. You just need to monitor your body carefully and rest when your body gives you the appropriate signs. One of the most common paths to both problems is performing a major upswing in fitness and piling more and harder work onto your training plate. Avoid this temptation! The same goes for the temptation to run numerous longer trail races at 100 percent effort in a short period. Another problematic situation occurs when a runner with a well-established and seemingly safe training routine encounters a ton of new life stress. The nonrunning and running stresses combine to overwhelm the body's systems, leading to burnout. Athletes need to minimize, monitor, and mitigate stress.

With this in mind, life balance is a worthy topic to close this chapter. Although difficult to define (and often harder to attain), life balance can mean that no aspect of your life should negatively affect another. You probably know this already: Running isn't everything. We all have jobs, friends, families, nonrunning hobbies, vacations, and many other ways in which we spend our nonrunning time. Running should make you happy and healthy and provide an outlet to challenge yourself. Symbiosis between running and the rest of life keeps trail running a positive experience.

You can certainly have short periods during which you focus on your running more than other aspects of your life, just as you surely have short periods in which you focus on something else that is important. New mothers and fathers, for example, know that the first year of their child's life requires extreme focus. During that time, other aspects of life are temporarily set aside. And students can attest to the fact that during finals time, hobbies must take a backseat to exams and essays. On the other hand, if you decide that a running goal is important, your preparations may require extra time and energy. To focus effectively on your trail running for a time, make sure you provide the space for it in your life by spending less time with other hobbies or by cutting back on socializing with friends.

Life ebbs and flows, just like a winding trail. Some trail runners find deep enjoyment in the unregimented freedom of trail running for whatever distances and times they are inspired to do on a given day, whereas others enjoy the sense of accomplishment derived from creating a training schedule and completing it before a goal race. The purpose of this chapter is to provide you with the knowledge and tools you need to create your own diverse training schedules that will suit your changing interests and needs. Whatever you do, enjoy the run!

DIPSEA RACE, CALIFORNIA, UNITED STATES

If you want to experience American trail running history, then head to California for the Dipsea. The first official Dipsea Race was held in 1905, making it the oldest trail race in the United States. The 7.4-mile (11.9 km) course traverses the equally famous Dipsea Trail connecting Mill Valley with Stinson Beach in the San Francisco Bay Area's Marin Headlands. From the starting line, the Dipsea Trail ascends and descends more than 670 steps through lush greenery, including towering coastal redwood trees and ornate ferns, before eventually yielding to endless views of the Pacific Ocean.

Each year, some 1,500 people run the race. Its unique age-handicapping system allows runners in all age groups to compete on an equal playing field. In recent years, the Dipsea has been won by an 8-year-old, a 56-year-old, and a 72-year-old, whose performances at their respective ages were superior to everyone else's. Olympian Jackie Joyner-Kersee once said, "Age is no barrier," and that's definitely true at the Dipsea.

The main barrier for competitors is the steep and staired terrain. During the race, things get wild and wooly. Locals who know the Dipsea Trail well or those who aren't afraid of a little (or sometimes big) fall do some seriously aggressive running. The trail itself is well used and in most places pretty wide, allowing racers who desire a more tempered approach the space to do so. This all results in one big, fast-moving party.

Even more, the 7.4-mile Dipsea Trail is open for proverbial business every day. You don't have to participate in the race to enjoy the Marin Headlands environs, the multi-thousand-foot hills that separate the Pacific Ocean from the inland territory of the northern San Francisco Bay Area. Aromatic eucalyptus trees, coyotes, the sounds and sights of the Pacific crashing against America, and raucous songbirds flitting among the forests are just a couple of the treats in store for you.

Chapter **10**

Trail Safety and Stewardship

With apologies to Dr. Seuss, oh the places you'll go! Trail running is a hall pass to adventure. The rewards of a grand adventure on the trails are endless: sunsets and sunrises that will take your breath away, views to the horizon and the heavens, glimpses of wild animals in their natural habitat, time spent exploring with interesting people, and more. But with adventure comes risk, the chance for an adventure to go awry. Because of remote locations, challenging weather, or inexperience in negotiating problems when they arise, a small issue can quickly escalate into a dangerous situation. Just because the proverbial trail to adventure has some potential bumps doesn't mean you shouldn't enjoy the run. As previous chapters have emphasized, the best way to deal with a problem is to prevent it from happening in the first place through planning, having the right gear, and acquiring the appropriate skill set for the adventures you wish to tackle.

This chapter addresses the most common risks—wildlife, thunderstorms, steep terrain, snow crossings, dangerous humans, and more—that trail runners encounter, and it dishes up the know-how for dealing with each. This chapter also describes the fundamental nonrunning skills you need to trail run safely, such as navigating effectively, obtaining and purifying water in the backcountry, taking the right actions if you become lost, and much more. Of course, this chapter can't fully prevent an adventure from becoming a misadventure, but it can dramatically decrease the chance that this will happen. We also address stewardship in this chapter, the important idea that we must take care of the places through which we run.

Basic Backcountry Skills

If you're planning to take your trail running to the backcountry, places we define as roughly 10 miles (16 km) or more from civilization, you need to take with you a small but crucial set of skills to help you negotiate unplanned situations and problems.

Trail Navigation

At first blush, finding your way on singletrack seems downright simple. Uh, you just follow the trail, right? In many cases, that's 100 percent true. You show up at the trailhead and start running. The trail twists and turns but eventually ends up back where you started. In this case, you can negotiate the trail on intellectual autopilot.

The setup of some trail systems, however, is not that simple. Often, you'll encounter unmarked trail intersections. Sometimes a trail continues for a long way until it simply fades out for a while. And, once in a blue moon, bad weather like fog can obscure your route even at close range. In these cases, you'll need to employ navigation skills. Navigation is often considered a difficult skill to master, but in fact, it's pretty darn easy.

First things first: Many trail networks are well marked with maps at trailheads and major intersections. Those maps are often decorated with convenient "You are here" labels. Some trail systems have signposts delineating divergent trails. These trail networks are nearly navigationally foolproof. So long as you have a plan and keep your head up at intersections, you'll have no trouble finding your way.

The farther you get from civilization on a trail or the more remote the whole trail network is, the greater the chances are that your trail will not have maps, signs, or other navigational aids. If you're traveling into the backcountry, be ready for this reality and always carry a map.

The main question about maps is, how do you read the darn things? Maps vary in layout, although most have a couple of features in common. First, trails and other prominent geographic features like roads, creeks, mountains, springs, and more are marked by symbols. For instance, a trail might be delineated as a dashed line. Almost all maps are scaled, meaning that a certain distance on the map corresponds to a distance in real life. For example, one inch on the map might represent a mile (1 cm would represent 625 m on a map of this scale). Most maps have a north symbol, which indicates which way is due north relative to the other map features. And almost all maps have a key that describes the symbols.

One feature of high-quality backcountry trail maps is topographic lines, which express in the two dimensions of the map the three-dimensional topographical features of the landscape. Each topographic line signifies a particular elevation with a specific amount of vertical change, such as 40, 100, or 200 feet, between each line. (Of course, maps that use a metric scale have intervals measured in meters.) The map key will tell you the amount of vertical change represented by the space between each line, as maps vary in their detail. You will notice that, on a map, the lines grow close together in some places and spread apart in others. Such areas on the map represent steeper and flatter terrain, respectively, in the real world. As a trail user, you can use these lines to determine how much climbing or descending awaits you on the trail and to navigate through the landscape by pairing surrounding topography with what is on a map. Further, understanding the topographic lines on a map is like unlocking a secret code: You'll be able to identify many smaller, real-life topographic nuances like mesas, ridgelines, gullies, and more.

A topographic map is a powerful navigation tool for trail runners.

Compass Basics

In the rare case when one of the other kinds of navigation described in this section won't work, a trail runner will need a compass to navigate. You should carry one on any run into the backcountry and know how to use it.

Liza Howard, a champion trail runner and instructor for the Wilderness Medicine Institute and the National Outdoor Leadership School since 2003, humorously explains, "a compass can be an intimidating piece of equipment. Fortunately, the only part that's tricky is compass vocabulary. Compasses themselves are entirely straightforward. A compass points north. That's all it does. Your toaster and coffee maker

Liza Howard demonstrates compass use.

are wildly more complicated. And once you know where north is, you can figure out all sorts of other things like what direction you're heading, where you want to head, or where you are."

If possible, bring a compass with at least two degrees of accuracy, meaning that each tick mark on the compass dial is two degrees apart, and one that allows you to adjust for declination, the number of degrees that magnetic north deviates from true north in a particular location. Declination is a funny reality of our world. Maps display arrows pointing toward the North Pole, what we call true north, but magnetic north, where the magnetized arrow in your compass points, isn't necessarily located precisely at the North Pole. This difference, the declination, varies by your location and is noted on quality maps.

If you want to use your compass to determine which way you are headed, follow these simple steps:

1. Set your declination as noted in the key of your map. On most compasses, this means adjusting a small dial underneath the regular compass dial.

2. Point the arrow extending away from the compass dial itself in the direction you're headed.

3. Look at the compass dial and notice where the magnetic arrow inside it is pointing. This magnetized arrow always points toward magnetic north. Taking care to keep the long arrow pointing toward your direction of travel and the whole compass itself flat (some compasses come with bubble balances to assist with this), rotate the compass dial until the arrow pointing toward magnetic north is between the two parallel lines inside the dial itself.

1. Read the number on the dial next to the small arrow pointing at the dial, which will be somewhere between 0 and 360 degrees. This number represents your direction of travel. For your information, zero equals north, 90 degrees equals east, 180 degrees is south, and 270 degrees is west.

You can use a compass in many other ways, the most common being the triangulation of your position in real life onto a map. You use a compass to determine the position relative to you of three known geographic landmarks—high points, usually, that you can identify both on a map and in real life. Doing this is simple. Point the arrow extending from your compass dial at the first landmark and follow the previous instructions. Then, draw a line on a map representing your sight line to that landmark. For example, if you determine that a certain mountain is located 270 degrees relative to you, you would draw a line on a map representing your sight line to it, which would be 180 degrees opposite on a compass, or 90 degrees. When you do that two more times, for two other landmarks, you will find that the three lines intersect at precisely one point. That intersection is exactly where you are. If you have nothing to write with, place a piece of grass or a tiny twig on your map to represent each sight line.

A one-day orienteering class or compass-use course at your local outdoor store will fully open the wide window of compass navigation. You might never need to use a compass to find your way out of the backcountry, but it's incredibly empowering to know that you can.

Finally, some detailed backcountry maps contain other features that indicate variations in terrain, like shading to indicate steep slopes or dense vegetation. Using the many features of a map and studying the way that your intended route spans them, you can gain authentic knowledge of where you're headed long before you get there.

The landscape through which you're running offers numerous navigation clues, too. For instance, if you know the trail on which you are running is headed toward a high pass between two mountains, you might be able to pick it out long before you begin your climb to it by looking for a low spot between two tall points. In places where sparse vegetation allows long views, a keen observer can often pick up the trail itself far ahead. Or, if you know that a certain mountain or a river should be on your right as you're running a trail, you can look for it before you get there. All this said, the landscape of the earth is extremely complex, and you'll commonly find yourself fooled by canyons not visible until you get close to them, ridges that ripple more times than you expect, and false summits.

In rare cases, weather can impair your view entirely, prevent you from seeing the trail just 10 or 20 feet (3 to 6 m) ahead, and not allow you to read the landscape at all. More common, however, is dense vegetation that does the same thing, like thick tree cover, tall grass, or overgrown shrubs. When this happens, rely on a map, compass, or maybe a GPS device, as needed.

Obtaining Drinkable Water

If you run in the backcountry enough, the time will come when you'll need more water than you've carried, perhaps when it's hotter than you expected, a run takes longer than you planned it to, or you accidentally spill your water. Therefore, you should always carry a means to treat water when you trail run in the backcountry.

First, you have to locate water. The difficulty of doing this depends on the environment and climate through which you're running. In a high alpine environment, small streams and cascades can be ubiquitous. In a desert, you'll have to plan your water acquisition at the rare water access points. In any case, the map you're carrying contains clues on how to find water. Check the map key for water-related symbols and then seek them out on your map. The best approach is to figure out the water-access points along your route in the planning process.

In any environment, look for valleys, big and small, or places where the land crinkles or creases downward, because water follows gravity on a downward path. The presence of deciduous trees and shrubs—cottonwoods, aspens, willows, and tamarisks, for example—is also an indicator of nearby water in many environments. Also, look for outcrops of solid rock, because water may collect in depressions.

Finding potable water from potholes in Canyonlands National Park's Maze District.

The water you find may be safe to drink untreated, but it may also contain any number of bacteria, parasites, and other creatures that can make you sick. You should presume that any water you find in the backcountry needs to be treated, either chemically or mechanically, before consumption. An array of water-treatment products are available, including filters, iodine, chlorine dioxide, and ultraviolet radiation, that will ready your water for safe drinking. Each water treatment product has pros and cons relating to the speed with which the treatment process occurs, the effort you must put into treatment, the taste of the water after treatment, and the weight of the water-treatment product.

Here are a few tips to help you find the best water source. Try to acquire water from a moving body rather than a still one, like a creek as opposed to a pond, so that the water has presumably had less time to interact with the microscopic creatures that can sicken you. If signs indicate that your water source has recently been used by wildlife or livestock, move upstream from where they've used it so that you collect water before it runs through more likely contamination. Look for water with good clarity, because suspended sediment can clog a filter, block ultraviolet treatment, or add grit to water if you chemically purify it. In a pinch, you can use a piece of fabric to prestrain cloudy water.

What to Do if You Get Lost

We hope you never need to use the information in this section, but knowing exactly what to do if you become lost can mean the difference between a mere misadventure and an unnecessary tragedy. Here's how to save your own bacon.

Don't Panic

"Take a deep breath. People get lost and then found a lot. The key when you're lost is not to get more lost," says Liza Howard. If you do become highly emotional, stop everything and ride out those feelings. Literally, don't move, make decisions, or do anything until your emotions settle and your rational side returns.

Stop Moving Forward

If you don't know where you are, you most likely have even less of an idea of where you are headed.

Consider Retracing Your Steps

Next, Howard recommends considering the possibility of retracing your steps in the direction from where you came. The goal here would be to backtrack to the last place you knew where you were. Are your footprints visible in dirt, sand, or snow? Are you nearly 100 percent confident that you'll recognize the features of the landscape that you passed through earlier? If so, carefully retrace your steps until you are again in familiar terrain.

Triangulate Your Location

If you have a map, compass, and a good view of the terrain, triangulate your location. How to do this is described in the "Compass Basics" sidebar earlier in this chapter. After you have located yourself on the map, plan your way from there back to your intended route. Do so by retracing your steps instead of taking a new route. Use a compass to guide yourself back.

Don't Take a Shortcut

Don't leave the trail to cut cross country in an effort to take a shortcut. Often, terrain deviations and difficulties aren't fully visible, and the shortcut may not be one after all. Also, if you will require rescue by professional search and rescue, they can more easily find you on a trail, even if it's not the one you're supposed to be on, than off trail. The only exception to this, explains Howard, is when you can see something extremely obvious and helpful: "If you can see an unmistakable 'handrail,' like a road, stream, or valley that will take you to a known location, you can try following it." But be prepared to turn around if you encounter dangerous terrain; do not add more risk into your already risky situation.

Don't Split Your Group

Two or more heads (and bodies) are better than one. Pooling resources and working together is much easier and safer than splitting into smaller groups or going solo. The only exception to this rule is if a member of your group is incapacitated and unable to move. Depending on the situation, you may have to leave someone alone so that you can get the needed emergency assistance.

Work Together as a Group

If you are part of a group, you can work together to create a search system of people looking for your last known location, but be certain to stay in voice or visual contact with each other. This method will allow your team to search a greater area than you could solo but keep you safely together.

Take Note of Your Supplies

Survey your emergency provisions such as food, water, fire-making tools, clothing layers, light sources, first-aid supplies, communications technology (and their power supply), and more. Make a plan for rationing them in a way that keeps you healthy now and for a reasonable period into the future. Gather emergency provisions from nature, such as water, kindling and wood for a campfire, and dry leaves or pine boughs that can be placed inside your clothing for extra insulation.

Personal Climate Control

Taking care of your personal climate control is of utmost importance if you become lost. Staying warm, cool, or dry, depending on your circumstances, is key. If you need to get warm or dry, make fire or keep moving and consume available food and water to keep your metabolism working. You can use leaves and pine boughs as extra insulation inside your clothing, and don't hesitate to huddle with your companions. Cold appendages can be warmed against your body or someone else's, especially in the armpits, between the legs, or against the torso. Friction creates heat, so work together with your companions to rub cold body parts.

If wet weather is an issue, you must find a dry place to get out of the elements. You may have to create your own dry place by building a shelter out of natural material if you can't find a rock overhang or a dense stand of trees. Don't forget to store your kindling and firewood in that dry place, too. Use fire and body heat to help dry wet clothing. Consider the wind and stay out of it to help stay warm.

If the temperature is very hot instead, find or make shade immediately and limit your activities during the heat of the day. Drink water if you have it to stay hydrated.

Seek Professional Rescue Assistance

If you can't resolve your situation independently, consider the access you have to the outside world. Do you have cellular or satellite communications service? If so, make appropriate outside contact with search and rescue (SAR) or a reliable person who can make such contact for you. Relay crucial information on your last known location, the number of people in your group, the condition of the group, your survival provisions, and the landscape features around you.

If you have requested the outside help of professional SAR or if the person with whom you left your trail running plan at home enacts a request for assistance when you don't return at your previously designated time, here's what you need to know about the process. If weather, time of day, and other risk factors allow, a SAR team first engages in a hasty search. A small, quickly assembled team goes out looking for you, by helicopter, foot, horse, or vehicle, shortly after they learn you are missing. As a hasty search is being conducted, other SAR professionals make plans for a full-blown search effort, which generally begins near dawn of the first day after they receive a request for assistance. A SAR team concentrates first on the area they determine you are most likely to be in and radiates outward if they find no sign of you.

Pros and Cons of Trail Running Alone

Deciding whether you want to trail run alone is a conscious decision you must make. First, you have the enjoyment factor to consider; some people prefer solo runs, whereas others enjoy the company of their friends. Next, you must decide whether you are willing to undertake the extra risk involved in trail running alone. Should you become incapacitated or lost, you have no one with you to provide or obtain assistance. A good rule of thumb for true backcountry travel is to travel with no fewer than three people in your group so that if someone is injured, one person can go for help and the other can care for the injured person. But some people, particularly those who have a lot of experience trail running in remote places, choose to run alone because they feel confident in their abilities or think that the rewards of the outing exceed the risks.

If you are awaiting rescue, Howard recommends that you make sure you're as visible as possible from the ground and air and that you're away from loud noises like rushing water that can keep you from hearing searchers. She adds, "It'll also help if you can make some noise to attract attention to yourself. Whistles do a great job of making noise and not sounding like anything but whistles. A lot of running packs have tiny whistles built into them now. You can also help attract attention by hanging something colorful up high."

Wildlife

Glimpsing a wild animal behaving naturally in a wild place—now that's a fantastic fringe benefit of trail running! Wild animals big and small deserve our utmost respect. Each of them is entitled to space to roam and be free. The backcountry is their home, so this section is designed to help you understand how wildlife behaves and how to be a deferential visitor where these wild things are.

Wild animals are not to be feared, but respected. With a little knowledge, you'll understand why certain animals behave the way they do and how to act in their territory.

The best thing you can do for a wild animal is to give it a wide berth as you pass. As you will see, most wildlife often goes to great lengths to get what they think is a safe distance from you. Give them space so that they don't have to expend extra energy flying off, running away, or becoming stressed by your presence. A good rule of thumb is to give a wild animal enough room so that it doesn't modify its behavior because of you.

Trail running offers special experiences in nature, like this glimpse of a sandhill crane mother and colt.

Follow these general tips on trail running among wildlife:

- Don't feed wild animals, intentionally or unintentionally. For a number of reasons, accessing human food is unhealthy for wildlife.

- Use great care when you spot young wildlife, because mothers will act defensively if they think your presence is threatening their young. Don't come between a mother and its young.

- Herd animals are called that for a reason. They feel comfortable living in groups. Avoid accidentally separating members from a group of wildlife because this may cause them behave erratically.

- Give ungulates like deer, antelope, and elk extra space during the time of year when females are in season, because male members of the species may act in defense of females they think are being threatened. This season happens during autumn in North America.

- If you're trail running with your dog, maintain control of it at all times. Don't allow it to harass wildlife. We'll address dog issues while trail running in greater depth later in this chapter.

- If you travel abroad and trail run in another country, get local advice on what wildlife you may encounter and how you should behave around it.

- Enjoy, enjoy, enjoy! Relish in the opportunity of seeing a wild animal.

A bull elk in Yellowstone National Park.

Deer, Elk, and Moose

All over the world, deer species commonly occur in wild and, often, not-so-wild places. Deer are usually harmless and almost always sprint away when they see you. The exceptions to this are males who will defend in-season females and mothers who will defend their young. Give these types of animals a lot of room. If a deer runs at you in defense, get away as quickly as possible.

Elk, which are common all over the western part of North America, are mostly harmless, as well. Although their flight response to humans is not as well developed as it is in deer, elk will generally trot away if you sight them at close range. Male elk, however, are extremely volatile during what's called the rut, when females are in season. Male elk separate females into protected harems with which they breed. Males aggressively fight with other male elk, sometimes causing injury because of their giant antlers and great strength, to defend their harems and add females to them. The power of these males is truly a sight to see, but you could be gravely injured if you get in their way. During the rut, give elk loads of room. Give a female elk with a calf or calves plenty of space, too. If an elk charges, run away and place trees or other substantial obstacles between you and it for protection.

Moose are found in many places throughout North America, mostly in wetland and woodland habitats. Generally, moose are gentle giants, but they do not like to be surprised at close range. When this happens, moose usually run away, but once in a while, a moose will charge whatever has surprised it. Use extra caution when running through their habitat, especially if your view is obscured. If a moose charges, get away as fast as you can and put trees or other big objects between you and the animal for protection.

The mothers of many ungulate species hide their young babies during the day. Mothers do this because they walk and graze for many hours, and babies don't yet have the endurance to do so. If you come upon a baby ungulate in hiding, leave it alone. The baby will likely freeze in place. If you touch it, there's a small chance the mother will abandon it because it has your human scent on it. Also, be aware that the mother may be near.

Venomous Snakes

Rattlesnakes, copperheads, and other poisonous snakes are relatively uncommon members of ecosystems all over North America. These snakes will strike at animals that make them feel threatened by coming too close, including humans. The venom they may inject upon biting is highly toxic and requires immediate emergency medical treatment.

Snakes are cold-blooded reptiles, so they need warm air or sun to be active. Trail runners running in snake habitat during warm, sunny weather need to be observant for snakes stretched across or coiled near the trail. If you're on steep terrain and are using your hands for assistance, use caution when placing them. Your powers of observation and avoidance are your best defense. If you see a venomous snake or hear the quintessential rattlesnake rattle, get at least six feet (2 m) away from it, beyond a snake's striking range, as fast as you can.

A black-tailed rattlesnake trailside in Texas.

Insects

Bees, wasps, biting ants, scorpions, and poisonous spiders all occur in the many places we trail run. Avoidance is the best measure for all of these wee beasts. Watch where you stand or sit for a break on your trail run, and look where you put your hands when raising or lowering yourself over steep terrain. Avoid swatting at a bee or a wasp that flies by you so that it doesn't sting or bite to defend itself. If you hear the distinctive hum of a beehive or see a beehive or wasp nest, get the heck out of Dodge. If you are stung by an insect, a small amount of pain and swelling is normal, but a large amount of either combined with difficulty breathing and swallowing constitutes a dangerous allergic reaction that may require immediate medical attention. Those who experience anaphylaxis because of insect stings should carry emergency epinephrine and have a plan for obtaining emergency medical treatment.

Bears

Black bears are regular members of many ecosystems around North America. Although they are much larger and stronger than we are, most black bears react to humans by running away. Black bears can become dangerous if they think you are threatening their food source or young. Put as much distance as you can between you and any black bear that doesn't immediately run away from you by walking backward as fast as possible. In only a few cases have black bears, which are omnivores, intentionally preyed on humans. If a black bear attacks you, fight back with all your might.

Grizzly bears live throughout Alaska and western Canada as well as in parts of Idaho, Montana, and Wyoming in the continental United States. In their habitat, grizzlies are truly the highest members of the food chain. Contrary to black bears' natural flight response to stress, grizzlies react to stress by fighting. We need not dwell on the fact that an altercation with a creature perhaps three times as big as you will not go well! Grizzlies charge and attack if they think that something threatens them, their food, or their young. But if a grizzly bear knows that a human is nearby and it has the opportunity, it will most often choose to leave the area.

Grizzlies that charge and attack are usually those that are surprised at close range, so avoid this situation by yelling to let grizzlies know you are around, scanning all around you for bears, and slowing to a walk when the view becomes obscured by brush, trees, or bends in the trail. Give them the opportunity to detect you and move away before you get too close. Carry bear spray, which is an oversized container of pepper spray made especially for humans to protect themselves in the event of a charging grizzly bear. A grizzly charge can happen in a split second, so carry that bear spray in an accessible location on the front of your hydration pack or in hand. If a grizzly bear charges at you, spray a cloud of pepper spray between you and it, creating a temporary barrier of the highly irritating chemical that you hope the bear won't go through. If a grizzly bear makes contact with you, cover your head and neck with your hands and arms and play dead. A grizzly bear's goal in this situation is to minimize what it perceives as a threat as fast as possible. If you lie motionless, the bear may believe that you no longer represent a threat. Don't move until you are certain that the bear is long gone.

Mountain Lions

Elusive, shy, and highly dispersed, mountain lions are the highest member of many food chains where they live across western North America and in some places in the central and eastern parts of the continent. Because of their lifestyle and small population, your chances of seeing them are slim. But mountain lions are predators that hunt by stalking and attacking. A mountain lion attack on humans is inordinately rare but possible. If you see a mountain lion, remember that it's a cat, a mammal that has an incredible chase-and-pounce instinct. Running away is likely to trigger that instinct, so resist your natural reaction to get away quickly. Instead, do things that make you look and sound big and aggressive: Yell, wave your hands over your head, and throw things at the cat. Walk backward at the same time to put distance between you and the animal. Generally, avoid bending over or otherwise making yourself look small or vulnerable. If a cat determines that an animal it is attacking could injure it, it may give up and flee, so fight back as hard as you can in the infinitely small chance you are attacked.

Other Wildlife

Wolves are rare members of some ecosystems in North America, and coyotes are common all over the continent. Only in an extremely rare circumstance will a wolf or coyote attack a human. Aggressive coyotes are typically those that have become acclimated to getting food from humans. If a wolf or coyote attacks you, react in violent defense of yourself.

Bison live in a very few ecosystems of the North American West. If you are lucky enough to trail run through their habitat, give them space. Bison charge animals that threaten them, and the few humans who have chosen to walk close enough to elicit that charging response have been gravely injured.

Mountain goats live on the high, alpine ridgelines and peaks of the North American West. Typically, mountain goats run away on seeing a

A mountain goat perched at 13,000 feet in the Colorado Rockies.

human, but occasionally they don't. Because mountain goats have limited access to water and salt in their high-altitude environments, some goats have become acclimated to getting liquid and salt from human urine. Yes, it's true. Mountain goats that have discovered such a "delicacy" will follow humans around. Occasionally, you might meet a stubborn mountain goat that doesn't want to move to allow you to pass on a trail. If you are in an alpine environment with no safe way around a goat, you may have to wait patiently or turn around.

Weather

We've discussed before how to deal with rain, snow, heat, cold, and sun in enough detail to make your trail runs through them as enjoyable and comfortable as possible. But you should be aware of two other kinds of weather before trail running through the backcountry.

Lightning

Sadly, every year a few outdoor recreationists are struck by lightning, even though such incidents are easily preventable. There is no reason for any trail runner ever to be struck by lightning. For the most part, lightning becomes a risk to humans when they are in exposed areas, like a high, open meadow or a ridgeline or mountaintop that doesn't have the protection of trees. Lightning occurs mostly during summer and fall thunderstorms, which tend to build up after midday and sometimes continue into the night. To avoid lightning, leave those exposed areas when thunderstorms are building or occurring. It's as simple as that.

If you are in the mountains of western North America, plan to be back down into the relative protection below treeline by noon, or earlier if thunderstorms form sooner. If you are in the other parts of North America, don't cross meadows, high bald hills, or other open areas during a thunderstorm. The same rule holds true for urban road running or trail running: Don't run through exposed areas during a thunderstorm.

If you find yourself in an exposed location and a thunderstorm approaches, use your trail running skills to sprint back to cover. If this isn't possible and you have to wait out the storm in a precarious place, get into the "lightning position." Separate yourself from any metal you have with you and your companions by about 50 feet (15 m). Squat with your feet together, keeping only your feet on the ground. Wrap your arms around your legs. Don't allow your butt or hands to touch the ground because this additional contact point can create a line through which electrical current can flow through your body should lightning strike. Maintain this position until the storm passes.

Lightning flashes during a desert storm.

Flash Floods

Flash floods occur mostly in North America's desert ecosystems after a significant amount of rain falls during a short time. Desert ecosystems generally lack absorbent soil, and solid rock allows rain to run off downhill, pooling into gullies and canyons. These gullies and canyons can become flooded within a matter of minutes in or after heavy rainfall. Avoiding flash floods is as easy as avoiding lightning. Don't go into a low place before, during, or even after a storm.

Because big drainage systems can extend for many miles, a flash flood can originate from a storm over a part of a drainage system that's far upstream from your location. If you are trail running through the desert during summer or early fall, when thunderstorms are common in the afternoon and evening, know the rough layout of the drainage systems through which you're traveling and take note of weather in the upstream direction.

Have a plan for getting out of a flood path in the event of a flash flood. If you hear a rumble reminiscent of a freight train approaching or observe water or debris starting to fill a drainage, seek high ground immediately.

Potential Terrain Problems

If you're unsure that you'll be able to retrace your steps backward through natural obstacles such as snowfields, cliffs, and disappearing trail, don't continue forward—even if you don't plan to return the way you came.

Surmounting terrain challenges is part of trail running. Some trail runners find terrain challenges so enjoyable that they seek out routes that include a great deal of elevation change, technicality, or other challenges. Although you'll have to practice negotiating most terrain challenges before you master them, the way to surmount obstacles is at least partly self-evident. In this section, you'll learn how to take on a couple of terrain challenges that might seem daunting at first (or 400th) pass.

Exposure

Some humans have it in their nature to be uncomfortable with exposure—an open and airy location—and heights, whereas others are unbothered. No matter your proclivity, you should use care when a trail travels through an area with steep drop-offs. Cliffs can warrant walking, because moving across one would be a very bad time to catch a toe! If you have some wiggle room in the width of the trail tread, use that space to stay away from the cliff. For travel through extensive exposure, the use of your hands or trekking poles can add stability. Look in the direction of where you're headed, not down the exposure. If you are the kind of person who goes weak kneed at the sight of steeps, that's totally alright. Seriously, your ego won't be damaged by avoiding what you don't like.

Once in a while, you might encounter a section of trail that makes you incredibly uncomfortable because of its combination of exposure and extreme technicality. Such a stretch of trail might make you think, "I could get up that, but I'm not sure if I could get down." In such situations, you will have to use your best judgment about whether to proceed. Do you have to return this direction, or are you continuing a different way? Even if you are continuing, what might happen if for some reason you have to turn around and come back through? Can you really get through the technicality in the first place? As you decide, let your backcountry skills be your guide, not your ego or your desire to see what's beyond that swath of trail.

Snowfields

Snowfields can be short or long bits of snow that are left over in high alpine locations from the previous winter. They are common during the early summer season on the north and east slopes of mountains or high passes. At first sight, they look like an absolute blast to play on and they very well may be. But in the wrong conditions they can be extremely dangerous.

The trail disappears into the snow high in the Spanish Pyrenees.

When you encounter a snowfield, observe the hardness and steepness of the snow. Generally, if a snowfield is flat or nearly so, it will be safe to cross, because even if it's slippery and you fall, you won't slide anywhere. If a snowfield is hard, that is, if the snow is frozen solid and doesn't give in any direction under your feet, and steep, crossing it is dangerous. A fall could turn into a slide that ends in serious injury. If you encounter a snowfield like this, scan the terrain for a way to get around the snowfield on bare ground or flat terrain. Get past the snowfield this way if it's safe and doesn't damage the environment to do so. With proper light mountaineering equipment including crampons and an ice axe, as well as the skills to use this equipment properly, crossing a frozen, steep snowfield is possible. Mountaineering is beyond the scope of this book, but you can take a class from a local outdoor store to learn how to do this.

Suppose that you encounter a snowfield that is steep but soft, and you are able to kick flat steps into it or follow the steps of people who have come before you. Before you decide to cross, consider a couple things. Be aware that some snow, even though it's soft, can still be quite slippery. Also, consider what might happen if you are going to a mountain peak and have to return the same way. Will the snow freeze and harden again before you return? You will have to use your best judgment to decide whether to cross the snow. As they say in mountain climbing, the journey doesn't end at the summit; it ends when you are safely down from the mountain.

Be aware that although the traction devices discussed in chapter 5 can aid in snowfield crossings, you must use them with care. Don't let extra traction on your feet embolden you past your skill and comfort level.

Finally, you need to exercise caution on snow bridges, the snow that covers creeks or streams, which is a common feature of many environments during winter and spring. You will be tempted to use such snow to cross creeks in lieu of submerging your feet in cold water. But these features are extremely dangerous because they can collapse, thereby flushing you into the water and underneath the snow downstream. When crossing snow, listen for the sound of water rushing below. Avoid crossing atop this snow and water at all costs.

Disappearing Trail

A good singletrack trail may occasionally disappear, almost as if some sort of black magic had been conjured. One minute you are running along an easily discernable trail, and in another minute—poof—you can't find it anywhere. You can lose the route when the trail opens into a meadow and grass covers the trail and meadow equally, where the trail crosses a section of solid rock, where a trail crosses an exposed area of talus (an extended field of rocks that can take up a whole hillside), on a trail recently exposed from snowmelt, or on a trail that isn't used often. Sometimes the trail disappears for only a short distance, but other times it's gone for good.

If the tread of the trail you're running on disappears, look for other signs of the direction you're supposed to travel. Stacks of rocks made by humans called cairns, paint or other markings on exposed rock surfaces, hash marks in the bark of trees, and small trail markers hanging from trees are all directional indicators. Keep your eyes peeled for details, because there is almost always a human-made hint of where you need to go.

If you can't find any indication of where you should go, you will have to look for the trail on the other side of the treadless space. For instance, if the trail disappears into a meadow, cross to the other side and look for its reentrance into the forest. You may have to scan the opposite margin of the meadow for quite a ways until you find it, because sometimes the trail angles across an open space in a way you don't expect. If you have to cross an area of talus or exposed, hard rock, remember that the trail will usually take the path of least resistance, even if the distance is a bit longer, using switchbacks, cliff bands, and the like. In this case, letting your natural instinct guide you over the terrain may lead you back to easily distinguishable trail.

As you are searching for the continuation of the trail, don't lose track of where you came from. If you can't find where you need to go, you'll have to backtrack.

Human-Related Trail Issues

Most people you encounter along the trail will be joyful and respectful of you. They will almost all inspire you to treat them the same way. A wave of greeting and a generally kind attitude toward others go a long way in creating good vibes among the people with whom you share the trail. What follows is a short discussion about how to keep the trail safe for yourself and the other people out there.

Trail systems usually have rules that govern rights-of-way for different kinds of trail users, and you should know these regulations before you set out. But even when the trail runner technically has the right-of-way, common sense, courtesy, and community relations can sometimes counsel toward yielding, such as when a mountain biker would have to unclip her or his shoes and dismount when a trail runner could let the rider pass in an instant.

Dogs—Yours and Theirs

Many outdoor recreationists enjoy time on the trails with their dogs. In fact, many breeds of dogs love trail running, are good at it, and are healthier and happier dogs because of the sport. Doggone it, trail running with your dog can be a truly pleasurable experience. But every dog owner has the job of preventing his or her dog from creating a dangerous situation for other trail users or harming the natural world. Dog lovers, here's how to create safe, enjoyable situations for everyone on the trails:

- Follow local regulations on dogs. Maintain voice control, leash your dog, and pick up your dog's poop. Don't bring your dogs on trails where they are disallowed.
- Don't allow your dog to chase wildlife. It can stress, injure, or kill wildlife, and you need to prevent this from happening. Letting your dog do any of these things is often illegal.
- Although you love your dog, remember that not all humans are comfortable with dogs and do not wish to interact with yours. Respect their rights by not allowing your dog to approach other humans or their dogs uninvited.
- If your dog displays aggressive behavior toward other trail users, other dogs, or wildlife, don't bring it trail running. You need to make sure that everyone out on the trail stays safe from your dog. You can teach your dog appropriate social skills off the trail.

On the other side of the leash, you may have an altercation with a dog. These confrontations often happen so quickly that it's hard for you or the dog owner to act in a way that will stop it. If a dog is threatening, you'll have to ward it off aggressively. If you are trail running and a dog threatens you, defend yourself by yelling, waving a trekking pole or stick, or by using pepper spray. Report details about the incident to local authorities as soon as you can safely do so.

Mechanized Vehicles

Many trails are open to mechanized vehicles like mountain bikes, off-road vehicles, and, possibly, jeeps. Depending on the nature of the trail, these vehicles may be moving quite fast or slow. When the terrain allows fast travel, keep your eyes and ears peeled and avoid surprise encounters. Use special care when you negotiate blind corners and when brush or rocks obscure the trail. Follow right-of-way regulations for the trail system you're on, but be mindful of your personal safety because you are unlikely to win in a collision with a machine, even if you have the right-of-way.

Hunting

On many trails, you will cross public lands that may offer hunting seasons for various animal species. In these seasons, you'll be sharing the landscape with people using guns or bows and arrows. State and federal governments enact rules to help keep hunting safe for hunters and others who share the trail. Nevertheless, a mistake made by a hunter can be lethal. You need to be extremely careful when trail running during hunting season. Stay safe out there using these guidelines:

- Wear safety orange or a similarly highly visible color.
- Stay on designated trails so that you are traveling in places where hunters expect to see you.
- Run during midday, if possible, because hunters prefer dawn, dusk, and, occasionally, night.
- Make noise if the view is obscured so that hunters know you are coming. Some hunters might find noisemaking bothersome if they perceive that it will scare their prey, but it is entirely your right to keep yourself safe and to make noise when running down a trail.
- If you see hunters and they don't see you, announce your presence until they do. Again, this action may bother some hunters, but it's the safest course of action and you can do it in a friendly way.
- Some hunters, like those hunting bears or mountain lions, use dogs to facilitate the hunt. These dogs run in packs, bark loudly, and seem incredibly imposing. But if you encounter them, they will likely be fixated on their job and oblivious to you. Although an attack on humans by hunting dogs is extremely rare, it's possible. An aggressive response of yelling, waving your arms, kicking your legs, waving sticks, or throwing rocks is warranted for your protection.

- If you run with your own dog, put safety orange on it. Keep it leashed and under your control.

Dangerous Humans

Most people on the trail seek experiences similar to yours. Very rarely, people are on the trails for malicious or illegal reasons. These people are wholly unpredictable, which makes offering advice about how to deal with them almost impossible. Instead, we'll say that you should treat interactions with potentially dangerous humans on the trails the same way you would in town. These few tips could help keep you safe around people who might be dangerous:

- Don't leave valuables in your car at trailheads. If you do, make sure that they're out of sight. Always lock your doors and leave your windows up.
- Don't give strangers your detailed trail running itinerary or contact information.
- Avoid people who are behaving in ways you don't expect of regular trail users or those who act secretive or nervous about your presence.
- If a person makes you feel uncomfortable, you don't need to have a conversation with him or her. You can simply keep going on the trail. Maintain your personal space.
- Use your cell phone or satellite device to report problems with people in a truly dangerous situation. Report the details of illegal or suspicious activities to authorities as soon as you can safely do so.
- Remember that you're a fit trail runner and can run fast and far. Use your skills to escape a truly dangerous human.

Pack Animals

Pack animals such as horses, mules, and donkeys have long been used to transport people and goods through wild places, and they, along with llamas, are commonly seen along the trails. Pack animals may behave erratically if surprised, and they could injure you or the humans with them if this happens. On almost all trail systems, pack animals have the right-of-way over every other trail user. Thus, you have to yield to them. Ask for and await instructions from their human leaders and help to create a safe passing situation.

If you come upon a pack animal or a train of pack animals from behind and you would like to pass, politely announce to the humans leading the animals as much, but stay at least 50 feet (15 m) back. The pack-animal leader will tell you when and how to pass safely. The leader may pull the pack animals to the side of the trail and tell you to pass, ask you to go off trail and around them, or offer another solution.

A mule carries supplies out of the Grand Canyon.

If you encounter a pack animal or pack train head on, step off the trail well before you meet and give the animals plenty of room to pass. Say hello and talk gently to the animals as they pass so that they know exactly what and where you are. If you meet a pack animal in exposed terrain and there's nowhere for you to safely step off the trail, you will have to back up until a pass can happen safely.

Pack-animal leaders are quite adept at caring for their animals and other trail users in passing situations. Let them lead your interactions.

Domestic Herd Animals

The public lands through which you run may be used for cattle, sheep, and goat grazing. Many times, these domestic animals behave similarly to their wild brethren: They run away when they see you. Although they are domesticated, they spend much less time around humans than those living on farms. You will find that cows are highly protective of their calves, especially young ones, and will charge you in defense if they feel threatened. Give them a wide berth.

Perhaps most dangerous are the dogs that live with and protect sheep herds. These dogs also have little experience with humans, and they are bred to protect sheep from potential predators. If they perceive you as a threat, they will charge, bark, and bite. Avoid sheep herds altogether. If aggressively approached by a sheep dog, firmly and exactly tell it, "Go back to the sheep," because this is the safety phrase with which some are trained.

Caring for the Trails

While trail runners are attracted to our sport for a number of reasons, most of us share a common motivator: the desire to experience and move through natural landscapes. We take to the trails for their clean air and water, abundant and healthy wildlife, diversity of plant life, quiet, lack of human impact, aesthetic vistas, and more. These resources are, in some cases, sensitive and rare. And these resources, in all cases, are finite. Impact by humans can and does change, damage, and destroy them.

It is, thus, a privilege as trail runners to be stewards of the lands through which we run. What does it mean to practice land stewardship? On an individual level, such as that of a single trail runner, a land steward is someone who takes care of natural places. Land stewards believe that all of the resources in a landscape as well as the people who use those places should be carefully cared for. Thus, our goal as trail runners is to travel with care, thereby minimizing the impact we have on natural spaces. As they say, knowledge is power, so here is the basic framework for responsible trail running.

The Leave No Trace Center for Outdoor Ethics (LNT), a non-profit organization that promotes land stewardship in everyone who recreates outdoors, developed seven core principles to help guide outdoor recreation of all kinds, including trail running. Here they are:

1. Plan Ahead and Prepare
2. Travel and Camp on Durable Surfaces
3. Dispose of Waste Properly
4. Leave What you Find
5. Minimize Campfire Impacts
6. Respect Wildlife
7. Be Considerate of Other Visitors

© Leave No Trace Center for Outdoor Ethics: www.LNT.org.

The balance of this chapter applies these principles to trail running and discusses the many ways you can be a caretaker of the places through which you travel.

Preparation

The legwork of a trail run begins before you reach the trail. Natural areas are administered by towns, counties, states, the federal government, or private entities. Each natural space has a unique set of rules designed by its land managers to protect and preserve its equally unique resources. Things get tricky for trail runners because, from wild place to wild place, rules change. That's because different resources need to be differently cared for. It's your job to know the rules of the natural spaces through which you run. Knowing and adhering to the rules helps trail runners avoid behaving in a damaging way.

Here are a couple rules commonly found in natural spaces that apply to trail running:

- **Opening and closing times.** Sometimes this rule is established to give space to wildlife that is active nocturnally. As an example, some of the trails through Yellowstone National Park close daily a couple hours before sunset and open a couple hours after sunrise so that humans don't impact grizzly bears at night, and vice versa. Other times, this rule is in place because natural spaces aren't staffed at night.
- **Group sizes.** The larger the group, the more the impact that group will have on the environment and the other people also using it. Many land managers establish a maximum group size that they believe is sustainable for a particular open space.

Another way that trail runners can plan ahead is to research the potential hazards and special qualities of natural spaces. Is there a certain type of wildlife to be watching for? Are there rare plants growing along the trail? Is the trail easy to follow or are there tricky intersections to navigate? Being prepared for the conditions you are about to experience will help prevent negative interactions. For instance, knowing how to react when you see a wild animal can prevent a negative interaction that might harm that wildlife or you. Being able to identify a sensitive plant should mitigate the chances of you accidentally damaging it.

LNT encourages trail users to consider the time of day in which you use a trail. Humans heavily use some trail systems, such as those in or near urban and suburban areas. And, at certain times of day, those trail systems receive even-heavier use. For instance, midmornings and late afternoons on urban and suburban trail systems, and weekend days on trail systems that are within a couple hours of an urban or suburban area are high-use times. Using the trail in off hours takes some of the pressure off those high-use times.

Substrate Impacts

Walking and running on trails, next to trails, at overlooks along trails, and off trail can have a negative impact if the surfaces over which you travel

Switchbacks prevent erosion on open mountainsides.

degrade as a result of your footsteps. Examples of the nondurable surfaces you might encounter include mud, riparian areas, alpine environments, and cryptobiotic soil. Cryptobiotic soil exists in many desert ecosystems with microscopic organisms that help fix soil in place and prevent erosion due to wind, water, and gravity.

LNT asks that trail users travel single file, on trail, and down the middle of the trail, even if it's muddy or wet. Walking along the trail margin or outside of the trail tread to avoid mud or water can cause the trail to widen and erode. In some deserts, land managers forbid off-trail travel to protect cryptobiotic soil, which can take decades to redevelop if damaged, and prevent erosion.

As a trail runner, you will shortly become familiar with switchbacks, or the bends trails make on hillsides so that you don't have to travel straight up or down that hill. Switchbacks are in place to prevent the erosion that would occur in a path that was as steep as a hill. It might be tempting to cut switchbacks, especially when going downhill, to save distance traveled and maybe time. However, cutting switchbacks leads to the erosion that the switchbacks themselves are trying to prevent. Please stay on the trail.

Proper Waste Disposal

By waste, LNT means everything you bring with you or produce while trail running: the wrappers of the food you're eating, leftover organic matter like apple cores and banana peels, and your body's waste products.

In terms of the trash produced, it's pack it in, pack it out, each and every time. Everything you bring for a run must be brought back out. We additionally encourage you to pick up any trash you find that was left by someone else. The reasons for this are self-evident: Trash isn't natural, it doesn't easily biodegrade, animals that eat it can become sick, and it's unsightly.

When it comes to bodily waste, always use a bathroom when it's provided. Here's Liza Howard's no-nonsense recommendation for dealing with your bodily waste on the trail, "You shouldn't poop in the middle of a trail. You'd think that could be one of those unwritten rules, but sometimes new trail runners equate the liberating feeling of running in nature with liberation from social norms, mores, and basic hygiene. So, just as you shouldn't poop in the middle of your neighborhood sidewalk, you shouldn't poop in the middle of a trail. The same goes for emptying your bowels right next to a trail. A mound of poop is about as attractive there as it is in the grass next to a sidewalk. The social impact is even worse if there's toilet paper wadded up in the fly-ridden mess. The best practice is to walk about 70 steps from the trail or water, dig a hole about six inches deep and big enough to accommodate your deposit, wipe with a smooth stone, stick, or snowball, and then fill the hole in and cover it up."

LNT asks us to carry out all toilet paper and sanitary products. Toilet paper and tampons, even those that have been labeled flushable or biodegradable, take many years to degrade and, thus, should not be buried. You can bring a couple Ziploc bags to carry out these things. Side note, baby wipes or hand sanitizer might make this experience more sanitary and comfortable.

Some natural areas have additional rules for trash treatment. For example, on the most popular approach trail to the summit of Mount Whitney in California, humans must carry out their feces along with their toilet paper and sanitary products. Don't worry; in unique cases like this, commercially available products assist you with doing so in a sanitary manner.

Take Nothing, Leave Nothing

There are plenty of interesting objects that will capture your attention along the trail such as fossils, plants, historical artifacts, and more. LNT asks that you leave everything just as you found it. Enjoy the heck out of whatever you find. Stop, take photos, dream about what the world was like when the artifact was made, whatever trips your trigger, but leave the objects exactly as you found them.

This is because not only is a fossil or artifact important, but also the situation in which it's found can help tell its story. For example, if a number of historic horseshoes are found in one location, this might indicate that the location was a historic camp where horses were kept and shod. If the horseshoes are moved away from their original location, part of their story becomes lost in that movement.

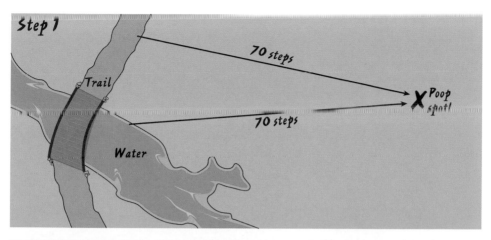

Step 1

Trail

70 steps

70 steps

X Poop spot!

Water

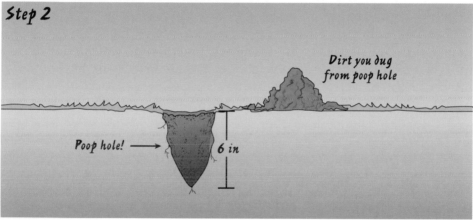

Step 2

Dirt you dug from poop hole

Poop hole! →

6 in

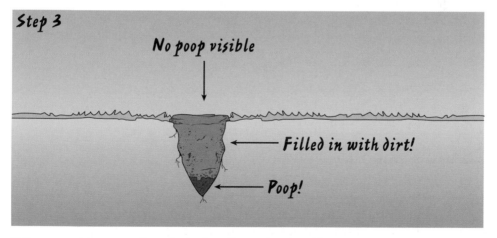

Step 3

No poop visible

Filled in with dirt!

Poop!

Where and how to dig a hole for disposing bodily waste.

Leave what you find on the trail—like this Native American projectile point—where you found it.

LNT asks trail users to additionally leave natural places unaltered. Rock cairns and wind shelters, made by stacking rocks atop each other, for example, leave unnecessary, long-lasting, visible, and unnatural reminders of your visit.

Liza Howard adds, "My son hates this principle. What's the point of finding arrowheads, antlers, cool-looking rocks, or even a really great stick if you can't take them home with you? He doesn't buy into the 'if everybody took one, there would be any left' logic. But he's young and he's still working on recognizing the impact of his behavior on others. If every trail runner took something interesting or beautiful home from a run, the scenery would change and the trails would lose their 'Wow!' factors. So be the example and preserve the 'Wow!'"

Consideration for Wildlife

As previously discussed, wildlife roams in the places you trail run. Birds, insects, reptiles, ungulates, and predatory mammals call open spaces home. To see a herd of elk grazing in a meadow, to watch butterflies pollinate flowers, to listen to birds chirp from treetops, to hear frogs croaking from desert oases, to see a bear searching for food, or to hear a pack of coyotes yipping at sunset: A glimpse of wildlife living free in its native habitat is an incredible benefit of trail running.

In being a land steward, it's your job to make sure wildlife have the continued opportunity to live unbothered by your passage. Most importantly, you must give wildlife its space. A national-park ranger once gave Meghan a wonderful recommendation for providing wild animals with the space they need to feel comfortable: If an animal modifies its behavior for you, you're too close. Different land managers have a variety of rules and recommendations for how far you should stay away from certain kinds of wildlife. Check those rules before you run.

Wild animals should never be allowed access to human food or trash. Don't feed animals and always supervise your food and hydration pack so that you don't unintentionally provide wildlife access to your food. Wild animals can become sick from the consumption of human food. Access to human food additionally makes many animals behave aggressively as they attempt to gain access to more human food. For example, bears in the Lake Tahoe region of California who access human food have been known to charge other humans, and squirrels that have been fed in Zion National Park in Utah have bitten other humans.

Dogs can be especially impactful to wildlife. Dogs love to chase and, in some cases, kill wildlife. Control your pet at all times by leash or voice. If you are unsure of your ability to control your dog by voice, kindly use a leash.

Finally, some wildlife species become especially sensitive to the presence of humans at certain times of the year, such as when they are mating or raising young. Land managers often set temporary closures to take the pressure of human presence off wildlife during these sensitive times.

Consideration for Other Visitors

Trail runners share the trails with all sorts of other human users, including other trail runners, hikers, dog walkers, mountain bikers, birders, backpackers, equestrians, hunters, ATV riders, motorcyclists, jeepers, astronomers, and more. Each legal trail user has a right to experience the trail, and none should behave in a way that degrades another's experience.

Most land managers for areas that are visited by multiple user groups have established rules to govern how these groups interact. Rules establishing right-of-way designations, one-way trails, limited-use trails, trails where motorized use is allowed, trails where motorized use is prohibited, and more are meant to help prevent negative and dangerous encounters among user groups.

For example, multiple user groups, including hikers, trail runners, and mountain bikers, heavily use Park City, Utah's trails. Some Park City trails have been designated as uphill-only or downhill-only trails for some or all user groups to prevent negative encounters between users. Also, some trails have been designated as pedestrian only to prevent dangerous interactions between pedestrians and mountain bikers.

LNT also asks trail users to respect other users' desire for quiet. If you would like to listen to music while you run, use headphones. Avoid extended bouts of shouting or other loud noises that can intrude upon another person's experience.

As previously mentioned with regard to wildlife, trail runners should control dogs via leash or voice so that other trail users don't have to interact with them if they don't want to.

LNT says that a trail user should keep courtesy and respect in mind each time he or she interacts with other trail users, that this simple but mindful approach can effectively guide our actions in a way that will help sustain strong, kind relationships between all trail users.

To learn about the rules, potential hazards, and special qualities of a natural space you would like to run through, consult that natural space's manager. Call them, check out their website, stop by a visitor center, or read interpretive signs at trailheads. Be aware that rules vary from location to location because of different resources, and that rules can change throughout the year to protect resources at seasonally critical times.

As much as we would like it to be, trail running isn't exclusively about gallivanting carefree through beautiful places. Trail running in wild places is a privilege. We believe that the more skills you take with you trail running, the more problem free and therefore the more pleasurable your experience will be. Running with as little impact as possible on the resources through which you travel and the other trail users you meet ensures that our wild places stay wild for generations of trail runners and other outdoor enthusiasts to come. You now have a solid set of knowledge and skills for beginner to intermediate-level trail runs. Get out there and use it, but remember to be a perpetual learner.

LAKE DISTRICT, ENGLAND, UNITED KINGDOM

In a group of British trail runners, whisper the words "Lake District" and watch eyes glimmer, lips curl into smiles, and minds disappear into dreams of big adventures in huge landscapes. Watch too as brows furrow and conversations turn to the inevitable weather-induced misadventures for which this region of the world is also known.

The Lake District refers largely to England's Lake District National Park, located in the country's northwest corner. Known by its name and by lower-altitude recreationists for its lakes and other water bodies, the Lake District is famous among trail runners for its fells, as the mountains of the area are known. In the Lake District, these fells reach as high as 3,209 feet (978 m) atop Scafell Pike, England's highest mountain. The fells are basically gargantuan piles of alpine rock rubble, making them a challenge to negotiate. The Lake District's infamous rain, wind, fog, and often even worse weather add difficulty to outings here. The lowlands offer challenges as well, by way of shoe-sucking mud and bogs.

These variables shouldn't deter you, however, because they haven't deterred the many generations of fell runners who have preceded you. Fell running is a bit different from trail running in that race courses or the places you run aren't necessarily on marked trails; rather, they are routes that you self-navigate. Fell racing has been taking place throughout the United Kingdom, including in the Lake District, since the 1800s. Fell running itself dates back farther than that.

(continued)

Lake District (continued)

You can join in the fun in many ways, such as by one of the dozens of fell races that take place each year in the Lake District, predominantly but not exclusively in the summer. Or, with a Lake District topographic map, you can choose your own fell adventure by linking one, two, or perhaps more summits together into an out-and-back or loop. Do use care with any adventures you undertake because England's notoriously bad weather is even worse in the Lake District. Scarily, clouds and fog can obscure the view even 20 feet (6 m) in front of you, making the navigation of an off-trail route a true challenge. You should probably tackle your first fell-running adventure on a clear day, even if it's cold or windy, when you can see where you're going. A couple starter outings in the Lake District are to England's tallest mountain, Scafell Pike, from the agricultural hub of Wasdell Head or to the top of Skiddaw from the village of Keswick.

Chapter **11**

Health and Injuries

There are no ifs, ands, or buts about it: If you trail run long enough, a physical malady of some sort will result. Maybe you will trip and fall. Perhaps you will run straight into a branch. You might take a poorly fitted pair of shoes out for too long a run. By reading this chapter you'll learn how to avoid many ailments with knowledge and planning. You'll also learn how to address issues as they happen with swift first aid.

Preventative Care

Throughout this book, you've read about the benefits of planning. A little knowledge, a good plan of action, and the right preparation yield positive trail running experiences. In this section you'll learn what you can do before you trail run to help keep yourself healthy.

Sunburn

The ultraviolet light of the sun can burn both your skin and eyes, so both require protection that can be found in sunscreen, protective clothing, and sunglasses. Head back to chapter 7, "Conquering the Conditions," to see how to prevent sunburn.

Chafing

One thing that can be awful about running is chafing. Exquisitely painful and not uncommon among trail runners, chafing refers to the repetitive rubbing of your skin against itself, your clothing, or your gear and the skin abrasions that result. Because the human body comes in all shapes and sizes, chafing happens in different places for different people. Examples from the top down include your shoulders or back against a pack; your underarms against your inner arms; anywhere a sports bra touches the skin; nipples against a shirt; shorts waistbands against your waistline; various genitalia against themselves or your shorts, tights, or liner within your shorts; and your inner thighs against themselves or your running bottoms. Ouch!

Chafing is a common runner ailment. Sports lube, tape, and properly fitting shoes, clothes, and gear will eliminate virtually all chafing problems.

But there's a solution for almost all kinds of chafing. Hurrah! By finding gear that fits correctly, pretaping, lubing areas that are apt to chafe, and reapplying lube when necessary during your run, you can eliminate almost all of your chafing problems. You might find portions of this section a bit forward—sorry about that. The goal here is to get right to the point and prevent a painful skin disaster.

Pretaping means that you cover the portions of your skin that may chafe with tape so that the tape takes the friction, rather than your skin. You'll need to use a tape that will stick even when you get sweaty and has a smooth outer surface. Lubing means that you cover your potential chafe points with a substance that will reduce friction. A number of commercial sports lubes out there are oil based, so you won't sweat them off for several hours. In a pinch, a petroleum jelly like Vaseline will do the trick, but it tends to wear off more quickly and is more prone to attracting grit. If chafing is a serious issue for you, carry lube on your longer trail runs and reapply as necessary. Don't run (and shower afterward) in pain.

Note that chafing becomes more common the longer you run. Also, in certain circumstances chafing is more common, such as in extreme heat and humidity, cold, and rain. Triggers vary by person. Over time you'll learn what conditions put you at higher risk for chafing, and you can take preventive action before runs in such conditions. You certainly shouldn't need to initiate preventive countermeasures before every run.

Pack

Packs shouldn't chafe. Occasionally, something might rub you the wrong way for a short time, but on a regular basis, the pack you run in should feel like part of your body. If that's not happening, first try to readjust the gear you're carrying as well as the various adjustment straps. If that doesn't work after a few attempts, you need to try a different kind of pack.

Underarms

Some people experience chafing of their upper arms against their armpits. You can avoid this by wearing a shirt that places at least one layer of clothing between your chafe points, by pretaping your chafe points, or by lubing as necessary.

Sports Bra

Unfortunately, many women have serious issues finding a sports bra that fits them like a glove. For some women, poor-fitting sports bras can result in chafing in any spot the sports bra touches skin, but it's most common in the small of the back, on the sternum, where the shoulder straps rest, or under the arms.

Fortunately, an immense diversity of sports bras is available these days. As with a pack, if you're wearing a sports bra that chafes (or otherwise pains) you, find one that feels good. There's no need to run like that! To address sports-bra chafing, pretaping your chafe points works best. Make sure to cut the tape large enough that the edges of the bra and tape don't overlap and cause the tape to rub off.

Nipples

Oh, men! If you've ever attended an endurance-running event, chances are you've seen that dude with two red streaks on the front of his light-colored shirt—right in front of his nipples. That's not sports drink from the aid stations; that's blood from his nipples rubbed raw. Men can completely avoid this problem by slapping a Band Aid or tape over each nipple. For the fancy, there are nipple covers made specifically for running. It might take a little trial and error to find the nipple protection you need, but find it and let your nipples run in peace.

Waistband

The chafing of a shorts waistband against the waistline is rare, but it can happen, especially when your clothing gets sopping wet. If you know that one small spot of your shorts waistband is apt to chafe against your waistline in certain conditions, pretape your skin accordingly.

Genitals

All kinds of chafing can occur in the genital region, and the issue varies between women and men, of course. But whoever you are and however it occurs, this sort of chafing is the most miserable. Genitals rubbing against skin or clothing can quickly make your entire life painful. If you chafe anywhere in the genital region, you'll need a heavy dose of lube, and you'll need to reapply it when you feel the friction start to increase again. The good news is that with adequate lube use you can prevent virtually all genital chafing problems. Use a lube that's recommended for sports use on the genitals, and use it externally only. That said, if this happens, you should seriously consider finding a new innermost layer for your running.

Inner Thighs

Both men and women deal with inner-thigh chafing. In fact, this form of chafing is the most common in running. It can be a huge problem for those who are prone. Folks who prefer traditional running shorts (i.e., a liner with a looser overshort) should opt for a skin lube in situations when thigh chafing is likely to occur. Alternately, runners might opt for some form of running short or tight that extends down to at least midthigh so that the fabric provides a mechanical barrier similar to taping.

Caring for Your Feet

On every run, your feet hit the ground thousands of times. They take a literal beating in this sport. Read on to learn how to ready your feet as much as possible to reduce the chances of foot problems.

Shoe Size, Fit, and Lacing Techniques

To keep your feet healthy for a lifetime of running, pick up the fantastic book *Fixing Your Feet: Prevention and Treatments for Athletes* by Jon Vonhof, which addresses dozens of foot issues that arise before, during, and after running.

If nothing else, use this chapter to help find a comfortable pair of running shoes. Hundreds of suitable running-shoe models are out there, and surely some of them fit your feet better than others. Seek them out!

Shoe sizing and fit is a matter of personal preference, but these tips should get your feet headed in the right direction toward maximal comfort. Some shoe experts recommend wearing a trail shoe that's a half size larger than your regular running shoe to accommodate your toes in the

What's not to love about running on soft singletrack through a sea of wildflowers?

front of the shoe on steep downhills, but that additional room can sometimes create too much extra space elsewhere in the shoe. A properly fitted shoe for trail running will provide about a half inch (about 1 cm) of space between the end of your longest toe and the front of the shoe's toe box. When you are running downhill, your feet may move forward a bit, and this extra space helps prevent your toes from banging against the front of the toe box. Your trail running shoes should otherwise offer the sort of toe box fit that you prefer. Some people find that they prefer a more glove-like fit in the toe box, whereas others want a looser fit so that their toes can wiggle and splay to help provide balance.

The rest of the fit of your shoe, through the midfoot to the heel, should be relatively snug. You will find that when the midfoot of the shoe envelops your own midfoot well, you will feel stable and as if the shoes are part of your feet rather than something foreign attached to them. You'll achieve that midfoot snugness through a combination of shoe fit and lacing, a topic to be addressed shortly. Your heel should sit snugly into the heel cup of your trail running shoe. Although you don't want to have too much movement of your heel in the shoe, you also don't want to have to wedge your heel in. If the fit of the heel is too tight or too loose, you are likely to suffer serious blistering problems on the backs of your heels.

You can attain a more custom shoe fit through varied lacing. For example, some trail shoes offer an extra top eyelet that, when you thread your laces through it, helps some people achieve a snugger shoe fit that feels more secure while trail running. Runners with low-volume or long, thin feet can especially benefit from this feature, as can those with small ankles. You can also alter the tightness of your laces in certain places across the top of your feet to achieve a slightly different fit. For instance, some people like to loosen the laces above the toes and tighten the laces over the midfoot. Others prefer the laces over the midfoot to be a little bit looser than the laces up toward the ankle, especially when they'll be descending a great deal. When you look at the tops of your feet, you'll notice an intricate array of muscles and tendons. You also have several nerves passing through the tops of your feet. Altering your lacing techniques ever so slightly can make the tops of your feet—with all those tendons, muscles, and nerves—more comfortable.

Although uncommon, the ankle collar, the upper ring of the shoe that contacts your lower leg, may bang uncomfortably into the bottom of your outer anklebone. If this happens more than once in a pair of shoes, you should find another shoe with a lower ankle collar.

Sock Choice

These days, choosing trail running socks is like going to a buffet. Just as you need to find a shoe that feels comfortable on your feet, you have to find a sock that works best for you. Trail running socks can do several major things while you are trail running:

- Wick foot sweat and other moisture away from your foot and into the upper of your shoe (where, ideally, it then evaporates out of the upper).
- Protect your foot with extra cushioning on the bottom of the sock as well as the ankle where a kicked-up rock might bite your ankle.
- Act as a mechanical barrier to the friction created by your feet making contact with the shoe and, sometimes, your toes making contact with each other during the running motion (think toe sock).
- Provide support to the arch of your foot, which is constantly rising, falling, and angling this way and that as the muscles and tendons of your foot contract and relax in the running motion.

Although not all socks do all things, these functions represent the diversity of your options, and you should choose a sock that matches your desired assistance. For instance, if your feet sweat a lot when you run, you should choose a sock that wicks appropriately for your needs. If you get friction blisters between your toes when you run, think about wearing toe socks, which encase each toe separately and help eliminate the friction caused by your toes making contact with each other. If you have pain in your foot arches, a pair of socks with extra arch support may help you.

Drying or Lubing Agents

Some trail runners find solace in using a drying or a lubing agent on their feet for their longest trail runs. When your feet sweat, that moisture can cause several problems, including a bit of extra friction as well as softened

Catching the light just right above the Pacific Ocean in Big Sur, California.

foot skin, which can more easily blister and break. Foot powders are meant to help absorb your foot sweat, and lubes are meant to take on friction so that the skin of your feet doesn't have to.

Pretaping

Some people swear by foot powder or sports lube, but others prefer to pretape areas of their feet that are prone to blistering for trail runs lasting several hours or more. In the same way that pretaping was discussed in reference to chafing, pretaping the feet at their friction points allows the tape, not the skin, to bear the brunt of any friction, thereby preventing blistering. Runners who use pretaping generally do so to their toes, the balls of their feet, or the backs of their heels, as dictated by their personal trouble areas. Again, if you're a trail runner who has persistent blistering issues on your long runs despite wearing a pair of shoes that feel good on your feet and socks that work well for you, consider the option of pretaping for blister prevention. Vonhof's *Fixing Your Feet* instructs on foot pretaping with incredibly helpful detail.

Acute On-Trail Issues and Injuries

No matter how carefully you prepare, accidents can still happen when you are trail running. Read on to learn about the most common accidents and acute injuries that occur in our sport and ways to care for them on trail. Although you can't predict when an issue will arise, you can know how to deal with one when it does.

Falls

Even if you're superbly coordinated and just plain lucky, as a trail runner you're going to fall. Falls happen, and here's what you need to know about them.

First, falls can occur in bad ways and in less bad ways. You can do more or less damage to yourself when you go down depending on how you do it. One of the worst things you can do is to lock out your arm and fall with it perpendicular to the ground. You can easily break your arm or wrist that way. Instead, you want your hands to hit the ground in either a semiextended state (i.e., with elbows bent) or, if you're flying face-first, fully extended but angled far enough in front of you so that you land superman style. Try not to tense up, because this can worsen the effects of the fall by concentrating the impact in one location and not allowing it to reverberate through the body. If a forward fall has you pitching at all to the side, consider tucking a shoulder and converting the fall into a tuck-and-roll to help spread out the impact and lessen the chances of a single major injury. Likewise, the superman fall (or, if you prefer, the headfirst slide) spreads out the impact over various body parts, ideally leaving you scraped up but unbroken. Both techniques demonstrate the valuable lesson of spreading out impact forces rather than landing full force on, say, one knee.

In most of your falls, you will be running one second and be on the ground in the next, shocked. It all happens so fast that you have no control over how your body goes down. In this case, you might land on your knees, elbows, hands, hip, or some combination of these.

Cuts and scrapes (often with embedded matter), as well as bruises, are the typical results of a trail running fall. Most of the cuts will be superficial. They may bleed some, but you've done no real harm and can continue running. Usually, by the time you're back to the trailhead, you have a nice dollop of blood dried on your knee or elbow, a badge of honor perhaps. After you get home—and this goes for any skin you break while trail running—you'll need to clean your wound well, making sure to remove any foreign matter. To prevent infection, you'll also want to apply an antibiotic cream a couple times a day until a protective scab has fully formed.

Occasionally, a serious cut can occur because of a fall or running into a sharp object like a tree branch or rock. This injury will require stitches or even more serious medical care. Deep cuts that expose part of a muscle, fat, bone, or some other subcutaneous body tissue, cuts that don't stop bleeding in a few minutes, cuts that open unnaturally wide because of their placement near a joint, and similar injuries will need stitches. If you cut yourself so severely that major bleeding occurs, you will have to compress the wound to decrease bleeding and evacuate to a medical professional for further treatment.

Bruising is another common result of a fall. In almost all cases, although the bruising of a muscle or other soft tissue is quite painful, and although you might develop swelling and discoloration, you will be able to resume running as soon as the initial pain has decreased. If you happen to fall on a bony part of your body, you can bruise that bone. These bruises are more serious, may require some medical treatment, and may mean that you'll need to take days or weeks off running until the pain subsides.

Your fall may occasionally involve a skid, as if you're sliding legs or arms first into home plate in baseball or slide tackling in soccer. This kind of fall tends to be more painful than serious because superficial scrapes occur over a large surface area. As with cuts, foreign matter can become embedded in the skin. Although an injury like this is painful at the outset, it doesn't look severe. In extreme cases, however, medical attention may be required to remove the embedded foreign matter. This process usually involves scrubbing the abraded surface and washing the wound with liquid through a high-pressure hose or syringe. Whoever does it, removing the foreign matter will be painful, but if it is not done properly, you risk unnecessary infection.

Finally, a fall can conceivably result in a broken bone. If you suspect you have broken a bone, get yourself off the trail as quickly as possible and visit an emergency room for an X-ray. Depending on the bone and your ability to move it, such evacuation can be difficult and painful, and you may need the assistance of others or a search-and-rescue (SAR) team. Use great care not to make your already serious injury any worse in going off trail. Use clothing and tree branches to help immobilize your injury, if needed.

Joint Issues

One extremely common on-trail injury is the old rolled ankle, when your foot tips to the outside as a result of landing on an uneven surface. Occasionally, trail runners roll their ankles the other way, tipping the foot severely inward toward the midline of the body. Depending on how badly you roll your ankle, you can do a variety of damage including a minor strain of some muscles, tendons, or ligaments all the way to a full tear of some of the soft tissues of the ankle.

If you sprain your ankle only slightly, you will probably be able to continue running after the initial pain subsides. If after a minute or two you can run on it without notable pain, you can do so, although when you get home you may want to ice it, take some anti-inflammatories, and lay low for a few days. If you have sprained your ankle severely—torn one or more of those ankle ligaments—you will have a hard time extricating yourself from the trail because you will likely be unable to run or possibly even walk. You may be able to limp slowly to the trailhead, possibly with makeshift immobilization. If you continue to experience severe pain or your ankle can't support your weight to walk or run in the days following your injury, you'll need to seek medical treatment.

Rarely, rolling an ankle can lead to breaking one of the bones adjacent to the ankle joint. As previously mentioned, if you suspect you've broken a bone, get yourself off the trail and to an emergency room. You'll need to immobilize your ankle, perhaps using a piece of your clothing and some sticks. Depending on your location and your ability to get off the trail without worsening your injury, you may require the assistance of a SAR team for evacuation.

Other joints can experience acute, on-trail problems, most often the knee. Although acute knee injuries are extremely uncommon in trail running when compared with other sports like soccer or skiing, they can happen when the foot missteps or the land underneath your foot moves unexpectedly. This circumstance can cause your upper and lower legs to do two opposing actions that end up severely stressing the knee joint. In the same way that injury occurs in the ankle joint, the muscles, tendons, and ligaments traveling across the knee or connecting the bones together can be strained or torn. A severe knee injury should be treated similarly to an injury resulting from an ankle roll: Get off the trail (using SAR, if needed) and seek medical treatment.

Painful Muscles

Most of the muscle pain we acquire because of running is overuse related. We work a muscle beyond exhaustion, and the muscle becomes tight, inflamed, and painful as a result. Because this chapter focuses on the acute, on-trail problems of trail running, we won't address chronic injuries any more than to say that they can and should be avoided altogether, but they should be treated professionally if they do occur.

Trail runners can also strain a muscle or a tendon while running as a result of falling or misstepping. The most common significant muscle strains are those that occur in the calves, quadriceps, and back, and they generally feel like a sudden pulling or ripping sensation followed by immediate muscle tightness and pain. Some muscle strains are insignificant, in which case you'll be able to finish your run. Others result in significant muscle tearing and might require you to walk or limp painfully home from your run and take several weeks off running while the muscle heals. Seek medical care if you have extreme muscle or tendon pain.

Snakebites

Snakebites were addressed in chapter 10, "Trail Safety and Stewardship," so be sure to page back for a look. If you are bitten by a venomous snake, seek immediate medical care. When venomous snakes bite, they may inject toxic venom that causes immediate and progressive damage to your body's tissues. Hospitals located where venomous snakes live generally keep antivenom on hand and may administer it to envenomated snakebite victims to counteract the effects of the snake's venom. Most people who are bitten by venomous snakes require hospitalization to assist the recovery process.

Insect Stings and Bites

The sting or bite of many insects is annoying but often benign, as discussed in chapter 10. Swelling and pain may occur at the bite site. But some insect bites and stings, as well as some humans' reactions to them, are serious. For example, those who experience insect-related anaphylaxis should always carry epinephrine and have a plan for seeking emergency medical assistance in the event of a bite. Also, scorpions and some spiders, like black widows, administer toxic chemicals into their victims when they sting and bite. This envenomation, like that of a venomous snakebite, requires medical assistance. Be sure to do your research about the dangerous insects you might meet before heading out on a trail run.

Injuries From Animals

In almost all cases, wild animals go to extreme lengths to avoid close contact with humans. Very rarely, a sick animal or one that is acclimated to getting food from humans might bite or scratch someone. If this happens, get away from the animal as fast as possible using the tips we described in chapter 10. Seek medical attention for wounds inflicted by a wild animal because the wound needs to be carefully cleaned to prevent infection. You may require medication or shots to counter potential diseases. Also, immediately report this unusual and dangerous animal behavior to the appropriate authorities, such as the local land managers.

The most common animal-induced injury is the dog bite. Chapter 10 addresses dog encounters in detail. Treat a bite or scratch from an unknown dog like you would that of a wild animal. Although serious infectious diseases are almost nonexistent in domestic dogs, a wound created by one of them needs thorough care to evade infection.

Altitude Sickness

You may have read about altitude sickness in detail in chapter 7, "Conquering the Conditions." If you have not, look back at the section about acute mountain sickness (AMS), which occurs in some people who visit high altitudes. With the exception of its more serious uncles, high altitude pulmonary edema and high altitude cerebral edema, both of which are extremely unlikely to occur unless you go to a very high altitude, AMS is merely an annoyance and a performance inhibitor. AMS sets in not long after arriving at higher altitude and may persist for several days until your body begins to acclimatize to its new environment. The nuisance headache, nausea, loss of appetite, and other AMS symptoms will slowly abate as your body gets used to being at altitude.

Any Life or Death Emergency

Sadly, oodles of (highly unlikely) scenarios can occur while trail running that are life threatening, such as a heart attack, a gaping wound, or a severe head injury. A life and death emergency that occurs on the trail needs two things immediately:

1. The condition incompatible with life must be treated immediately. A person who is choking needs the Heimlich maneuver. Someone who has stopped breathing is in need of cardiopulmonary resuscitation (CPR). A giant open wound needs compression to slow the bleeding. A person who could have a head or spine injury needs to be immobilized.

2. Emergency medical services (EMS) must be summoned immediately. Someone, preferably not the person or people administering life-saving care, needs to get EMS on its way to the injured person. If you are doing this job, you need to explain calmly where you are and what the life-threatening issue is. The faster, more efficient, and more precise you can be, the better assistance you can be to the person in need.

As they say, safety first! The preventative care addressed in the first half of this chapter is crucial to comfortable and enjoyable trail running, and the how-to explanations for acute on-trail issues will help you negotiate a difficult or potentially life-threatening situation should you encounter one while on the trail. Knowledge is certainly power when it comes to problem-free trail running, so let this chapter be a jumping-off point to a lifetime of learning.

LANTAU ISLAND, HONG KONG

As Hong Kong's largest and least-developed island, Lantau Island is an excellent outdoor playground. Home to a number of tall peaks stretching more than 3,000 vertical feet (900 m) into the sky, the popular 43.5-mile (70 km) Lantau Trail, and many shorter trails, the island is a magnet for trail running.

The Lantau Trail, the best known place to trail run on the island, is a well-organized loop that starts and finishes in the village of Mui Wo on the east side of the island. The trail is divided into 12 sections of varying distances, and signposts with distance markers are found every half kilometer. You'll always know where you are on the Lantau Trail. Also, along this organizational vein, many of Hong Kong's trails are different from trails in other parts of the world in that pavement and stairs are frequent fixtures. Development aside, the Lantau Trail can take you to some spectacular places, including the island's highest peak, Lantau Peak, at 3,064 feet (934 m) above sea level, the giant Tian Tan Buddha and associated Po Lin Buddhist Monastery, as well as many small mountain and fishing villages.

If you're in the mood for trail racing, you're in real luck because the Hong Kong trail racing scene is robust. A trail race is almost always happening on Hong Kong, although the races are clustered from October through May, the region's cooler season. On Lantau Island, try the Lantau 2 Peaks 23 km event, which is run every October. Some locals call it the hardest half marathon they've ever run. You could also try one of the three race distances at TransLantau in March: the, 25 km, 50 km, or 100 km.

Whether you plan to trail run or race on Lantau Island, be prepared for major vertical. The trails are never flat and often climb or descend steeply; grades of over 1,000 vertical feet per mile (200 m per km) are common. Heat and humidity are also a factor on Lantau, so be prepared with water and appropriate clothing.

Winning the 2015 Western States 100-Mile
Run brings a big smile to Rob Krar's face.

Chapter 12

Trail Racing

If you have come all this way with trail running, you might find yourself
interested in participating in a trail race. Racing may help you search for
your own top speed, measure yourself against others, or become a part of
the wider trail running community. Whatever your proclivity, this chapter
explains how to choose and what you can expect from a trail race.

Choosing a Race

Trail races come in many shapes and sizes. Races of any distance exist, from a few miles to 100 miles (160 km) or more. Many trail events host races of several distances as well, such as a 5 km (3.1 miles), half marathon, and marathon, all offered from the same starting line. You will also find that trail races take place on a variety of surfaces, from the grass of a local high-school cross-country course to up, down, and around some of the world's most imposing mountains.

You'll also have to choose the size of race you wish to participate in, from a small one with 40 or 60 participants to those with thousands of runners. Although you'll find very big races in Europe, the latter is still quite uncommon in North America, at least for now. That said, trail running is growing quickly in popularity, and an evolving race scene is surely part of that.

A trail race in proximity to your home or at an inspiring destination may also factor into your decision. Because of other life commitments, some trail runners desire races that are close to home. Others like to use a trail race as a getaway or a reason to go on vacation. A trail race can make a lovely excuse to explore new places both near and far.

> If you want to run a race, check its registration procedure. As trail running increases in popularity, some races require participation in lotteries and sign-ups months in advance.

Some communities frequently host trail races, as often as every weekend, whereas other areas with less developed trail running communities might have trail races only a couple times per year. Thus, the actual existence of trail races might help you make the decision about which race you will run. If you live in a place that becomes snowbound in the winter, you will notice that the trail racing scene tapers off when the snow flies.

To find trail races, check out your local running store, ask other runners, search one of the many online trail race calendars, or search online for trail races in a particular geographic area. After you discover your desired race, note the registration procedure. Some small trail races allow you to sign up on the day of the race, but the most popular races may require you to qualify, sign up far in advance, or enter a lottery that determines who can race.

Prerace Preparations

Trail racing can be one of the most enjoyable expressions of our sport. Most people find it at least as pleasurable as trail running in general, and others enjoy it even more for the added competitive challenge and community immersion. Adequate preparation can seriously boost the fun factor, so get ready to race!

Course Familiarization

The course—the ups, downs, curves, climbs, rocks, and views—is perhaps the best part about a trail race. Knowledge is power in just about everything in life, and the same is true in trail racing. If you know what's ahead on the course, you're likely to find it a little easier to manage.

Almost all trail races have websites on which you can learn about the course, including the actual route, climbs and descents, aid stations (places where you can restock on water and food), as well as crucial intersections. For longer races with too much crucial information to remember, you can make and laminate a cheat sheet to carry with you as a reference tool.

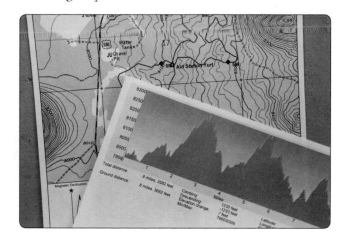

Review course maps and elevation profiles on a race website to help plan your race.

Climate and Weather

Knowing the climate—the typical weather in terms of temperature, humidity, precipitation, cloudiness, visibility, and wind—for the region where you're racing will help you plan all your needs such as water and fuel intake, gear, clothing choices, racing strategy, and more. For example, knowing when and how hot the weather will get on race day will inform when and how hard you decide to push during the race.

Fueling Plan

Whatever your racing goals, your water and nutrition intake is important. For a primer on general trail running hydration and fueling, check out chapter 6.

The first thing you should do is decide how much water and fuel you will need for your trail race using the estimated time it will take you to complete the course, your effort level, and the likely weather. Some races are short enough that you won't need water or fuel during the event, whereas races that last several hours require careful planning to ensure that you have the water and fuel you need. Apply the knowledge you've gained during training to develop your fuel plan.

A trail race longer than a couple miles will generally have at least one aid station where you can get water, at a minimum. Some aid stations, especially those at longer races, offer additional drinks and food. Generally,

The 2014 UTMB® begins in a torrent of rain.

aid stations are spaced 45 to 90 minutes apart. Occasionally, aid stations are spaced farther apart.

For races in the 10 km (6.2 miles) to half-marathon range, you might get your appropriate fuel and fluid intake by carrying one or two gels in a shorts pocket and drinking water or sports drink from the aid stations along the way. At longer races, if the weather or terrain is extreme or if the aid stations are far apart, you will need to carry and consume water and nutrition between aid stations. In this case, use your trail running gear to carry what you need—a handheld water bottle or a hydration pack. Most people use the same gear for racing that they use in their regular trail running, but a few use lighter-weight versions of their usual gear. If you are looking to race at the top end of your capacity, lighter gear will allow you to run a tiny bit faster.

Shoe Choice

If you are the type of runner who has one pair of general-purpose trail shoes that you wear in all conditions, you need not worry about race-day shoe choice. If you have multiple pairs of shoes, however, choose the one that best meets your personal needs and the trail conditions. Running your fastest might inform wearing your lightest pair of shoes. Rocky terrain might mean that you need shoes with a good rock plate to protect the bottom of your feet. Mud or snow indicates wearing shoes with aggressive lugs for increased traction. Chapter 5 discusses trail running shoes in detail, so make sure to look back as you decide what shoes to wear for your trail race.

Other Gear

For some races, you will have to carry additional gear such as a mandatory kit or extra clothing. Mandatory kits are a type of safety gear that a race requires you to carry in case an emergency occurs on the course. Examples of mandatory gear include a whistle, emergency blanket, headlamp, knife, and waterproof jacket.

The weather may necessitate that you carry extra layers of clothing to help you keep warm and dry, such as a wind jacket to guard against a breeze, a rain jacket to stay dry, or a hat and gloves for warmth. As you decide what gear you need for race day, be sure to check back on chapter 5 for a full discussion of trail running gear.

Some races are run, in part, under the cover of darkness. In this case, you'll need a light or two to lead the way. Refer back to chapter 5 for a detailed discussion of lighting choices.

Finally, a recent movement in trail racing is to make races more environmentally friendly. Among many aspects, these races often aim to produce less garbage at aid stations. Some do this by being "cupless," by offering their provisions—which you'll read about in detail later in this chapter—without cups, so you will need to bring your own, ideally something that is small, collapsible, and reusable.

Race Strategy

Even if you aren't planning to race your hardest or even if your race plan is to have no plan, you can still benefit from at least briefly considering your race strategy. Race strategy is, very simply, a plan of how you would like your race to unfold from start to finish. Let's call it an exercise in visualization and implementation.

If, for instance, you want no plan other than to adapt to whatever the event throws at you, spend a few minutes reminding yourself of your intent to run with flexibility and adaptability, and imagine what that will look like. If you would like a more developed race strategy, think it through ahead of your race, remind yourself of the particular skills you will need, and visualize yourself enacting that strategy. Among the many strategies for trail racing, here are a few to consider:

- Start slow, speed up midway, and push hard at the end of the race.
- Negatively split the race by running the second half faster than the first.
- Run and walk in alternating, even intervals, particularly on flatter courses.
- On hillier courses, run the flats and downhills and powerhike the uphills.
- Keep the pace conversational from start to finish.
- Run at a certain heart rate for the whole race.

. . . and they're off at the 2015 U.S. Mountain Running Championships outside Bend, Oregon.

Crew Plan

Longer trail races, like a marathon or ultramarathon, sometimes allow you to have a crew made up of family and friends who travel to designated aid stations to deliver you drink, food, and gear. If you're running a race that allows a crew, make a plan for where and how you will use them, such as at which aid stations they'll assist you and what materials they'll provide you at each location. Make sure to give them directions to aid stations and a complete list of duties ahead of time. Planning your crew's tasks will make their experience easier and more fun.

Starting Lines

By its nature, trail running takes us to remote places off the beaten path. Accordingly, you might need to follow a convoluted and confusing route to the starting line of a trail race. Just getting to it may feel like a twisty, winding trip on singletrack. Most race websites provide good instructions for getting to the start with maps and written directions. If you navigate to the starting line with a GPS device, use it to confirm your location relative to the instructions provided. Don't rely entirely on your GPS unit because GPS devices aren't always able to route you correctly through remote areas. Make sure to leave plenty of extra time for the meandering and mistaken turns that might be part of this journey.

Parking for all but the largest trail races, which we discuss later, is typi
cally straightforward, if occasionally messy. Usually, race volunteers point
you toward an empty parking spot, but be prepared for this parking spot
to be off road, maybe in a grassy or muddy field. Depending on the layout
of the starting line and the parking area, you might have to walk a fair
distance from your car to the line. Budget time for this.

Those who are familiar with road racing will have a similar image come
to mind when we mention starting-line restrooms: a long row of portapotties with a longer line of waiting runners. The restroom situation at
the starting line of a trail race might be similar to this or quite different.
Sometimes you will encounter that same line of portapotties, whereas other
times you will have access to a restroom at a trailhead or visitor center. You
will likely have to wait your turn, so build some restroom time into your
prestart plan. You may or may not have a way to clean your hands after
using the bathroom, depending on how simple the facilities are. Consider
bringing hand sanitizer or baby wipes just in case. To prevent an unnatural
and unnecessary concentration of human waste in one spot, please don't

Big Races Versus Small Races

As mentioned earlier in this chapter, trail racing is growing by the minute, and
with it comes a changing racing scene. For the most part, trail races are still small
endeavors, but there are maybe a dozen or two very large trail races around
the country, and even more outside the United States. Those of you who are
looking to test your mettle against the other fast people in our sport will naturally be drawn to the increased competition of these races. Others might find
themselves at the big races out of simple interest in the terrain or the desire to
be part of something that represents a larger part of our trail running community.

Larger trail events often have events that occur before and after the headline
race itself, like a prerace question-and-answer session where you can meet the
top participating runners, kids' races, shorter-distance races, a festival with
booths and shops, and more.

Sometimes the larger trail races have an elite starting corral. Predetermined
access to the corral is granted to the projected fastest runners.

Larger trail races are timed with timing chips rather than being manually
recorded by volunteers. You'll be given a timing chip to wear on your shoe or
race number that registers as you cross timing mats along the course.

You might notice the presence of photographers and media at the starting
and finish lines of larger races and sometimes on the courses themselves.

The biggest difference you'll probably notice in running a larger trail race is
simply the larger number of people. You'll encounter more runners on the trail,
you might have to park farther from the start and take a shuttle to the starting
line, and the finish-line festivities are likely to be amplified. The race website
generally explains all these unique details.

use the natural area around the starting line for defecating. Even if you bury your waste and carry out your toilet paper, too much human waste in one location can contaminate the soil and ground water. Use the provided honey bucket if you have honey to deposit prerace.

At a trail race start, you will need to check in as well as pick up your bib number and maybe some swag like a shirt or a hat. Sometimes races offer check-in the night before at a local running store or hotel, but others offer check-in only at the starting line. Even if you've checked in before race morning, you may need to check in again on race day so that the race has an accurate list of who is on the course. Make sure to note all this from the race website. Again, check-in can take time, so arrive with enough time to accomplish it.

For the most part, North American trail race starting lines are casual setups that have no corrals to hold runners of differing speeds. Because trail races often funnel straight onto singletrack with little room for passing, you need to seed yourself among your peers. Should you seed yourself too far ahead in the pack, you'll likely be stuck running in a train of runners who are too fast, which could make the second half of your race a painful, slow slog. If you seed yourself too far back, you're apt to waste time waiting for those ahead of you to negotiate the terrain. To seed yourself appropriately, estimate the size of the crowd and place yourself in it according to your previous race results. For example, if you often finish around the top 30 percent, place yourself behind roughly one-third of the runners. If you don't have any racing experience, exercise courtesy by not starting on the front line unless you've been training successfully alongside others who are up there.

When you find yourself needing to negotiate a pass or to allow other runners to pass you, err on the side of caution and respect for others. If you would like to pass another runner, politely ask the person ahead of you for permission. When the trail allows, the person should step aside to let you go by. If another runner wants to pass you, offer the same little step off the trail as soon as it's safe to do so. A little kindness goes a long way, in life and on the trail.

Staying on Course

The thing that varies the most from trail race to trail race is how courses are marked. Although you won't find consistency from race to race, the website or the prerace briefing are perfect places to find out exactly how a course will be marked. Most courses are marked at least in part with inch-wide (2.5 cm wide) colored ribbon known as flagging. Flagging is hung from trees, shrubs, grass, and permanent trail markers. Most often, flagging is hung to delineate the path you are to travel. Flagging comes in many colors, but pink, orange, and yellow are frequently used at trail races. Generally, race directors use the same-color flagging from start to finish to delineate the course. Some events hold races of multiple distances, so race directors often use flagging of different colors for the different races. Make sure you know the flagging color you are to follow. Occasionally, races use small flags or reflective markers hanging from flagging or attached to thin metal stakes in the ground.

A race director might supplement flagging with additional markers, such as flour arrows or plastic plates with arrows directing where you should go, particularly at intersections. Sometimes, wrong-way signs, differently colored ribbons, or branch barricades are placed on the trails you shouldn't take.

In an ideal marking situation, a race director marks the course at regular intervals with what we call confidence markers, say every quarter or half mile (every half or full kilometer). These markers provide affirmation that you are going the right direction over expected and regular periods. In such cases, if you don't recall seeing a marker for a while, you can begin actively looking for one. If you then don't see one in slightly longer than the intervals you have previously, you may want to turn around if no other runners around you can confidently say that you're still on course.

Above all, pay attention. If you keep your eyes peeled, you are unlikely to have issues navigating.

Aid-Station Expectations

Aid stations are beacons of hope that offer water, food, and friendly faces in remote locations. Although aid-station layouts vary from race to race and even from station to station within a single race, you'll find certain mainstays among them all.

Most likely, volunteers will record your passage manually or by chip and timing mat, so that the race can track each runner's location. This usually happens as you enter or leave an aid station. Do what you can to facilitate this process.

A simple aid station is ready for trail racers.

Next, address your hydration needs. You'll generally find that drinks are available from already poured cups and from large jugs. Water, sports drinks, and soda are common hydration offerings at aid stations. At a short race, you may just want to stay a moment and sip on a glass of water or sports drink. For longer races, you want to do the same while also refilling a handheld water bottle or hydration pack from a jug. Swigging a bit of soda can add a jolt of energy for the coming section, although many runners save this for late in a race. Sometimes, aid stations offer ice for longer or hotter races. If so, add it to your bottle or hydration pack. Note that if you're participating in a "cupless" race, you'll need to provide your own drinking and water-storage containers and you won't find drinks awaiting you in cups.

You'll likely find a table full of easy-to-eat snacks, usually including salty foods like salted potatoes, chips, and pretzels, and sweet foods like gels, gummy bears, cookies, and hard candies. At longer trail races, like a trail marathon, you might find more substantive food like soup, grilled cheese, bacon, and pancakes.

Aid stations supply garbage bags or cans. Use them. Don't drop your garbage on the ground. If recycling or composting containers are provided, use them appropriately. Keep the natural places through which you're running trash free.

Some aid stations will have a restroom, whether it's an outhouse, porta-potty, or backcountry setup. Also, many aid stations are staffed with medical personnel. Ideally, you won't need their services, but knowing such help is available provides peace of mind.

Finally, be kind to the volunteers who help you at aid stations. Even better, volunteer to work at an aid station of another race to give back to those people who have helped you.

Finish Areas

Most trail runners love finish-line areas. You are done with the challenges of running. You can hang out with your compatriots, compare notes on the day, have a picnic with your family and friends, and enjoy food and beverages offered by the race. Sometimes races have live music and other activities that enhance the experience. Many people find themselves having so much fun at the finish of a trail race that they stay there longer than the time it took them to run the race itself. Be sure to pack supplies that will allow you to hang out after the race if you wish, be it clean and warm clothes to change into, a blanket or camp chairs to sit on, some of your own food and drink, and extra sunscreen.

Trail races are incredibly social places. Racing them is a great way get to know your local trail community.

François D'haene crosses the finish to win the 2014 UTMB®.

At most trail races, all finishers get some sort of prize, which is given out when you cross the finish line. A low-key award ceremony for the fastest runners will take place as part of the finish-line festivities. The number and kinds of awards vary from significant prize money for the top men and women to small gifts that extend through top age-group finishers.

Wherever the trail takes you—whether it's to a race every weekend, on your hometown trail network, or to an adventure on the other side of the world—we hope you enjoy learning and growing, gaining confidence and endurance, and generally having a blast!

BRIDGER RIDGE RUN, MONTANA, UNITED STATES

The Bridger Ridge Run, which takes place north of Bozeman, Montana, is perhaps the best unknown mountain race. The 20-mile (32 km) course with 6,800 feet (2,100 m) of ascent and 9,500 feet (2,900 m) of descent traces the spine of the Bridger Mountains from north to south.

When we say that it follows the range's spine, we mean this literally. The race begins by climbing Sacagawea Peak, a mountain in the northern part of the range. Next, the course either follows the crest of the range or contours just below it. From the spine, the views are grand and far-reaching, unless the range is shrouded in fog and clouds as it occasionally is; the view can then be something along the lines of fairy-tale spooky. The trail is mostly rocky and technical, and the exposure factor is moderate to extreme. After you make it to the south end of the range at the summit of Baldy Mountain, you drop straight off the range, at times in sane, switchbacking fashion and at other times more precariously. It's truly a riotous race.

Within its region, the Bridger Ridge Run is no secret. Almost every trail runner within a 500-mile (800 km) radius wants to run this iconic race. The only way to get one of the 250 bib numbers allotted each year is through a lottery.

But if you don't get in, you can enjoy the course outside the racing environment. Doing it point to point, north to south, just as the race does, is the way to enjoy this route. Don't expect to pop off a 20-mile (32 km) run on the Bridger Ridge with any speed. This route will take you anywhere from 4.5 to 8 hours at a recreational effort. Also, given the high, remote reaches of the route and the tendency for summer thunderstorms to ravage the range, you'll want to start early and finish before the skies erupt. The route is bucket-list worthy, but you need to know that it's intermediate- to advanced-level trail running.

Resources

Beyond this book is a wealth of additional information on trail running. We share some of our favorites here.

General Online News and Information

iRunFar.com

Website with global trail running news, reviews, and additional resources founded and operated by the authors.

TrailRunnerMag.com

The online extension of North America's trail running magazine.

Magazines

Trail Runner (US) (trailrunnermag.com)

Ultrarunning (US) (ultrarunning.com)

Trail Running (UK) (www.trailrunningmag.co.uk)

Fellrunner Magazine (UK) (fellrunner.org.uk)

Trail Run (Australia) (trailrunmag.com)

Trail (South Africa) (trailmag.co.za)

Asia Trail (Pan-Asian) (asiatrailmag.com)

Kiwi Trail Runner (New Zealand) (www.kiwitrailrunner.co.nz)

Revista Trail Run (Spain) (www.trailrun.es)

Trails Endurance (France) (www.trails-endurance.com)

Trail (Germany) (www.trail-magazin.de)

Trail Running Books

The Ultimate Guide to Trail Running by Adam W. Chase and Nancy Hobbs
A basic introduction to trail running.

Trailhead: The Dirt on All Things Trail Running by Lisa Jhung
A trail running book with a lighthearted, conversational voice.

Relentless Forward Progress: A Guide to Running Ultramarathons by Bryon Powell
An ultrarunning how-to, which includes principles applicable to trail running.

Training and Physiology

Lore of Running by Timothy Noakes
An exhaustive treatment of many running principles, many of which can be applied to trail running.

McMillanRunning.com
Training resources, many of which can be applied directly to trail running.

Daniels' Running Formula by Jack Daniels
Renowned training book on endurance running, the principles of which can be applied to trail running.

Racing Weight: How to Get Lean for Peak Performance by Matt Fitzgerald
Nutrition for endurance running.

Waterlogged: The Serious Problem of Overhydration in Endurance Sports by Timothy Noakes
A deep look at the science of hydration and endurance running.

Metabolic Efficiency Training: Teaching the Body to Burn More Fat by Bob Seebohar
Principles of metabolic efficiency training.

Medical Aspects of Harsh Environments, Volumes 1 and 2
The U.S. Army Medical Department's guide to harsh environments. Volume 1 focuses on extreme heat and cold, while volume 2 examines high-altitude environments.
Volume 1: www.cs.amedd.army.mil/borden/Portlet.aspx?ID=eebb9338-2027-46d5-a5f2-f245e2019b6c
Volume 2: www.cs.amedd.army.mil/borden/Portlet.aspx?ID=7c0ebab2-6720-4e15-883b-dbfaafa960f9

AltitudeMedicine.org
Resources about physical exertion at altitude.

Fixing Your Feet: Prevention and Treatments for Athletes by John Vonhof
Foot treatment before, during, and after running and other endurance sports.

Barefoot Running: How to Run Light and Free by Getting in Touch With the Earth by Michael Sandler and Jessica Lee
A good resource for barefoot and minimalist running.

Outdoor Ethics

LNT.org
The Leave No Trace organization's website, which includes much information on ethical outdoor play.

TrailRunner.com/trail-news/trail-running-rules-run
The American Trail Running Association's "Trail Running Rules on the Run."

Online Race Calendars

TrailRunnerMag.com/races/race-calendar
The magazine's website has an extensive calendar.

TrailRunner.com/race-calendar
The American Trail Running Association has an online calendar.

I-TRA.org/page/290/Agenda.html
The International Trail Running Association website has a calendar with many international race listings.

UltraSignup.com
Race registration and results website with a focus on ultramarathons.

Index

Note: Page numbers followed by italicized *f* and *t* indicate information contained in figures and tables, respectively.

About the Authors

In 2006 through a set of fortuitous encounters with trail runners, **Meghan M. Hicks** learned about the sport of trail running. In doing so, she realized that she could combine her formerly dueling loves of road running and exploring wild places on foot within one activity.

Meghan was the 2013 winner of the Marathon des Sables in Morocco, the world's largest, oldest, and most competitive expedition-style trail running race. She has many other wins and podium finishes at trail races around the world.

Meghan loves the people, places, and races that compose the trail running community, and she's passionate about telling the stories that define it. She is the senior editor of iRunFar.com, the world's premier trail running website, and a contributing editor for *Trail Runner* magazine.

Hailing from Moab, Utah, Meghan is still most enthusiastic about using the sport as a means for fast-moving explorations of the earth's wildest places.

Bryon Powell started running trails behind his parents' house in central New Jersey more than 20 years ago, and he hasn't stopped since. He's twice finished in the top 10 at the Leadville Trail 100-Mile Run, twice won the under-30 age group at the Western States 100-Mile Run, and finished the Hardrock 100-Mile Run. He still gets a thrill toeing the line at shorter trail races, too.

In 2009, his love for the trails and writing about them led Bryon to stray from the well-traveled path of a Washington, D.C. attorney and begin working full-time on iRunFar.com. He's previously written *Relentless Forward Progress: A Guide to Running Ultramarathons* in addition to many magazine articles on trail running. He's a contributing editor at *Trail Runner* magazine and an advisory board member at the American Trail Running Association.

He calls the trails above Moab, Utah, home. They make him feel like a kid again.